TRAVELERS SERIES GUIDE TO THE TOKYO DISNEY RESORT®

WWW.TRAVELERSSERIES.COM

Also available and coming soon from TRAVELERS SERIES:

<u>Special Destination Memory Books</u>
    Disneyland Resort
        Disneyland
        Disney's California Adventure

    Walt Disney World Resort
        Magic Kingdom
        Epcot
        Disney's Hollywood Studios
        Disney's Animal Kingdom

<u>Metro Area Memory Books</u>
    San Diego, CA
    Orange County, CA
    Los Angeles, CA
    Santa Barbara, CA
    Monterey, CA
    San Francisco, CA
    Sacramento, CA
    Nashville, TN
    Phoenix, AZ
    Las Vegas, NV
    Austin, TX
    Denver, CO
    Seattle, WA

<u>Themed Memory Books</u>
    California Baseball Stadiums
    California Missions

TRAVELERS SERIES GUIDE TO THE TOKYO DISNEY RESORT®

By Travis Medley

Travelers Series Publishing

Published by:
Travelers Series Publishing
10531 4S Commons Drive, Suite 513
San Diego, CA 92127

ISBN 0-9830184-0-7

Editor: Michelle Medley
Cover Design: Matthew Bowers

To view and purchase our other products or for additional information, please visit www.travelersseries.com.

CONTENTS

OVERVIEW 1
    Notes on the Travelers Series Guide to the Tokyo Disney Resort................... 3

SECTION 1: YOU'RE GOING TO JAPAN! 5
    Overview 5
    Air Transportation 5
    Communicating 7
    Cultural Tips.. 8
        Bowing... 8
        Directions 8
    Eating 9
    Electricity 10
    Emergencies 10
    Insurance... 10
    Internet Access... 11
    Money.. 12
    Packing.. 14
    Passport... 15
    Phones 15
    Restrooms.. 17
    Time Zones.. 18
    Transportation – Getting Around Tokyo 18
        Plan Ahead 19
        Tickets... 19
        Entering and Exiting.. 20
        Metro Lines 21
        JR Lines... 21
    Travel Warnings... 22

SECTION 2: PLANNING FOR TOKYO DISNEYLAND 23
    When to Go 23
        Weather... 24
        Holidays 25
        Tokyo Disney Resort Festivities... 28
        Park Hours... 28
        Ride Refurbishments 29
        Tickets... 29
        Length of Stay 30
        Travel Budget.. 30
        What Travelers Series Recommends 31

SECTION 3: WHERE TO STAY 32
    On Property– An Overview of the Disney Hotels...................................... 32
        Overview... 34
        Seasonal Pricing 34
        Disney Hotel Benefits 34
        Reservations.. 34
        Rooms – Beds and Baths.. 35
        Smoking 35

Internet Access 35
Disney Ambassador Hotel **35**
Overview 35
Theme 36
Getting to the Parks 36
Rooms 36
Dining 40
Shops 41
Reservations 42
Tokyo DisneySea Hotel MiraCosta **42**
Overview 42
Theme 43
Getting to the Parks 43
Rooms 43
Dining 48
Shops 49
Reservations 50
Tokyo Disneyland Hotel **50**
Overview 50
Theme 51
Getting to the Parks 51
Rooms 52
Dining 57
Shops 58
Reservations 59
Tokyo Disney Resort Official Hotels **60**
Overview 60
Pricing and Packages 60
Tokyo Disney Resort Official Hotels Guest Benefits 61
Reservations 61
Getting to the Parks 61
Sunroute Plaza Tokyo 62
Tokyo Bay Maihama Hotel 63
Tokyo Bay Hotel Tokyu 63
Hilton Tokyo Bay 64
Hotel Okura Tokyo Bay 65
Sheraton Grande Tokyo Bay Hotel 65
Travelers Series Recommends 66
Tokyo Disney Resort Partner Hotels **67**
Overview 67
Pricing and Packages 67
Tokyo Disney Resort Partner Hotels Guest Benefits 67
Reservations 67
Getting to the Parks 68
Contact Information 68
Tokyo Disney Resort Good Neighbor Hotels **68**
Overview 68
Pricing and Packages 69
Tokyo Disney Resort Partner Hotels Guest Benefits 69
Reservations 70
Getting to the Parks 70
Other Tokyo Hotels **70**
Overview 70
Travelers Series Recommends 72

SECTION 4: ARRIVING AND DEPARTING TOKYO 74
  Hotel Transportation Options 74
    Trains and Subways.. 75
    Limousine Bus 75
    Rental Car 76
    Taxi. 76
    Travelers Series Recommends... 76
  Getting to Tokyo Disney Resort Hotels via Airport Limousine Bus 76
  Getting to the Airport via Airport Limousine Bus.. 77
  Getting to the Tokyo Disney Resort from Central Tokyo....................................... 78

SECTION 5: UNDERSTANDING THE TOKYO DISNEY RESORT 80
  Ikspiari 80
  Bon Voyage 81
  Cirque du Soleil Theatre Tokyo 81
  Dining at the Tokyo Disney Resort.. 82
  Hidden Mickeys 83
  Pin Trading.. 83

SECTION 6: UNDERSTANDING THE TOKYO DISNEY RESORT PARKS 85
  The FASTPASS Factor 87
  Single Riders 89
  Experience the Difference 89
  Eating Your Way Through the Parks 90
  Guests with Disabilities 91
  Mickey Mouse and Friends... 92
  Rated and Reviewed 93
  Shopping Around 93
  Subtitles... 93

SECTION 7: TOKYO DISNEYLAND 95
  Overview 95
  Shows and Parades... 98
  Stroller and Wheelchair Rental... 100
  Main Entrance 100
  World Bazaar... 101
    Overview 101
    Attractions 103
    Dining 105
    Shopping 108
  Adventureland 112
    Overview 112
    Attractions 113
    Dining 119
    Shopping 124
  Westernland... 126
    Overview 126
    Attractions 127
    Dining 133
    Shopping 136
  Critter Country... 137
    Overview 137
    Attractions 138

Dining 140
Shopping 141
Fantasyland **141**
Overview 141
Attractions 142
Dining 152
Shopping 154
Toontown **155**
Overview 155
Attractions 157
Dining 163
Shopping 164
Tomorrowland **165**
Overview 165
Attractions 166
Dining 175
Shopping 178
Upcoming Attractions **179**
Mickey's PhilharMagic – 2011 179
Cinderella's Fairy Tale Hall – 2011 180

SECTION 8: TOKYO DISNEYSEA **181**
Overview **181**
Shows and Parades **184**
Stroller and Wheelchair Rental **184**
Main Entrance **185**
Mediterranean Harbor **186**
Overview 186
Attractions 187
Dining 192
Shopping 195
American Waterfront **198**
Overview 198
Attractions 200
Dining 208
Shopping 212
Port Discovery **213**
Overview 213
Attractions 214
Dining 217
Shopping 218
Lost River Delta **219**
Overview 219
Attractions 220
Dining 224
Shopping 226
Arabian Coast **227**
Overview 227
Attractions 228
Dining 231
Shopping 232
Mermaid Lagoon **232**
Overview 232
Attractions 233

      Dining 239
      Shopping 240
   Mysterious Island 241
      Overview 241
      Attractions 242
      Dining 245
      Shopping 246
   Upcoming Attractions 246
      Jasmine's Flying Carpets – 2011 246
      Fantasmic! – 2011 246
      Toy Story Mania – 2012 247

SECTION 9: TOKYO HIGHLIGHTS **248**
   Overview 248
   Riding on the Metro 249
   Tsukiji Fish Market 249
   Meiji Shrine 249
   Sensoji Temple 249
   Sumo Wrestling 250

APPENDIX A – JAPANESE WORDS TO KNOW **251**

APPENDIX B – LIST OF WEB SITES **253**

INDEX **255**

Overview of Travelers Series Guide to the Tokyo Disney Resort

Tokyo Disneyland has long been an enigma for Disney fans, especially Americans. The park has been around for more than 25 years, features many attractions and technologies not found in any other park and is among the best of what Disney has to offer. Tokyo Disneyland has often been the second or third most visited theme park in the world. The Tokyo Disney Resort is an amazing complex consisting of two theme parks: Tokyo Disneyland and Tokyo DisneySea. Tokyo DisneySea opened in 2001 and has consistently ranked #4 or #5 in the world in annual visitors (behind the Magic Kingdom at Walt Disney World Resort, Disneyland, Tokyo Disneyland and at times, Disneyland Paris). The Tokyo Disney Resort, with two world–class parks, ranks second only to Disney World in annual visitors; the only reason it is in second place is that the Walt Disney World Resort has twice the number of theme parks. Where the Walt Disney World Resort is an international destination, the Tokyo Disney Resort is supported almost entirely by Japanese visitors. Combined, Tokyo's two Disney parks had more than 25.8 million visitors in 2009 for the second–highest attendance levels in Tokyo Disney Resort history (down 5% from the record 27.2 million visitors in 2008). All told, more than 489 million people have entered the Tokyo gates since April 1983. So why are there so few books – especially in English – about this magical world? This is fodder for endless speculation and conspiracy theory on blogs, forums, chat rooms, and web sites where Disney fans gather. The answer may not be too complicated....first, the parks are not owned by Disney (more on this later)

1

and, therefore, not part of its world renowned marketing machine. Second, the parks are crowded year–round with local visitors as more than 97% of 2009 guests were Japanese! That said, more than 700,000 non–Japanese guests visited in 2009 and many others would like to visit.

Forgive us, at times, if we fawn a bit over this resort. For those who frequent the Disneyland Resort and Walt Disney World Resort, and even Disneyland Paris, they are used to seeing the parks "borrow" rides and shows from each other. Disney fans get truly excited when something new and unique is available. The Tokyo Disney Resort parks offer plenty of originality coupled with exquisite attention to detail. On every level, these parks are "Disney done right" and you are bound to come away wondering why every park built in the last 10 years isn't as awe–inspiring as Tokyo DisneySea.

Disney magic, with some help from the Imagineers in California, permeates throughout the resort and this is a trip that will definitely not disappoint. This book is dedicated to helping you experience the magic and wonder of Tokyo Disneyland and Tokyo DisneySea. Whether you are determined to visit every Disney theme park across the globe, considering a day trip during your stay in Tokyo or want to "travel" to this magical destination from the comfort of your living room, just give a little whistle and let this book be your guide. We'll help you decide if you should attempt this

---

TOKYO DISNEY FUN FACT

Tokyo Disneyland was a long time in the making. Multiple Japanese companies approached Disney about building a park in Japan. Most sites were 60 miles or more from Tokyo – Japan's population center. The Oriental Land Company, however, owned a 200 acre plot of land on Tokyo Bay located a scant six miles from the city (the Tokyo Disney Resort currently occupies approximately three times that acreage). Disney, at the time, was reeling from significant cost overruns at Epcot during that park's four–plus year construction and was not enthusiastic about investing in another theme park. The Oriental Land Company proposed a licensing deal whereby Disney Imagineers would design the park and Disney would be paid royalties based on performance. The initial offer was to pay Disney 2% of all gross revenues (i.e. 2% of every Yen spent in the park on admission, food, souvenirs, etc.). In the final deal, signed in 1979, Disney agreed to invest a paltry $2.5 million in the park. In return, Disney received 5% of the gross revenue on food and merchandise sold in the park and 10% on admissions and corporate sponsorships for 45 years. This deal earned Disney $40 million in royalties the first year alone!

---

adventure – a resounding YES! – to providing the essentials of getting there. From packing to arriving, to getting around the parks, you will learn about the Tokyo Disney scene...right down to how rides compare with other Disney parks. Fasten your seat–belt, this e–ticket ride is about to begin.

The intrigue of the Tokyo Disney Resort is enhanced by the history and culture of Japan. Japan is a nation–island steeped in tradition. Cultural values run deep with the Japanese and it is a culture very different than that of the western world. Add to this the drastic oral and written language barriers for the average American and Japan appears mysterious. Areas in North or South America, Australia or Europe have stronger language ties to the U.S. Words in Spanish, French or German often share similarities with English words and a very similar alphabet of letters A through Z is used; whereas in Japan symbols make up entire words and more often than not, the origin or root of a word is nearly indistinguishable. In addition to the language barriers, Japan is home to Sumo wrestling, samurai swords, geishas, karate, giant pagodas and ancient shrines. Japan and U.S. relations have changed dramatically over the past 60 years. These nations have gone from mortal enemies in the wake of the attacks at Pearl Harbor, U.S. internment camps for people of Japanese descent and the dropping of an atomic bomb at Hiroshima to end World War II, to the strongest of allies. Within 20 years of the war ending, America had become a large tourist destination for the Japanese and Disneyland was a tremendous draw. Roughly 30 years after the war ended, the Japanese were beginning to approach Disney about building a theme park in Japan. In many ways, we need to look no further than Tokyo Disneyland to see how strongly allied these countries have become; American flags can be seen throughout the park and "U.S.A." is prominently displayed for all to see on the StarJets attraction. It is interesting to witness firsthand how fascinated the Japanese are with American and western culture while Japan remains widely unknown to many Americans.

Notes on the Travelers Series Guide to the Tokyo Disney Resort

The Travelers Series Guide to the Tokyo Disney Resort is independent of the Oriental Land Company, The Walt Disney Company or any affiliated firm. This guidebook was created in direct response to the limited information available on the Tokyo Disney Resort – primarily for English speaking Disney fans. The Tokyo Disney Resort, because of this lack of information, has often been considered somewhat of a mystery. Our team's focus was to uncover the intricacies of this magical place and to share it with people who would be interested in reading and learning about the Tokyo Disney resort.

Prices quoted throughout this guide are in U.S. dollars ($) in order to make it as simple as possible for you, the reader. Currency fluctuations exist, and prices constantly change at the Tokyo Disney Resort. The prices quoted are based on current prices at press time and actual prices will vary depending on price changes and currency fluctuations. In essence, prices in guidebooks are outdated the moment the book goes to print and we felt this approximation in U.S. dollars would have more impact on you rather than quoting outdated prices in Yen. We assumed an exchange rate of $0.0111 U.S. to ¥1 Yen or ¥90 to $1 U.S. While it is not perfectly accurate, removing the last two digits from any Yen price, will give you a quick idea of how much something will cost in dollars. For example ¥2,300 could quickly be approximated as $23 by dropping the last two numbers (it's actually $25.50) or ¥162,300 could be quickly approximated as $1,623 (it's actually $1,801.53).

Yahoo! Finance Currency Converter is a user–friendly and can be found at http://finance.yahoo.com/currency–converter.

Our team strives to provide a comprehensive review of attractions, restaurants and shops within the Tokyo Disney Resort hotels and theme parks. Additionally, this book contains in–depth reviews of each attraction, restaurant and store within the parks. Wherever possible, we attempted to compare the offerings of the Tokyo Disney Resort to the Disneyland Resort in California and The Walt Disney World Resort in Florida. The hope is that you will have a better understanding and create a clearer mental picture of the Tokyo Disney Resort with these comparisons. Additionally, these comparisons show the unique aspects of the Tokyo Disney Resort and why we believe it is a trip that is absolutely worthwhile for any Disney park fan. The reviews are comprehensive enough for someone who has never been to a Disney park (though we doubt they are reading this book!).

Lastly, we refer to a lot of websites throughout this guide. There is a comprehensive list of every site referred to in the book in the Appendix.

SECTION 1: You're Going to Japan!

Overview

Planning a trip to Japan, the Land of the Rising Sun, can be a lot of fun and any Disney trip comes with a certain amount of anticipation and excitement. We want to provide you with the basics of what you can expect and some tips to remember while you plan. We've also included a preview of some of the many wonderful things you will experience, including cultural differences between Japan and the United States. These will range from basic information (like hotel room prices in Japan include taxes and fees) to cultural insights (like how and when to bow).

The key to enjoying your trip abroad is planning. If you research the country where you plan to travel – especially a non–English speaking country – and think through the hurdles you may face, you will find yourself prepared to deal with the unexpected. Rest assured, the unexpected *will* occur. With basic planning (and hopefully the items you will learn in this book), this will not be scary, but rather a bit of an adventure. Any time you visit a foreign country, expect that communication will be more difficult. Expect that things that are easy at home will take more time abroad as you will be unfamiliar with local customs and requirements.

Air Transportation

The main airport in Tokyo is the Narita International Airport (NRT). It is also the most convenient airport when traveling to the Tokyo Disney Resort. Flying to Tokyo's Narita International Airport is a relatively simple process from any major airport. Flight time is about 11 ½ hours from Los Angeles or 13 ½ from New York and many airlines fly these routes. American, Delta, United, Northwest, Continental, U.S. Airways, British Airways, Lufthansa, Singapore Air, Korean Air, China Air, Japan Air, Air Canada and Qantas are among the many. As with any vacation, once you have determined your dates, it's time to get to work on finding a price and schedule that works best for your party. You can call up a travel agent and let them do the work or spend some time online to book the flights yourself. Rest assured, this is no more complicated than booking a trip from LA to Chicago…but if that overwhelms you, call your travel agent. If you have the interest and a little time, you will likely find the best rates by searching yourself.

TRAVEL TIP
Most Japan–bound flights from the U.S. leave in the morning. Because you will be following the sun through multiple time zones, you will find that it will be sunny outside your plane for a solid 18 hours or more. It can be quite a surreal experience to arrive in Japan the afternoon of the next day, having never seen nightfall.

Flight prices are determined by many elements including time of year, length of stay, days of the week for travel and advanced purchase. Typically, it is less expensive to fly during non–holiday times (this applies to Japanese holidays as well as U.S. holidays) and to fly on certain days of the week. There are a myriad of travel sites including:

Expedia – www.expedia.com
Travelocity – www.travelocity.com
Orbitz – www.orbitz.com
Priceline – www.priceline.com
Yahoo! Travel – travel.yahoo.com

Run searches on these sites and compare what prices and schedules you find. An important and quick "cross–check" is to compare what you find to the airline's web site. For example, if you found that the schedule that matched your needs best was found on Korean Air through Expedia, take the time to go directly to Korean Air's site to see if there are any special offers (typically under a specific Special Offers section separate from the Reservations tab) or discounted fares that make your flight more affordable. Likewise, if several airlines were comparable in price, you may consider inspecting each of those sites individually to compare what you found on the travel sites. These same sites can be instrumental in helping you review your options for hotels. Accommodations are discussed in depth in the Planning for Tokyo Disneyland section.

There are countless travel agents who specialize in tours to Japan and Tokyo. They range from online discount agencies to full–service travel experts. However, travel agents who focus on trips to the Tokyo Disney Resort from the U.S. are rare. By the time you finish this book, you will likely know more about the Tokyo Disney Resort than most travel agents. This is a trip that you can absolutely plan on your own. If you are accustomed to working with Travel Agents, we recommend you utilize this guide to determine elements of your trip including where you want to stay, length of your visit and other vital information and then let the travel agent handle booking of your Tokyo trip. Do not expect them to know the differences between the Disney Hotels, Tokyo Disney Resort Official Hotels, Tokyo Disney Resort Partner Hotels and Tokyo Disney Resort Good Neighbor Hotels. They will likely need specific direction from you on accommodations.

Communicating

The biggest question on most travelers' minds will be how they well they will be able to communicate in Japan. If you are at all worried about communicating, don't be. If you are not fluent in Japanese, you will probably not be able to hold a conversation with many of the people you encounter. However, the Japanese are very helpful and do an excellent job communicating with some English and a lot of hand gestures. They do their best to help foreigners and often go out of their way to do it. During our most recent trip, we had one person who spoke fluent English recognize we were lost and walk us a couple of blocks out of his way to get us back on track. On another outing, we were struggling to find our hotel and a very delightful young lady who spoke very broken English walked us, in the rain, 20 minutes out of her way to the front of our hotel. Most Japanese people are very kind and will not allow your inability to speak Japanese to get in the way of communicating.

Now that you know you will be able to get to the park with relative ease, even without speaking the language, rest assured that you'll also have no problem navigating the Tokyo Disney Resort. Maps are available in a variety of languages including Japanese, Chinese, Vietnamese and English. Many of the announcements and soundtracks for the rides at Tokyo Disney are in Japanese. While this may prevent you from following the intricate dialogue, it adds to the cultural experience and to the feeling that you are truly somewhere special. Where else in the world could you navigate Sinbad's Seven Seas in a language completely foreign to you and be relaxed knowing you are sharing the adventure through the common bond of storytelling…and leave having understood the essentials of what was being communicated. An overview of basic word translations may be found in the Appendix.

Cultural Tips

There is no limit to the cultural nuances in Japan. From the seemingly innocuous to the extreme, the Japanese culture is unlike any other. We've included a few tips throughout this book. This is by no means a comprehensive list but it will help you in the most common interactions. These tips are designed for those who need to know enough to get by.

Bowing

Bowing – called ojigi – is a Japanese custom that may appear intimidating to visitors. This custom is extremely user friendly and is very easy to pick up while traveling in Japan. Bowing is used to signify many things from "hello", "good bye", "thank you", "excuse me" and others. Bowing can also come in many forms from a simple head nod to a full bow where you will be staring at your feet. There are many rules that, as a tourist, do not apply the same way they would in a business setting where status, position and age impact how or when to bow. For example the younger person or person with lower status would bow longer and deeper as a sign of respect. As a tourist or "guest" in Disney terms, status will not be an issue as you are the customer. The easiest rule of thumb is to bow to others as they bow to you. If someone gives you a head nod, reciprocate with a head nod. If someone bows lower, try to bow in approximately the same manner. Typically, you will see men bow with their hands on their sides while women put their hands on their upper thighs or lower abdomen with their fingers intertwined or hands overlapped. It is not going to be a surprise to anyone you interact with that you are a tourist and they will be very appreciative if you attempt this custom. It is considered impolite if someone were not to bow when they were bowed to, but you are not going to send a shopkeeper into a frenzy or start an international incident if you do not perform the ojigi correctly. As a general rule, the Japanese do not shake hands, though they have grown more accustomed to this practice from foreigners.

Directions

Tokyo is a very confusing city. There is seemingly little logic in the structure and layout of streets; street numbers are a mess and often out of order and postal addresses would confuse even the most educated people. Therefore, we recommend you always obtain directions before you venture out – but be forewarned. The Japanese are very considerate and helpful people. In general, they want nothing more than to help. However, they also consider the inability to help to be very rude. They would rather give you bad directions than no directions at all; and they will appear confident as they give you inaccurate directions. There is no malice or ill–will in this practice, it is truly their desire to help that causes this anomaly. For the best results, ask for directions from your hotel and then ask someone else to verify. Ask for a map or have them show you the location on a map, but do not assume it is 100% accurate. Getting somewhere on your own is all about attitude – if you view it as an adventure, you will probably have a good time even if it takes a bit longer to find your destination. If you get stressed out or angry, you will spend a lot of time in a bad mood!

Eating

For many, a trip to Tokyo will be a delectably palate–pleasing experience. For others, it will be a test in patience and may force them to expand the foods they would normally consider "acceptable". Most of the restaurants throughout Tokyo are, as you probably expected, Japanese. There are occasional restaurants that serve other types of food and, of course, there is a never ending supply of fast–food options – "Big Mac" translates in any language! Different Japanese restaurants specialize in different foods, but the vast majority of offerings are a mix of local fare. For Japanese cuisine connoisseurs, this provides a virtually limitless culinary adventure. The chicken teriyaki crowd – those who, like one member of our team, always only want a teriyaki chicken bowl and shun sushi – will have a bit of a tougher time in and around Tokyo. For one thing, chicken teriyaki is surprisingly difficult to come by, while meals covered in brown gravy are not. Japanese restaurants generally have a plastic food display (creating plastic food is big business in Japan!) in the front displaying the different items on the menu. Those restaurants that do not have displays almost always have menus with pictures. The ability to see your options will make settling on a restaurant a bit easier…though the chicken teriyaki member of your party can also veto choices more easily!

If you have ever visited a sushi restaurant in the U.S., you know it is impossible to walk into a restaurant in Japan inconspicuously, as the employees loudly greet guests as they enter or exit the establishment. This practice extends to fast food and it is quite an experience to walk into McDonald's and be greeted by a half a dozen cheerful employees. As a rule, be prepared for serving sizes that are small (compared to American standards) including "large" drinks that are served in small cups and not filled all the way to the top. Sadly, refills are not a common practice.

There are many eating establishments located on the city sidewalks or in the Metro stations. Those places with seating or standing tables available generally make their food and serve it warm. Those that are stands with no place to eat typically sell their food at room temperature or cooler. For example, you may walk through the Metro and see some large food courts or open markets where people walk through and buy any number of cooked items. These items are fresh and will be wrapped immediately "to go", but they are usually served cold. It is not unusual to buy Gyoza (a Japanese pot sticker) from a vendor where you can see them cooking the food. However, because it is assumed you will not be eating it immediately – since there are no seats or counters at which to stand – you will not receive the items "hot off the grill", but will receive food that was prepared a bit earlier.

Most of these insights extend to the Tokyo Disney Resort with one major exception – the food options at the Tokyo Disney Resort are far more diverse than Tokyo at large. Here, guests will find a much larger selection of American–type cuisine available in both parks and around the resort. Also, food is all served warm because there are always places to sit and eat at Tokyo Disneyland and Tokyo DisneySea.

A word of advice when eating out – most restaurants throughout Japan are stingy with their napkins. It is not unusual to find one napkin with your sushi, gyoza, burger or any other item you might have ordered. So, be prepared! If you need more, ask. If you are getting food to go, be sure to grab extras because there will not be many in the bag when you stop to eat.

Electricity

You do not need to bring any electrical adapters on your trip to Tokyo. Most hotels run on two different kinds of electrical plugs. 110 outlets (like those in the U.S.) are located throughout the room and though you may find a couple of higher voltage outlets that often have rice cookers or hair dryers plugged into them.

Emergencies

Small stations are located throughout Tokyo called Kobans. These allow people to have a direct line to the police in the case of an emergency. They look like small ATM machines, but they will have the word Koban written on them in addition to the Japanese characters. Also, dial 110 from any cell or pay phone in an emergency. It is the equivalent of 911 in the U.S.

Insurance

There are a variety of insurances available to travelers. All travelers, domestic or international, should review their options in order to make informed decisions about what coverage they do or do not need. First things first – be sure to contact your medical insurance provider and ask how your coverage extends to Japan. Ask specifically what you need to do in the case of an emergency and in instances where you need non–emergency medical attention (i.e. the flu, a sore throat, ear infection, etc.). Be sure to ask your provider what information you need to bring with you, who pays for these visits (many times you will be asked to pay and then file for reimbursement through your insurance carrier) and any other pertinent information should you need to seek medical attention in Japan.

Next, review and consider travel medical insurance. This coverage is generally very low cost ($10–20 per person for a week) and serves as supplemental insurance for serious issues or injuries. This insurance typically covers transporting someone who has become very sick back to the United States and covering additional medical claims. We have traditionally used Nationwide Insurance's travel medical insurance on our international trips (www.nationwide.com), though we recommend checking with your current insurance providers (health, auto, home, etc.) or travel professionals for recommendations.

The other type of insurance you should review is trip cancellation insurance. This coverage will often reimburse you for the cost of your trip – airfare, hotel, etc. – if you must cancel for an "approved reason". We are not big fans of trip cancellation insurance because many of them have very stringent guidelines as to when the insurance applies, and it can be pricey (up to 5% or more of the cost of the trip). Also, some credit cards will offer similar protections at no additional cost. At any rate, be sure to do your research before you decide whether or not to purchase trip cancellation insurance.

Internet Access

Internet access works in Japan just as it does in the U.S. Many places charge for internet access and hotels and airports offer instructions in English. If your laptop is set up to detect wireless connections, no changes are required while traveling in Tokyo other than to select the appropriate network and start surfing. We think it is important to have internet access while traveling abroad for a myriad of reasons. This access will generally provide you with English–language access to information you may need regarding your trip as well as allow you to keep abreast of any important news. Likewise, the internet can be an inexpensive communication tool with people at home via email or calling/video conferencing programs like Skype (www.skype.com).

Money

Japan's currency is the Yen (¥). Banknotes are offered in denominations of ¥1000, ¥2000, ¥5000, and ¥10000 while coins include ¥1, ¥5, ¥10, ¥50, ¥100 and ¥500.

It is essential for any traveler – foreign or domestic – to have cash on hand. We are also firm believers that credit cards and/or debit cards are the best method of payment while traveling.

Cash is crucial because you never want to find yourself in a situation where you cannot pay for something you need – food, hotel, transportation, etc. Likewise, it is rarely a good idea to travel with large amounts of cash for safety reasons and because you have no recourse if it is lost, misplaced or stolen. We start our trip with approximately $400 worth of Yen (in addition to U.S. currency) for emergency use and incidentals. While exchange rates at airports are not very good for the traveler, converting a relatively small amount will have little impact on the unfavorable exchange rates. Additionally, it is worth the peace of mind to arrive in Tokyo knowing you have enough cash to get to your hotel. Once you are in Tokyo, you can exchange more money at the airport, at exchange shops throughout the city, at your hotel or at the Tokyo Disney Resort. However, you are likely to get a much better exchange rate by utilizing an ATM. The machines work the same as they do at home, but they spit out Yen instead of Dollars. Most banks charge a nominal fee (generally less than the cost of exchanging money at an exchange booth) for accessing the ATM. Be sure to check with your banking institution before you leave home so that you know what fees your bank will charge you for such transactions. Although you will get a better exchange rate using ATM machines, many U.S. ATM cards are not compatible with ATM machines throughout Tokyo and the Tokyo Disney Resort. In fact, none of the cards in our party worked at any Tokyo Disney Resort ATM machines including those at the parks or in our hotel. You can, however, use credit cards to charge almost everything during your trip to Tokyo and the Tokyo Disney Resort. It is still important to travel with some cash. We highly recommend that you get Yen at the airport. Whether you exchange cash at the airport in the U.S. or in Japan or use an ATM machine at the Tokyo airport (if the first machine you try does not work, try another), be sure to get enough

> **TRAVEL TIP**
>
> It is very common for travelers to have ¥10,000 banknotes for small purchases. It does not carry to same stigma as trying to pay for a pack of gum with a $100 bill in the United States. ¥10000 notes are regularly given at exchange counters or out of the ATM.

12

cash to cover food kiosks, short metro tickets and some "walking around money". If you have U.S. currency, it may be exchanged at Tokyo Disneyland and Tokyo DisneySea Guest Relations and likely at your hotel. Both of these locales generally offer a better exchange rate than the airport. So long as you have dollars, you will be able to quickly get your hands on some Yen.

If you are out exploring Tokyo and need cash, try a 7–11 convenience store or a post office (signified by a white sign with what looks like a red upside down "T" with two horizontal lines at the bottom) as they typically have machines that will work with U.S. bankcards.

TRAVEL TIP
When paying for items at a retailer, you do not hand your money or card directly to the cashier. Instead, there is a small tray near the cash register. Set your money on the tray and the cashier will take the money and put your change on the tray.

As you probably know, Yen is not widely accepted at U.S. retailers – so be sure to exchange any leftover money at Narita International or upon arriving at your home airport. We recommend utilizing your home airport in case you need to purchase any incidentals before you board your plane.

Visa and MasterCard are widely accepted throughout Tokyo and the Tokyo Disney Resort and represent both a convenient and safe method of payment. Additionally, your bank will convert the money on your statement and the exchange rate, like the ATM exchange rate, is generally more favorable than the currency exchange booths. Sometimes, your credit card company will add a small currency conversion transaction fee; so be sure to inquire with them before you leave home. Just as you would at home, be sure you

TRAVEL TIP
Alert your bank and credit card companies to your upcoming international travel before you leave home. This will help ensure fraud is not suspected and that the charges will be approved.

check your receipt carefully before you sign to ensure you were charged the proper amount. It is always a good idea to check with your credit/debit card company to find out what your responsibility is should your card get stolen or overcharged. The large hotel chains and the Tokyo Disney Resort also accept AMEX, but you should not rely on its acceptance in outlying areas and even all of the places around the parks.

Exchange rates fluctuate, but as a rule we found ATM and credit cards offer the best deal. Below is an overview of what we paid during a trip to purchase ¥10,000 – the lower the number, the better the exchange rate!

San Francisco International Airport – $130
Tokyo Disney Parks Guest Relations – $118
Hilton Tokyo Bay Hotel (Tokyo Disney Resort) – $118
Narita International Airport (Tokyo) – $115
ATM – $113
Credit Card – $113

A note on tipping: don't do it! The Japanese culture does not participate in the custom of tipping – this applies to food service employees (waiters and waitresses), hotel staff (concierge, bellhops, masseuse). However, don't be surprised to see a service charge added to your bill in some establishments.

Packing

Traveling to Tokyo provides an interesting dilemma when it comes to packing. First and foremost, you want to pack light because space is at a premium in hotel rooms, and it will make "getting around" much easier. On the other hand, Tokyo's weather can be unpredictable. Here is a general overview of important items to remember. Be sure to adjust these if you are a "cold–blooded" or "warm–blooded" person. Our team has members at both extremes and the items members packed varied wildly for the same seasons.

> **TRAVEL TIP**
> Confirm! Confirm! Confirm! Be sure to have a comprehensive checklist of things to do in the 24–48 hours before you leave home: confirm your air reservations and check–in online, confirm your hotel reservations as well as the best route to get to the hotel from the airport and check the weather forecasts and alter your packing accordingly.

No matter when you travel, bring a pair (or two, in case one gets wet) of good walking shoes. Do not bring new shoes on a "walking" vacation. Bring broken–in shoes that are comfortable to wear when walking very long distances. Additionally, bring a light jacket regardless of the season and bring a heavy coat in the winter (consider brining one in the spring and fall, too). No matter the season, always bring a small, collapsible umbrella and sunscreen. Also consider packing a plastic poncho. Pack light clothing in the summer. The weather is often muggy, though it can rain. Likewise, bring plenty of warm clothes in the winter as it does snow in Tokyo.

Don't forget that you are going to Tokyo Disneyland! Be sure to pack the theme park basics from snacks to sunscreen to hats and fanny packs. Bring your favorite Disney paraphernalia and wear it proudly – the vast majority of guests will be wearing theirs, too.

One interesting note is that you will very rarely see Japanese people in shorts. Even on the coldest days, you will see school girls with knee–high socks and very short plaid skirts (freezing their rear–ends off), but you will be hard pressed to find guests wearing anything other than pants.

If you are checking luggage, be sure to pack your basic "must haves" in a carry–on. This may include a change of clothes, medication, passports, laptop, money, etc. – anything that you cannot live without if your luggage were to be lost or delayed.

Passport

Passports are required in order to enter and exit Japan. Understandably, this document is very important and must be safely kept with you at all times. It is common for hotels to ask for your passport at check–in, just be sure to get it back. Should you lose your passport, immediately contact the United States Embassy in Japan for assistance. They can be reached at 03–3224–5000 from Japan or 011–81–3–3224–5000 from the U.S. The official State Department web site for the U.S. Embassy in Japan is tokyo.usembassy.gov.

> **TRAVEL TIP**
> Before you leave home, make two color copies of your passport. Bring one with you and keep it separate from your passport. Leave the other copy with someone at home. These copies will aide you should something happen to your passport.

Phones

Staying in touch with your travel party and people back home is important. In recent years, we have witnessed a dramatic dependence on cell phones, smart phones and any other device that allows for constant communication including email, internet access, texting, etc. At the same time, we have become accustomed to low–cost, unlimited plans. A trip to Japan will have an impact on how "connected" you feel unless you plan to spend a lot of money. Be sure you contact your cell phone carrier and ask specific questions about traveling to Japan. Ensure your phone is compatible and inquire about the costs of making and receiving local calls as well as international calls (they often have different prices). Additionally, ask specifically about texting costs, costs to utilize your internet access and costs for email. Lack of information will only lead to national headlines like

"Tokyo Disneyland Traveler Racks Up $18,364 Cell Phone Bill". If you will be using some features on your phone, but not others, ask your cell phone carrier how to disable the features you will not use (in some instances, you will be charged for receiving voicemails internationally – even if you never retrieve them!).

Cell phones have become a staple and many people are lost at the thought of traveling without one. Additionally, there is a sense of security and comfort knowing that you can reach someone or be reached easily in the event of an emergency. Japan's hi–tech network, once incompatible with U.S. phones, is accessible to 3G capable phones. Another option is to rent a cell phone. Phones may be reserved and even received before you leave home. Others may be delivered to your hotel and rental shops are readily available inside the Narita Airport. We highly recommend bringing your phone (disabling every feature if you have to) in case of emergencies.

> **TRAVEL TIP**
> Skype (and other similar services) are a great way to communicate while abroad. The service is free and you can make unlimited voice and/or video calls for no cost if you are connected to the internet. We highly recommend you set up your system and practice making calls from home to ensure everything works properly.

As with most things, you will find a larger selection at a lower price if you plan ahead and book a phone before you leave home. Several providers are listed below:

www.phonerentalusa.com
www.gomobile.co.jp
www.rentafonejapan.com

Most rental providers offer free incoming calls and you may also forward your U.S. number to the Japanese phone. Be sure to check the rates with your own provider for doing this. Internet and email/data packages are also available. Rates vary from service to service depending on your usage and length of rental. The overall cost is not exorbitant, but it isn't cheap either. A typical plan on a Go Mobile phone will cost $26 for a week and about $1/minute for calls to the U.S. while incoming calls are included at no additional charge. Additional fees will be charged for insurance ($1.50/day), delivery of the phone ($10) and for any internet or data packages. If your personal phone is not compatible with Japan's network and you can work a mobile phone into your budget, we highly recommend it as a "just in case" item and to be used to check in with people back home.

There are several easily identifiable cell phone rental kiosks at the Narita International Airport that charge $1.25–$3.50 or more per day for phone rentals and approximately $2/minute for international calls. They also have pre–paid packages if users have an idea of how many minutes they need.

> **TRAVEL TIP**
> You may need to make a few phone calls to Japan while planning your trip. Be sure to check with your home phone or cell phone provider about international rates before you call. If they are expensive, a calling card may be a good option for placing calls from the U.S. to Japan.

In case of emergency, keep in mind that dialing 911 will not do you any good. In Japan, the emergency number is 110.

Whether or not you choose to carry a cell phone, calling cards are a great option. They are generally far less expensive than cell phones, fit in your wallet and can be used with any hotel phone or pay phone. There are ample pay phones that may be used throughout Tokyo and the Tokyo Disney Resort. Before you use your hotel phone, be sure to inquire about charges for placing toll–free calls. We highly recommend securing a calling card before you leave home. Check with your phone carrier, search the internet, and look at stores like Costco or Wal–Mart for discounted calling cards.

Restrooms

Overall, there are very little differences between restrooms in Japan and the United States; they are clearly marked for men and women. While most have regular toilets, some restrooms (both men's and women's) have stalls containing what appears to be a horizontal urinal built into the floor. While this may cause a bit of a shock at first glance, a little bit of balance will go a long way in helping you lean, squat and bend to utilize these facilities. Often times, there are "regular" toilets in other stalls in case this is just too much "culture" for you. One of the most "comforting" things you will find in nicer restrooms and most hotel rooms is a heated toilet seat. Many also have a spray function to help clean your undercarriage after completing your business. And some stalls have their own fan to provide a noise buffer. Be sure to try each feature – you never know what your favorite bathroom experience will be!

The shopping experience in Japan is unique in that, if nothing else, the service is far superior to U.S. standards. Customers are greeted by any staff who sees them enter or exit. Many stores have umbrella bags outside (it rains a lot in Tokyo!) and customers are expected to place their collapsed umbrellas in these plastic bags to avoid getting the floor wet. Likewise, some establishments (generally hotels) will have umbrella locks outside where customers can lock their umbrella handles, set their own PIN, and leave their umbrella outside when they enter.

After you have completed your shopping and are preparing to pay, note that there will be a small tray for your money or credit/debit card. Once the cashier provides you with a total and points to it – to help the non–Japanese speakers understand what they are saying – place your method of payment into the tray. They will put your change or the credit card signature receipt in the tray. While the cashier will generally use a cash register, they may show you a total on a calculator; this is standard practice and it is okay to pay that amount. A consumption tax (similar to the VAT used in European countries) is levied on most goods at a rate of 5% (4% national tax and 1% local tax). You can expect to receive a receipt with every purchase.

Time Zones

Japan's time zone is significantly different from those in the United States. Japan does not recognize "Daylight Savings", so times will vary depending on the time of year. Below is a quick overview of the time difference in Tokyo from the U.S. Time Zones as well as a snapshot of the time conversions based on a Monday at 2 pm in Tokyo:

Time Zone	Daylight Savings	Standard Time	Monday 2 pm Tokyo Time in:	
			August	September
Hawaiian	Not Observed	+19 HST	Sunday 7pm	Sunday 7pm
Pacific	+16 PDT	+17 PST	Sunday 10pm	Sunday 9pm
Mountain	+15 MDT	+16 MST	Sunday 11pm	Sunday 10pm
Central	+14 CDT	+15 CST	Monday 12am	Sunday 11pm
Eastern	+13 EDT	+14 EST	Monday 1am	Monday 12am

Transportation – Getting Around Tokyo

In general, the more you know, the less intimidating things seem. Understanding what to expect from the metro is crucial if you are planning time to sightsee in and around Tokyo (which you should do, since you just traveled halfway around the world!). Even for experienced travelers, it is confusing to travel – by metro, train or foot – through Tokyo. The difference between enjoying yourself and getting angry or frustrated is your state of mind. Allow three times as long to get somewhere the first time as you think it should take. The great news is that Tokyo is safe and the people are very helpful. We recommend mapping out your trip as best as you can –

perhaps confirm it with the concierge if you are still at your hotel – then take a deep breath and head out on your adventure. Expect that things will not go as planned. The worse thing that may happen is that you end up somewhere you didn't intend to be. In the right mindset and if you are not pressed for time, this is no big deal. Simply exit the train or metro, and get on the train or metro that is going the opposite way. This will always get you back to where you have been. If you are feeling overwhelmed, get off the train or subway at the next stop where you can do some research without the pressure of not knowing if you are headed in the right direction. Above all else, have fun and be sure to experience and enjoy the people and the culture around you. Your best or your worst memories will come from "exploring the town". Many Tokyo trips will require you to switch train lines and metro lines multiple times and separate tickets are required for the trains and Metro lines. Additionally, each metro line has some nuanced differences. These can include the look and comfort of the cars, different route maps within the trains, and different announcement systems (though you will be happy to know that most are in English). There are two subway lines plus multiple train lines throughout Tokyo. The subway/metro lines are the Toei Line with four routes/lines and the Tokyo Metro Line with nine routes/lines. In addition to the metro, you will use the Japan Rail (JR) trains to get around Tokyo. If you are departing from the Tokyo Disney Resort, you will have to use the JR line for at least one leg of your trip to reach the metro lines, which will allow you to explore Tokyo.

Plan Ahead

Before you step foot on a train, take a couple of minutes to review the Tokyo Subway Route Map and decide which lines you will take to reach your destination. Remember, if you are ever unsure about where you are, just disembark and catch the next train/subway once you regain your bearings.

Tickets

We recommend purchasing JR tickets one at a time for each one–way trip. The JR ticketing machines are a bit confusing. First, study the map and look at the sectors (these will be identified on the map) you are traveling through to determine which ticket to buy. If you cannot figure out which ticket you need, find a ticket window or station employee and they will help you. Be sure to have Yen available and feed money into the machine until the buttons light up, allowing you to select the ticket you want. Your ticket and any change due will drop to the slot at the bottom. Machines accept banknotes up to ¥10,000 as well as coins. If necessary, you could even say the name of your destination to a traveler near you ("Tokyo station?") and shrug – they will probably help you buy the right ticket. It is very important you keep your ticket as you will need it to enter the station as well as exit the station. If you purchase the wrong fare or travel further than the value of your ticket, you will not be able to exit the station without paying the difference. Fear not – this is a quick process. Find a fare adjustment machine or fare adjustment ticket window. If you use the machine, just insert your ticket, pay the difference and be on your way. One–way tickets or tickets with no fare left are kept by the machine when you insert your ticket to exit the station.

For the Metro, play it safe and buy an unlimited day pass for both subway lines ($11 for both lines vs. $8 for one line). This unlimited pass allows access to both the Toei and Tokyo Metro Lines. In addition to making your travel much less frustrating, it will likely be the most cost–effective ticket. It will certainly avoid any frustrations for wrong turns or switching lines since you can enter and exit the stations as often as you like

> **TRAVEL TIP**
> Always have your JR or Metro ticket in hand as you approach the exit gates to avoid causing a major bottleneck for those around you and adding unnecessary stress to your trip.

throughout the day. With an all day pass, your ticket will be returned to you when you exit – hang onto it since it is your ticket for the entire day.

Entering and Exiting

When entering the Metro and/or JR stations, insert your ticket into the electronic machine, walk through and collect your ticket as the machine spits it out on top. You will need this same ticket to exit. When exiting the station, follow this same procedure. If you have an all day pass, collect your ticket and keep it with you. If you purchased a one way ticket, your ticket will not be returned to you as you exit. Most of the train and Metro stations have multiple exits and some have well over a dozen. Throughout the station, there are yellow and black signs with a number on them. These signs indicate which exit you are about to walk through. There are also yellow and black maps that show all of the exits, their numbers and some of the notable destinations and streets to which they lead. These are always helpful in finding your way. If you happen to exit out of the wrong area, you can either find your way on surface streets or head back into the station and find a different exit. It is extremely helpful if you exit in the right place as it can be much more difficult to navigate on the city streets rather than in the station tunnels where maps and signs are readily available.

Metro Lines

Each Metro line has a colored circle with a letter in it – this indicates the line. Each of the stops along the line is numbered in the same color. The station signs are typically horizontal and indicate which stop you are at and which stop is next along the line. The Metro signs are different in Japan than those in other countries including much of Europe. Where in Europe, the Metro sign shows the current station and the last stop on line, in Japan the Metro sign shows the current station and the next stop on the line. Metros run frequently – generally every few minutes.

JR Lines

The Rail lines in Japan are often accessible in many of the same stations as the Metro lines, but they are completely different from the Metro. They require different types of tickets. Rail lines run on a schedule, though the most popular routes and largest stations have trains cycling through at regular intervals. We find the JR lines a bit more difficult to navigate than the Metro lines, though with some patience you will soon navigate these like an expert. The JR signs are typically vertical and have the name of the station written in English on the bottom. They do not have a letter, color and number system like the Metro. Instead, once you arrive on the platform, you will need to study which train to board to ensure you are headed the right direction. If you are ever unsure, enter the train near the front or back since there are conductors on both ends, and say the name of your destination as a question with a slight shrug – "Tokyo station?" and point to the train. They will quickly tell you yes or shake their head and point to the opposite side of the platform.

> **TRAVEL TIP**
> Chivalry is alive and well! If you are healthy and spry, please give up your seat to someone who is elderly or has trouble standing when traveling on crowded subways, trains with unassigned seating, or monorails. This is a sign of respect to the person and they will be very grateful. Keep in mind that you are always a representative of the United States and showing respect when traveling abroad reflects well on our nation.

It is extremely rare to see people eating and drinking while they are walking or riding the Metro though it is fairly common to see people eating on long–distance trains. Whether someone has ordered sushi, fast food, an ice cream, or just purchased bottled water, they will sit or stand at a table/counter, eat their food (sometimes devouring their food quickly), dispose of their trash and continue on with their journey. It is considered rude to eat and drink while walking. This even applies to items from vending machines. People who purchase items from vending machines generally stand next to the machine while they consume their purchase (generally drinks), dispose of the trash and continue on.

Whether you are in the Metro station, the Tokyo Disney Resort or walking the streets of Tokyo, you will find that the Japanese will constantly offer help if you look lost or confused. Likewise, if you spend too much time trying to understand how an ATM or subway ticket computer works, you can expect someone to offer help. They will not be angry that you have taken too long, but instead will genuinely do their best to help.

Additional information on the Metro system may be found at http://www.tokyometro.jp/global/en/index.html and to review rail times and prices, visit http://www.hyperdia.com/.

Travel Warnings

It's always a good idea to review the State Department's information and/or travel warnings concerning any foreign country. You may review them at www.travel.state.gov and search under International Travel. In addition to travel warnings, the State Department provides a comprehensive overview of the country as well as issues facing travelers, from crime rates to crime penalties (HINT: do not commit a crime while traveling abroad) and items to consider for children traveling to these areas.

SECTION 2: Planning for Tokyo Disneyland

When to Go

There are many things to consider while deciding *when* to visit the Tokyo Disneyland Resort. Just a few include the weather and the crowds which, in turn, impact cost and availability (not to mention your personal schedule and when you can get away to fly 5,400 miles across the Pacific!). All of these factors must be considered and weighed based on personal preference. In the end, no matter when you go, once you arrive you will be lost in the fantasy and you will thoroughly enjoy yourself.

> **TOKYO DISNEY FUN FACT**
> Tokyo Disneyland was a smash hit drawing nearly 10 million guests in its opening year, when it nearly reached the attendance levels at Disneyland in California. Tokyo Disneyland drew 16 million guests in its 10th year (compared with 13.6 million in 2009).

Never forget the universal, international, inter–galactic Disney park formula:

No School = Crowds

This formula transcends all borders, geographies, weather patterns, and price points. If kids are out of school for holiday, summer vacation, the weekend, or just the evening, you are sure to experience longer lines. The great news about the Tokyo Disney Resort (vs. the Disneyland Resort or Walt Disney World Resort) is that some U.S. holidays are not shared by the

Japanese. Thos will allow you to leverage your school/work vacation and avoid the heaviest crowds simultaneously.

Weather

Japan's weather varies significantly throughout the year. There are distinct seasons – from hot and muggy rain showers to the freezing snow. Being prepared for your trip is crucial. With 100+ rain days per year, odds are you are going to get wet during your stay.

MONTHLY AVERAGE DAILY HIGHS (F) / AVERAGE DAYS OF RAIN

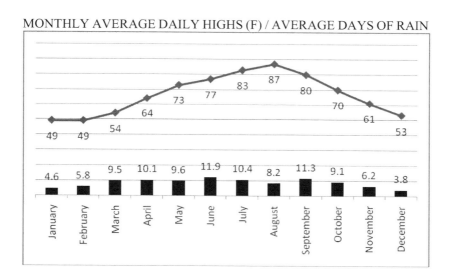

Summer brings hot, muggy temperatures and a lot of rain. The rainy season is June through mid–July. Fortunately, the city and the park are set up to handle the rain and a small umbrella should do the trick. It is humid throughout the summer in Japan and many locals use this time to get away. As such, the crowds at the Tokyo Disney Resort, like its U.S. counterparts, grow substantially during the summer. The Japanese summer vacations tend to dominate July and August so while Tokyoites are heading for the country, many vacationers from around the country are headed into the city and the Tokyo Disney Resort. Like the U.S., this is an energetic time in Tokyo with festivities, festivals and fireworks throughout the season.

Fall is a wonderful time to visit Tokyo. The temperatures become comfortable – sometimes cool – and the leaves begin changing colors. The end of summer and early fall (primarily in September) is typhoon season and can bring intense thunderstorms to the area.

Winter can be chilly. January is the coolest month when temperatures are 40 degrees cooler than the hottest August days. The air is crisp and the humidity is very low. Though temperatures rarely reach the freezing point, some snow fall will occur.

Spring is stunning and the cherry blossoms are the highlight of the season. Everywhere you look, you see pink and white blossoms during March and April. The temperatures are still cool (but not as cold) and the rain picks up slightly.

Make sure you layer clothing so you are prepared for any weather changes. During the cooler times of the year, the breeze off Tokyo Bay can be downright frigid and give guests quite a chill throughout the Tokyo Disney Resort; scarves, gloves and heavy jackets are called for during these times. However, it should be noted that areas of the parks serve as a wind break and, if the sun is out, you may quickly find yourself overheating. Likewise, the interior of buildings – restaurants, attractions, stores, etc. – tend to be kept very warm. You will freeze as you start to wait in line for It's A Small World, only to find yourself sweating five minutes later as you enter the inside portion of the queue. Those with layered clothing will survive these changes the best. We recommend an ensemble consisting of shirt, sweatshirt/sweater, and jacket combined with scarf, hat and gloves. Inside of twenty minutes, you may find yourself going from "fully bundled" to just a t–shirt, but the layers will allow you to help regulate your heat and stay comfortable.

Holidays

Holidays and other important times of the year impact crowd levels. Below is an overview of Japanese holidays. Those that are bolded are most likely to **increase** park attendance. A quick note on Japanese holidays: If a national holiday falls on a Sunday, the holiday will be observed on Monday. If two national holidays are separated by only one day, that day in the middle will also be observed as a holiday. In addition to these specific days, Golden Week (April 29 – May 5) and summer vacation (mid–July through August) will have a tremendous impact on crowd levels.

January
1 – New Year (shogatsu): National holiday with many businesses closed through January 3.

Second Monday in January – Coming of Age (seijin no hi): National holiday when men and women who have come of age (20 years old) are celebrated.

February
3 – Beginning of spring (setsubun): Not a national holiday, although it is celebrated at shrines and temples throughout Japan.
11 – National Foundation Day (kenkoku kinenbi): National holiday celebrating the day in 660 BC when the first Japanese emperor was crowned.
14 – Valentine's Day: Not a national holiday, though on this day Japanese women give chocolate to the men.
Mid–February – Entrance Exams: Not a national holiday, though hotel rooms may be in short supply as students throughout Japan flock to Tokyo to take their college entrance exams. While these dates will not likely impact crowds as the students will be focused on studying, it will drive down the availability (and can raise the prices) on hotel rooms. Plus…the day the exams are completed would not be a day to visit!

March
3 – Doll's Festival (hina matsuri): Not a national holiday and is also known as Girl's Festival.
14 – White Day: Not a national holiday, though this time it is the men's turn to give sweet treats to women.
20 or 21 – Spring Equinox Day (shunbun no hi): National holiday, like Autumn Equinox Day, when graves are visited throughout the week (ohigan) of this Equinox Day. The date can vary slightly.

April
29 – Showa Day (Showa no hi): National holiday celebrating the birthday of former Emperor Showa. This holiday is part of the Golden Week spanning four holidays from April 29 through May 5.

May
3 – Constitution Day (kenpo kinenbi): National holiday remembering the new constitution. This holiday is part of the Golden Week spanning four holidays from April 29 through May 5.
4 – Greenery Day (midori no hi): National holiday celebrating former Emperor Showa's love
for plants and nature. This holiday is part of the Golden Week spanning four holidays
from April 29 through May 5.

5 – Children's Day (kodomo no hi): National holiday and is also know as Boy's Festival. This holiday is part of the Golden Week spanning four holidays from April 29 through May 5.

June
N/A

July
7 – Star Festival (tanabata): Not a national holiday, but a Festival celebrated on the 7th day of the 7th month. Depending on the calendar (solar vs. lunar), this could mean July (solar calendar) or August (lunar calendar). This festival is celebrated on July 7 in some parts of Japan and August 7 in others. Tokyo Disneyland recognizes the holiday in July with a week–long celebration.
Third Monday in July – Ocean Day (umi no hi): National holiday that celebrates the ocean and the return of Emperor Meiji in 1876 from an oceanic trip to Hokkaido.

August
13 through 15 – Obon: Not a national holiday, but rather a festival to commemorate ancestors and is celebrated from the 13th to the 15th days of the 7th month. Depending on the calendar (solar vs. lunar), this could mean July (solar calendar) or August (lunar calendar). The weekend before and the weekend after this festival tend to see heavy traffic in the cities as these are travel dates.

September
Third Monday in September – Respect for the Aged Day (keiro no hi): National holiday to celebrate respect and longevity for the elderly. With the birthrate in Japan decreasing, the Tokyo Disney Resort actively markets to these people to visit and bring their families.
23 or 24 – Autumn Equinox Day (shubun no hi): National holiday, like Spring Equinox Day, when graves are visited throughout the week (ohigan) of this Equinox Day. The date can vary slightly.

October
Second Monday in October – Health and Sports Day (taiiku no hi): National holiday commemorating the opening of the 1964 Olympic Games in Tokyo.

November
3 – Culture Day (bunka no hi): National holiday promoting culture and the love of peace and freedom.

15 – Seven–Five–Three (shichigosan): Not a national holiday, but a festival celebrating girls of ages three and seven and boys of ages three and five. Prayers are said for their good health and strong growth. Odd numbers are considered lucky in Japan.

23 – Labor Thanksgiving Day (kinro kansha no hi): National holiday honoring labor.

December

23 – Emperor's Birthday (tenno no tanjobi): National holiday celebrating the birthday of the current emperor. The Emperor's Birthday is always a national holiday and the date changes with the Emperor.

24 through 25 – Christmas: Not a national holiday, though Christmas is increasingly celebrated by the Japanese.

31 – New Year's Eve (omisoka): Not a national holiday. December 31 is not a national holiday, though many businesses close from December 31 through January 3.

Tokyo Disney Resort Festivities

Halloween is celebrated at both Tokyo Disneyland and Tokyo DisneySea from early September through early November. In 2009, the Oriental Land Company launched a Halloween event at Tokyo DisneySea. According to their reports, this event added to their attendance during this season.

Christmas is celebrated at both Tokyo Disneyland and Tokyo DisneySea from early November through late December.

Celebrating holidays at the Tokyo Disney Resort can be a lot of fun with special decorations, parades and events. However, these "extras" come with larger crowds.

Park Hours

The operating hours for Tokyo Disneyland and Tokyo DisneySea do not vary much throughout the year. Whereas the Disneyland Resort and Walt Disney World Resort often fluctuate their schedules by as much as 4–6 hours or more, the Tokyo Disney Resort does not typically alter their operating schedule by more than 1–2 hours. It is a good idea to review park hours by visiting the Tokyo Disney Resort web site and selecting "Park Calendar" on the right hand side under Resort Schedule (www.tokyodisneyresort.co.jp/index_e.html). Tokyo Disneyland and Tokyo DisneySea operating schedules are generally available six months in advance, although they are subject to change and should be verified up to the day of your visit.

Ride Refurbishments

Like all Disney parks, Tokyo Disneyland and Tokyo DisneySea undergo regular refurbishments of their shows, shops, restaurants and attractions. Unlike the Disneyland Resort in California or the Walt Disney World Resort in Florida, planned closures are listed up to a year in advance and occur almost continuously throughout the year. They are listed in the "Temporary Closures" section of the Tokyo Disney Resort web site (www.tokyodisneyresort.co.jp/tdr/english/plan/schedule/stop.html). If there are particular attractions that are extremely important to you, consider aligning your travel dates to avoid these closures. Keep in mind, however, that refurbishment schedules can change and attractions can be closed for unplanned reasons as well.

Tickets

Theme park tickets at the Tokyo Disney Resort are called Passports. There are a variety of Passport options and they are pretty straightforward. The main decision is whether to purchase a one, two, three or four day ticket (this is nothing like navigating the myriad of ticket options at the Walt Disney World Resort!). The rules of use are a bit different from either the Disneyland Resort or the Walt Disney World Resort.

Multi–day tickets can offer a good value, but offer little in the way of rest or breaking up your theme park visits. Multi–day Passports must be used on consecutive days. If you buy a 4–Day Magic Passport, it is only good for 4 consecutive days (i.e. you cannot go Monday and Tuesday, take a break Wednesday and go back Thursday and Friday). Also, when purchasing multi–day Passports, the first two days are only good at either Tokyo Disneyland or Tokyo DisneySea while any additional days will allow access to both parks within the same day. When you purchase your tickets, you must decide and tell the cashier which parks you will visit on the first and second days.

> **TRAVEL TIP**
> Ask for multiple English language maps for both parks when you purchase your tickets. This will help save time at the turnstiles as Cast Members generally do not have them immediately available. They will find them as quickly as they can, but it's a bummer to have to wait when you are anxious to begin your day at Tokyo Disneyland!

Make the most of your time and be sure to buy your tickets before heading to the theme parks. The lines at the ticket booths outside of Tokyo Disneyland and Tokyo DisneySea can be quite long, while the lines at the hotels (our preferred purchase method) and the Welcome Center are likely

29

to be much more reasonable and their operating hours extend beyond those of the park ticket booths.

Passports may be purchased before you leave home on the Tokyo Disney Resort web site and picked up at the Welcome Center. We recommend using this option only if you are concerned the parks may reach capacity (i.e. if you are traveling during periods of high attendance and not staying in a hotel that sells tickets).

Length of Stay

How many days do you need at the Tokyo Disney Resort? In the slower times of the year, you can experience all the major attractions in both parks comfortably in three full days. Four days would allow your party to pace itself as well as experience some of your favorite attractions multiple times. If you are a touring maniac, you could do each park in one day, but you will miss a lot of the more intimate details and nuances within the parks. There are far fewer attractions at Tokyo DisneySea than there are at Tokyo Disneyland. Tokyo DisneySea can be toured in about a day. Tokyo Disneyland will take closer to two days.

If you only have time to visit one park, we highly recommend Tokyo DisneySea. The park is unlike any other Disney park in the world and has some of the best attractions Disney has ever designed (some of which can be found only in Tokyo!). Additionally, the park itself is a marvel. If your greatest desire is to visit all the "Disneylands" in the world, Tokyo Disneyland will certainly not disappoint, though the layout and attractions are quite similar to the parks in California and Florida.

If you are visiting during peak season, you may only be able to experience 10–15 attractions in a full day. Considering there are 36 attractions at Tokyo DisneySea and 46 attractions at Tokyo Disneyland, visiting during these times will force you to be extremely selective on which attractions you visit.

Travel Budget

Question: What will it cost to visit Tokyo Disney Resort?

Answer: It depends ☺

There are four main cost elements to your trip that will be impacted by time of year and length of stay:

Flight / Accommodations / Meals / Entertainment

Most of these elements can vary wildly in price. We recommend you invest time assessing each of these areas and their importance to you. Some people will want to splurge on business class tickets for the flight, while others may want a park–view room at the Tokyo DisneySea Hotel MiraCosta. Some folks will want to take in a Sumo match and see Cirque du Soleil while others will be content with just theme park tickets.

What Travelers Series Recommends

Back to the universal formula: No School = Crowds.

Weekdays are less crowded than weekends. The Tokyo Disney Resort offers discounted ½ day tickets that are valid only on weekends and national holidays. This causes an influx of visitors in the afternoon hours.

Days are less crowded than evenings. The Tokyo Disney Resort offers discounted evening only tickets.

The lowest attendance at the parks occurs in January through March while the summer months have the highest attendance. Wait times can exceed two hours or more for many popular attractions during this time.

With more than 25 million people passing through the turnstiles each year, Tokyo Disneyland and Tokyo DisneySea will never be "empty". Popular attractions will maintain 40+ minute waits throughout the year.

But what does "crowded" mean? Tokyo Disney Resort tickets can be suspended due to large crowds and wait times can exceed two hours or more for popular attractions. Tokyo Disneyland's capacity is roughly 85,000 guests and this capacity can be reached by noon on the busiest summer days. These "attendance control conditions", as expected, occur far more frequently during the summer, Golden Week, national holidays and weekends.

So…when should you visit the Tokyo Disney Resort? We would plan a trip in October, November, January, February or March. You will thoroughly enjoy yourself no matter when you go, and if the choice is to visit in early August or not at all, go! Enjoy. It will be a memorable trip.

SECTION 3: Where to Stay

"Where should we stay?" This question is crucial for any vacation. The real question when planning a trip to a Disney park is: Do I stay in the resort hotels or the hotels outside the resort? This question is made far more difficult at resorts like Disneyland, Disneyland Paris, Hong Kong Disneyland and Tokyo Disneyland versus Disney World. At the Walt Disney World Resort, there are 22,343 Disney–owned and themed rooms (compared to 1,711 at the Tokyo Disney Resort) that start as low as $70 per night. At these other resorts, the Disney offerings are much more limited and, as a direct result, much more expensive. Staying in a Disney resort makes you feel much more intimately involved with the Disney fantasy – let's face it, Disney sells "feelings" and "memories" as much as entertainment. You will enjoy yourself immensely whether you stay "on property" or "off property". This book will cover, in detail, your "on property" options and provide an overview of the countless "off property" hotels are a short train ride away from the Happiest Place in Tokyo.

On Property– An Overview of the Disney Hotels

There are two classes of hotels on the Tokyo Disney Resort's 494–acre property – the three Disney Hotels and the six Tokyo Disney Resort Official Hotels. Additionally, the Tokyo Disney Resort includes the Tokyo Disney Resort Welcome Center, the Bon Voyage Disney shop, Ikspiari – a Downtown Disney style shopping and entertainment area, and Cirque du Soleil Theatre Tokyo. You can view the latest maps of the Tokyo Disney Resort, Tokyo Disneyland and Tokyo DisneySea by visiting www.tokyodisneyresort.co.jp/index_e.html and clicking on "Map Download" in the lower right–hand corner. The Official Hotels are situated around Tokyo Disneyland, and the three Disney Hotels are centered near the parks' main entrances and Ikspiari. There are three primary transportation methods within the Resort: walking, Disney Resort Line, and the Disney Resort Cruiser. The Disney Resort Line is a monorail that shuttles guests along four stops throughout the resort for a fee. The Disney Resort Cruiser is a complimentary bus service from the hotels to the Bayside Station of the Disney Resort Line practically requiring that guests purchase a monorail ticket. Tickets are complimentary for guests of the three Disney Hotels. Additionally, most of the nine "on property" Resort hotels – 3 Disney and 6 Official – allow you to check–in at a Service Counter at the JR Maihama rail station where you are likely to arrive. You can leave your luggage with them and they will deliver it to your room when it is ready so that you can immediately begin exploring the Tokyo Disney Resort. All hotels are western–style hotels with private bathrooms and traditional amenities (phone, alarm clock, TV, etc.).

> **HIDDEN MICKEY ALERT**
> Once aboard the Disney Resort Cruiser, you will no doubt notice the not–so–hidden handles for standing passengers in the classic Mickey shape, the Mickey ears in the bus' front grill, on the orange reflectors, the taillights and even those on the side rails as you enter the bus. However, take a close look at the vents near the ceiling and see if you can spot the Hidden Mickey.

There is a fee to utilize the Disney Resort Line. A single one–way ticket is $2.80 while unlimited passes range from $7.20 to $15.55 and are good for up to four days. Children ages 6 to 11 are half price and children under 6 are free.

The premier service you will experience throughout the Tokyo Disney Resort carries over to the hotels. Hotel staff will immediately greet you and ask to take your bags. They will keep them close while you check in and insist on accompanying you to your room. You do not have to let them do this, but it is best to allow it as they are expressing their gratitude that you are staying in their hotel. Remember, tipping is not customary in Japan and the bellhop will likely be embarrassed or confused if you try. This is one of the great things about being in Japan; enjoy the terrific service at no additional cost!

> **DID YOU KNOW?**
> There are an additional five Tokyo Disney Resort Partner Hotels located just outside of the resort and 15 Tokyo Disney Resort Good Neighbor Hotels spread throughout Tokyo.

Overview

There are three Disney hotels including the original Disney Ambassador Hotel, the Tokyo DisneySea Hotel MiraCosta and the Tokyo Disneyland Hotel. Each is as distinctive in its architecture and ambiance as the lands within Tokyo Disneyland. They are impressive and beautiful and the service is top–notch.

Seasonal Pricing

The pricing for the Disney hotels is broken down into four categories based on historical crowd levels. These include Value (least expensive), Regular, Peak and Top (most expensive). The Value pricing is typically available for mid–week stays in January, February, April, May, June and the first part of July. Peak and Top rates are generally in effect during July and August, around national holidays and many weekends throughout the year. Top prices can add as much as 60% to the already hefty hotel prices, so visiting in the Value season can save you a lot of Yen.

Disney Hotel Benefits

Tokyo Disney Resort cites 13 "benefits" to guests staying at the three Disney hotels. These benefits include Disney characters being interwoven into the décor of the hotels from the lobby to the hallway. Other features for guests staying at the Disney hotels are complimentary Baggage Delivery Service (they will deliver your bags form the train station) and Shopping Delivery Service (items purchased in the parks can be delivered to your hotel). Hotel guests will be guaranteed entrance to Tokyo Disneyland and Tokyo DisneySea – even during times of "attendance control". For the child in all of us, the Disney Channel is provided free of charge.

Reservations

You can make reservations online for the Disney Hotels, at www.tokyodisneyresort.co.jp. The Tokyo Disney Resort Vacation Maker will require that you create an account with username and password. It is a relatively simple planning tool to navigate, and the options are quite clear. Like all Japanese hotels, room rates include tax. You may also call the Tokyo Disney Reservation Center at +81–45–683–3333 between 9 am and 6 pm Tokyo time. Calling the resort is quite an experience! First, check with your phone carrier to confirm the international charges, as there are no "toll free" options when calling Tokyo. Second, remember that to access out of country numbers from the U.S., you must first dial 011 – so the number as you would dial it from the U.S. is 011–81–45–683–3333. Third, be patient. This line is often busy – especially when the Reservation Center first opens. When the call is answered by the automated system, it will be answered in Japanese. Be prepared to hear some "Japanenglish" here, like "Main Menu" mixed into the recording. Patience is a virtue; if you hang on the line for about 1 minute, the recording will repeat in a very clear and crisp English voice. You will be prompted to select "91" and, unfortunately, it will not do any good to try and select these prompts early. From there, you will be given instructions on speaking with an English–speaking agent. Be advised that odds are good your call will be terminated if there is no English–speaking agent available for your call. It's not unusual to call 5+ times before reaching an English–speaking agent. Once you do reach them, their English is excellent and they are delightful and incredibly helpful. In fact, during our research we asked a question that the Cast Member did not know the answer to and, after confirming we were making an international call, they asked for our number and called us back! Reservations may be made up to six months in advance. Saturday nights throughout the year quite often sell out a full six months ahead of time.

Rooms – Beds and Baths

All Disney Hotel rooms include a shower and tub or a shower/tub combo. The standard bed size is a "regular" bed which measures in at 120cm/47in and is roughly halfway between the size of a twin bed and a double bed. Many rooms also include a slightly smaller trundle which is the size of a twin bed 100cm/39in and some include a cruise bed for the very small; only 80cm/31in wide. The number of people each room can accommodate is established based on the number and sizes of beds.

Smoking

The Disney Ambassador Hotel and the Tokyo DisneySea MiraCosta offer both smoking and non–smoking rooms. The newer Tokyo Disneyland Hotel is 100% non–smoking. When making reservations online, you will have the option to select between smoking and non–smoking rooms.

Internet Access

Can't enjoy your Disney vacation without checking in at work? Internet access is available for no additional charge.

Disney Ambassador Hotel

Overview

The Disney Ambassador Hotel was the first "Disney" hotel to be built at the Tokyo Disney Resort. It opened in July 2000 under a license by the Walt Disney Company and, like the Tokyo parks, is owned and operated by the Oriental Land Company.

Contacting

You can reach the hotel directly at +81–47–305–1111 – don't forget to dial 011 first from the U.S. Your call will be answered by someone speaking Japanese. Ask to speak with someone in English and they will politely ask you, in English, to hold while they transfer your call.

HIDDEN MICKEY ALERT
The band that runs around the canopy of the hotel incorporates Hidden Mickey's throughout.

Theme

This Art Deco–themed jewel is situated in the heart of the Tokyo Disney resort. The Ambassador features 500 guest rooms, five restaurants, a stunning pool themed to the glitz and glitter of Hollywood's Golden Age, two shops and banquet and wedding facilities. Walking into the lobby is a treat and the chic décor is accented by constellations that highlight the lobby ceiling. Look close and you will find these "constellations" are Disney–made with many of the most beloved characters shining bright.

NOT SO HIDDEN MICKEY ALERT
Mickey is woven into the ironwork of the curved staircase located at the opposite end of the lobby from the elevator.

Location

The Disney Ambassador Hotel is located about halfway between the entrances to Tokyo DisneySea and Tokyo Disneyland and is nestled between the Cirque du Soleil Theatre Tokyo and Ikspiari. There are beautiful courtyards surrounding the hotel that, in typical Disney fashion, help transition guests into the 1930s art–deco theme.

HIDDEN MICKEY ALERT
Each of the tall vertical lights in the lobby sport a Hidden Mickey on the bottom.

Getting to the Parks

Guests have complimentary access to the Disney Resort Cruiser – a bus that provides transportation from the Disney Ambassador to the "Bus & Taxi Terminal" located in front of each park. Guests may also use the Disney Resort Line for a fee.

Rooms

The Ambassador offers five different types of rooms and five different types of suites. You have probably heard that Japanese hotel rooms are small relative to U.S. hotels. You won't find this to be the case at the Ambassador. The rooms range in size from 34 sq meters (365 sq. ft) to 97 sq meters (1,044 sq ft) – for reference, this puts the smallest rooms on par with the Walt Disney World Resort's Deluxe resort room size, or they are the same approximate size as the Standard Rooms at the Disneyland Hotel in California.

All rooms are well–appointed and comparable to a 4–star hotel. The room's amenities include a special touch of Disney with Disney characters incorporated into the furnishings and décor. Each room type is decorated in essentially the same motif. Prices range from $311 to more than $3,300 per night. Room options include:

> **HIDDEN MICKEY ALERT**
> There is a large mural by the curved staircase located at the opposite end of the lobby from the elevator. The mural depicts a castle. Look at the flag at the top of the highest turret. Just to the right of the flag is a Mickey hidden in the clouds and sky.

Standard Room

These rooms are very comfortable; the décor is light and rooms well–lit. These rooms include two "regular" beds, a trundle bed, two chairs and a small table. There is a television, phone, closet and drawers for clothes. These rooms generally accommodate up to three guests.

> **HIDDEN MICKEY ALERT**
> The decorative band around the lamps in many rooms is really a collection of dozens of Hidden Mickeys. Likewise, "full" Mickeys and Minnies may be found hidden in the wall paper band around the top of the rooms.

Superior Room

The difference between the Superior and Standard is size; the bed count is the same. The Superior rooms include a small sofa. The space is very generous, but considering you are at the Tokyo Disney Resort to enjoy the parks, we don't think it's worth the extra money.

Triple Room

Triple Rooms contain all the amenities of the Superior room but include a third regular bed instead of a trundle. The trundle is included with Standard and Superior rooms, so you have to weigh the extra $20–80 per night to upgrade a trundle to a regular bed.

> **HIDDEN MICKEY ALERT**
> The hotel has two types of bell carts. One sports a hidden Mickey at the top while the other showcases Mickey on the side.

Deluxe Room

These are beautiful and spacious rooms. There is plenty of room to relax and the lighting is terrific due to the additional windows.

Family Room

The Family Room is larger than most apartments. Clocking in at over 1,000 square feet, the room includes four regular beds and a trundle. The bathroom is very large and will accommodate three or more just in there! The rooms are set up with two full-sized beds on each side of the room separated by a living area with chair, couch, television, and a table for four. An additional bed – for a grand total of six with the trundle – may be requested for roughly $63 per night. The price per bed is higher in this room than the Standard or Deluxe rooms. While the living space is wonderful, you may prefer to get away from your traveling companions – especially if they are your in–laws – after a long day at the parks.

> **HIDDEN MICKEY ALERT**
> There is a large white mural atop the main entrance. The three circles of a Hidden Mickey may be found just left of the center and just to the upper right of the sea snail shell.

AMBASSADOR HOTEL ROOM OVERVIEW

Room Type	Size (sq ft)	Beds	Value ($)	Regular ($)	Peak ($)	Top ($)
Standard	365–409	2+	311–511	377–566	455–655	500–699
Superior	441	2+	411–544	488–622	611–733	655–777
Triple	484	3	488	533	633	677
Deluxe	484–603	2+	533–611	588–666	677–755	722–799
Family	1044	4+	1,177	1,299	1,443	1,476

+denotes a trundle bed is included in addition to the number of regular beds

Ambassador Lounge

The Ambassador Lounge allows guests staying on the Ambassador Floor (Concierge Floor) or in a suite to utilize the services offered in the Lounge. These services include complimentary beverages and continental breakfast. Additionally, the staff will handle your check–in and check–out procedures. Standard and Superior rooms are available on the Ambassador Floor for a 20% – 46% premium. In those instances where the price gap is lower (+/– 20%), the price of breakfast and drinks can easily offset the cost increase.

Special Rooms and Suites

In addition to the rooms reviewed, there is one special room type and five types of suites at the Disney Ambassador Hotel. All suites except the

Panorama Suites and some Garden Suites are located on the Ambassador Floors, and all suites allow guests access to the Ambassador Lounge. These suites with their living areas, large bathrooms and unique décor (Fantasia, Mickey and Ambassador) will knock your socks off and empty your wallet. Suites range in price from $910 to more than $3,300 per night.

Donald Duck Room

These rooms are located on the second floor and have a view of the Palm Garden Pool. They are "decked out" – sailor pun intended – in Donald Duck colors. The bedspread looks like Donald's clothing, complete with a red bow–tie pillow. The headboards of the two beds look like Donald's feet and a picture Donald and Daisy dancing is etched into the mirror. Custom Donald Duck wallpaper lines the suite and everything is decorated in Donald's colors – yellow, blue, and red. The Donald Duck Room ranges from $533–$722 per night.

Garden Suite

The Garden Suites have a view of the chic Palm Garden Pool. They are available on Standard and Ambassador Floors. These suites range between $910–1,465 per night.

Panorama Suite

The Panorama Suites, as the name would suggest, sport an enormous panoramic window running nearly the entire length of the suite. These suites are available on Standard Floors only and range between $1165–1465 per night.

Fantasia Suite

This tastefully appointed room showcases designs, art and décor celebrating the Disney film *Fantasia*. The Fantasia Suite costs $1,940 per night.

Mickey's Premiere Suite

Stylized like the 1930s, like the rest of the Ambassador, Mickey's Premier Suite features portraits, statuettes, and "hidden" Mickey designs. Mickey's Premiere Suite costs $1,940 per night.

Ambassador Suite

This suite has it all. It features a full living area, dining area, working area, a king–sized bed and breathtaking views of Tokyo Disneyland. The suite also carries the heftiest price tag at the Ambassador Hotel, at $3,330 per night.

Pool

The Disney Ambassador's Palm Garden Pool is an oasis taken directly out of 1930s Hollywood. Complete with cabana style coverings, this pool sports a main swimming area and lap pool. This is a delightful place for an evening stroll when the pool's lighting really shines. The pool, along with the Palm Garden Bar, is open only during the summer. There is no fee to use the Palm Garden Pool and lockers and towels are available to guests at no additional charge.

Workout Facilities

There are no workout facilities at the Disney Ambassador, though going for a jog is always free!

Dining

There are five dining options at the Disney Ambassador Hotel – each with very different offerings. Other than breakfast at Chef Mickey, you do not need to be a guest of the hotel to dine at these restaurants.

Chef Mickey

Like Goofy's Kitchen at the Disneyland Hotel in California and Chef Mickey's at the Contemporary Resort in Florida, Chef Mickey at the Ambassador Hotel is a character buffet. During meals, a varying cast of Disney characters will make the rounds to each table to play with kids and adults, pose for pictures, and sign autographs. This is a unique experience where the characters

> **NOT SO HIDDEN MICKEY ALERT**
> Mickeys, hidden and not, abound in this restaurant. Be sure to take a look at the medal around the neck of Chef Mickey's statue.

come to you. There are three price points for the buffet including ages 4–6, ages 7–12, and ages 13 and older (there is no charge children 3 and under). For adults, prices are $35, $40, and $45, respectively, for breakfast, lunch and dinner buffets. The 4–6 year old children are about half that price while the 7–12 year old children are about two–thirds the price. Attire for this restaurant is theme–park casual.

Empire Grill

The Empire Grill is the premier restaurant at the Ambassador Hotel. It is only open for lunch and dinner. This restaurant proclaims itself as California–style Cuisine offering fusions of Italian, Mexican and Asian cooking. Cocktails and wine are served in this elegant and formal restaurant and it is open for lunch and dinner. Prices start at $52 for the buffet.

Hana

This Japanese offering provides a true Tokyo experience. The restaurant offers Teppan–yaki grill (an iron griddle is used to cook the food) options as well as traditional Kaiseki (meals served in courses). Additionally, Hana offers private rooms for families or groups preferring a more intimate atmosphere. Hana offers breakfast, lunch and dinner. Set course prices start at $50.

Tick Tock Diner

This diner is decorated in contemporary art deco and has music notes decorating the floor. They offer Mickey Shaped rolls, sandwiches, soups, coffee and sweet snacks – they even offer it to go. The restaurant serves breakfast, lunch and dinner. Prices range from $9 for sandwiches and $5.50 for snacks.

Hyperion Lounge

Hyperion Lounge is located just off the lobby and is a beautiful area to snack on light appetizers or cakes, sip afternoon tea, or enjoy cocktails. Breakfast is available each morning and the Lounge is open through lunch and dinner. Prices range from $11.50 for an ice cream float to $6.50 for a soda.

Shops

There are two shops located within the Disney Ambassador Hotel.

Sunset Sundries

Sunset Sundries is a tiny shop providing traditional hotel lobby shop items such as sundries, snacks, baby food, and medicine.

Festival Disney

Festival Disney is a large Disney souvenir shop offering Tokyo Disney Resort memorabilia, Disney character souvenirs, toys and clothing, and original merchandise which is only available in the Disney Ambassador Hotel.

Parking

Parking is $11 per day.

Currency Exchange

Foreign currency exchange is available at the Front Desk for hotel guests only. The exchange rate offered is the same as the rate at Tokyo Disneyland and Tokyo DisneySea's Customer Relations. Utilizing your credit card for charges or ATM card for cash will provide a more favorable rate.

Baggage Storage

The Disney Ambassador Hotel's Guest Service Counter will store your baggage prior to check–in and/or after check–out so that you can enjoy the Resort on your day of arrival and day of departure without worrying about your luggage.

Reservations

Reservations may be made online at www.tokyodisneyresort.co.jp or over the telephone at +81–45–683–3333 (see Reservations under Disney Hotels for details). The Tokyo Disney Reservation Center is open between 9 am and 6 pm Tokyo time and all rates quoted include tax. Remember, you must first dial 011 – so the number you would dial it from the U.S. is 011–81–45–683–3333 – and it may take several attempts for your call to go through. Listen through the prompts until you can select "English". Reservations may be made up to six months in advance and Saturday nights throughout the year often sell out a full six months ahead of time.

Tokyo DisneySea Hotel MiraCosta

Overview

Stunning. Elegant. Luxurious. Mediterranean Paradise. These are just a few words to describe the MiraCosta – the only Tokyo Disney Hotel actually *inside* a theme park. Words alone cannot describe this incredible hotel. It's as if the finest hotel on the Mediterranean Coast were picked up and delivered to Tokyo Bay and then the Disney Imagineers went to work adding the Disney touch to an incredible piece of art. This hotel will make you feel like you are walking in an Italian painting. The MiraCosta opened in September 2001 on the same day as Tokyo DisneySea. The hotel is owned and operated by the Oriental Land Company.

> **HIDDEN MICKEY ALERT**
> Intricate iron work decorates the glass doors outside the Hotel MiraCosta's main entrance. Look closely at the iron work for a number of Hidden Mickeys.

Contacting

You can reach the hotel directly at +81–47–305–2222 – don't forget to dial 011 first from the U.S. Your call will be answered by someone speaking Japanese. Ask to speak with someone in English and they will, in English, politely ask you to hold while they transfer your call.

Theme

The Tokyo DisneySea Hotel MiraCosta is an Italian–themed masterpiece. From the moment guests arrive at the sprawling courtyard that makes up the front entrance and stroll through the columned promenade into the marble lobby, they know they have arrived somewhere truly spectacular. The lobby boasts a stained glass duomo, vibrant murals, richly decorated Italian marble columns and a hand–carved ship. This homage celebrates the sea and the rich history of the Mediterranean.

> **NOT SO HIDDEN MICKEY ALERT**
> The ship in the center of the lobby sports Mickey Mouse as the Captain and Minnie Mouse as the mermaid on the front. Stand back a ways to see Mickey.

Lost in the décor, guests will immediately forget they are in Japan's largest city at its most popular tourist destination. The façade is flawless and highlights the sea–side architecture next to DisneySea's Mediterranean Harbor. Every hallway and walkway feels like part of a nautical adventure. The rooms that face Tokyo DisneySea and its centerpiece, Mount Prometheus, are sublime. Guests will not regret staying in any room in this magnificent resort.

Getting to the Parks

The MiraCosta is located inside Tokyo DisneySea and offers quick and easy access to the park. Guests staying at this hotel have access to a special entrance to Tokyo DisneySea. Guests will receive complimentary access to the Disney Resort Line monorail to access Tokyo Disneyland. The monorail provides easy access to Ikspiari and the Tokyo Disneyland Main Entrance. Complementary passes can be picked up at the Tokyo Disney Resort Welcome Center or at the Hotel MiraCosta.

Rooms

The Tokyo DisneySea Hotel MiraCosta offers three different types of rooms and five different types of "Speciale" rooms and suites. These rooms are very nicely sized ranging from 37 sq meters (398 sq ft) to 43 sq meters (463 sq ft). For reference, the smallest rooms are larger than rooms at Walt Disney World Resort's Deluxe resorts, and quite a bit larger than Standard Rooms at the Disneyland Hotel or Disney's Grand Californian Hotel in California.

All rooms are five–star quality. The rich and vibrant colors are accented with cherry and mahogany furniture. Like all Disney rooms, the MiraCosta's amenities include a special touch of Disney with Disney characters incorporated into the furnishings and décor, albeit in a much

HIDDEN MICKEY ALERT

The dome in the center lobby boasts eight magnificent murals. Each of these murals ties into one of the themed ports at Tokyo DisneySea and sports a Hidden Mickey. If you have trouble finding any of them, the staff of the Hotel MiraCosta will be happy to assist. Begin with the mural depicting a woman in red and gold holding a masquerade mask in front of a building that looks like the Tokyo DisneySea Hotel MiraCosta with a Venetian gondola on the left side. From there, the descriptions move clockwise.

1. Masquerade Woman (Mediterranean Harbor): The woman at the center of this mural is standing in front of a semi–circle wrought iron fence. Located on the right hand–side of this iron work is a full Mickey profile.

2. Red–Haired Goddess with Fire (Mysterious Island) – On the far right–hand side of the mural, just below the dome and bridge is a Hidden Mickey.

3. Mermaid and Sea Dragon Mural (Mermaid Lagoon): A full profile Hidden Mickey may be found on the left hand–side, just to the left of the sea dragon's tail and just above the coral shaped like Ariel's castle from the Little Mermaid. This full profile Hidden Mickey is incorporated into the undersea bubbles.

4. Woman and Smoking Lamps Mural (Arabian Coast): At the base of mural are a number of plants and reeds at the edge of the water. Just to the right of the right–hand smoking genie lamp is a full profile Hidden Mickey in the open space between the plants to the right of the lamp and the tall set of plants just to the right of the open space.

5. Sailor with Orange Flags Behind and Flanked by Two Ships Mural: Take a look at the top sail of the ship to the left of the center character. There is a circle on the top sail and a dark Hidden Mickey within the circle.

6. Tribesman in Jungle (Lost River Delta): Located on either side of the center character near the top is an ancient design. The design to the right has a Hidden Mickey profile incorporated into the circular design.

7. Winged Goddess Mural (Port Discovery): The center character is standing in front of an ornate metal design just above the bottom golden border of the mural. On the right–hand side of this metal design, there are three circles near the top that form a classic Hidden Mickey. It's tough to spot, but it is there.

8. Lady Liberty in front of Red and White Flag (American Waterfront): This is among the toughest to find. There is a building to the left of the center character with two flags. Find the flag closest to the center character and follow it down to the base of the building. Immediately to the right of the base and at the base of the skyscraper next to it is a full profile Hidden Mickey.

more subtle fashion than most. Each room type is decorated in essentially the same luxurious motif. Prices range from $377 to more than $5,500 per night.

In addition to room type, the view plays a tremendous role in determining price at this hotel. There are three "sides" to the Hotel MiraCosta:

Tuscany Side
These rooms overlook the Tokyo Disney Resort and the grounds and garden of the hotel. Specifically, the views include the entrance to the hotel or the entrance to Tokyo DisneySea. The views are beautiful.

Venice Side
These rooms overlook the Palazzo Canals inside the Tokyo DisneySea park. As you might imagine, the picturesque view is enhanced at night as "Venice" comes to life.

Porto Paradiso Side
The name says it all – paradise. These rooms overlook the Mediterranean Harbor area of Tokyo DisneySea. Some rooms have a breathtaking view of Mount Prometheus including the bay with the fortress at its base.

Room options include:

Superior Rooms
These luxurious rooms are spacious and include two "regular" beds, a trundle bed, two chairs, and a moderate sized table; most include a sofa. The bathrooms are well appointed. The rooms have a television, phone, and armoire with drawers. These rooms generally accommodate up to three guests.

Balcony Rooms
The primary difference between the Balcony rooms and the Superior Rooms is, well, the balcony, and the view. The Balcony rooms have the best views on the Porto Paradiso Side of the hotel. It's hard to justify the extra $100–300 per night for these rooms until you see Mount Prometheus from your room at night. It is Disney magic at it's finest.

Triple Rooms
Triple Rooms contain all the amenities of the Superior rooms plus a third regular bed. The trundle is included with Superior and Balcony rooms

and not available in the Triple, so the bed count remains the same. The Triple Room is not available with a Harbor View (only the Piazza View on the Porto Paradiso Side). As such, Superior Rooms can easily cost more than the Triple Rooms. The biggest difference is size and that a larger regular bed has replaced the trundle. However, since the Superior Room's trundle can be stowed, usable square footage is about the same.

The range of prices reflects the range of views associated with each room. The most expensive are those on the Porto Paradiso Side, followed by the Venice Side and then the Tuscany Side of the Tokyo DisneySea MiraCosta.

TOKYO DISNEYSEA HOTEL MIRACOSTA ROOM OVERVIEW

Room Type	Size (sq ft)	Beds	Value ($)	Regular ($)	Peak ($)	Top ($)
Superior	398–431	2+	377–744	455–810	566–910	633–966
Triple	463	3	444–555	522–644	633–766	699–833
Balcony	398–463	2+	655–744	722–810	821–910	877–966

+denotes a trundle bed is included in addition to the number of regular beds

Salone dell' Amico

The Salone dell' Amico is reserved for guests staying in one of the two "Speciale" room types or three suite types. This refined and upscale version of a Concierge Suite – complete with oil paintings, rich furniture, columns and divine rugs – is located on the hotel's highest level. As such, it has one of the best views of Mediterranean Harbor anywhere in the Tokyo Disney Resort. The Salone's services include complimentary beverages and continental breakfast. Additionally, the staff will handle your check–in and check–out procedures. The Superior Room Harbor View on the Porto Paradiso Side of the hotel is the only room with optional access to the Salone at an 11–28% premium. The savings on breakfast and drinks may easily offset the additional cost.

"Speciale" Rooms and Suites

In addition to the rooms reviewed, there are two "Speciale" room types and three suite types. With the exception of the Terrace room, each of these spectacular accommodations is located on the Porto Paradiso Side. They range in price from $640 to more than $5,200 per night:

Terrace Rooms

The only "Speciale" room with an option of the Venice Side or Porto Paradiso side, these rooms are appointed like the Superior or Balcony rooms, but include a 30 sq meter (323 sq foot) terrace complete with plants, a bistro table for four and a unique way to enjoy an afternoon break or to enjoy Tokyo DisneySea at night. These rooms range from $688–910 per night.

Harbor Rooms

These rooms are very large and feature open spaces, a large bed, living area, and table for four as well as outstanding views. These rooms range from $1,032–1,288 per night.

Porto Paradiso Suites

These expansive suites are located on the third and fourth floors of the MiraCosta and feature large bathrooms with a separate walk–in shower and tub, spacious living area and a separate bedroom. The views from the Porto Paradiso side of the hotel are unmatched! This suite costs $1,942 per night.

MiraCosta Suites

A larger version of the Porto Paradiso Suites, these rooms offer unobstructed views of Mediterranean Harbor, Mount Prometheus and Tokyo Bay. This suite costs $2,775 per night.

Il Magnifico Suite

If the Tokyo DisneySea Hotel MiraCosta is luxurious, then the Il Magnifico Suite is divine. This room's centerpiece is an inset mural above the elegant living space. You may actually decide not to visit the parks if you stay in this room at a whopping $5,550 per night.

Pool, Spa and Workout Facilities

There are two pools at the Tokyo DisneySea Hotel MiraCosta. The pools, along with the sauna, jacuzzi and workout facilities make up the Terme Venezia and may be enjoyed by guests for $33 per person per day in the summer, and $22 during other seasons when the Outdoor Pool is closed. Children ages 4–11 are half price.

Outdoor Pool

This "Summer Only" pool is situated in the heart of "Venice" and showcases Italian marble statues around the property featuring Disney characters.

Indoor Pool

The indoor heated pool is situated among towering columns, cavernous alcoves, and intricate mosaic tile. The hot tub – big enough for a party of 20 or more – is situated next to the indoor pool among frescos and columns while the sauna provides a much–appreciated respite from a day (or days) of theme–park going. This indoor facility is beautiful and even if you are not a guest of the MiraCosta, it is worth a look.

Workout Facilities

A state–of–the art workout facility is available.

Dining

There are four places to dine at the Tokyo DisneySea Hotel MiraCosta and each is a testament to it's grand style. The MiraCosta actually requests guests limit their visit to 120 minutes at two of these restaurants, since guests have been known to linger excessively enjoying their surroundings.

Oceano

The marquee restaurant of the hotel serves Mediterranean cuisine and Faces Mediterranean Harbor in Tokyo DisneySea. The restaurant is styled to enhance the oceanic them found throughout this hotel. Each dining room is themed for an undersea adventure. The main dining room will make you feel as if you are "under the sea" as the décor, aquariums and stylized furniture combine to transport guest to the bottom of the ocean for a delicious meal. Other rooms include the Pearl Room, whose

> **HIDDEN MICKEY ALERT**
> Several dishes including the "bamboo" bowls served to guests have Hidden Mickeys.

walls are fashioned to look like the inside of an oyster complete with pearl–shaped chandelier. Oceano is opened for breakfast, lunch and dinner and meal options include buffet or a course menu. Prices start at $33.

Silk Road Garden

Silk Road Garden offers excellent Cantonese Chinese fare. Guests are surrounded by a mural showcasing Marco Polo's journey. The oversized columns have layer after layer of intricate Chinese carvings and Chinese lanterns hang from the ceiling. The ambience makes guests feel they have been whisked away and the food is terrific. Silk Road Garden is open for lunch and dinner and dishes are offered as a buffet or a la carte. Lunch buffets start at $22 and dinner starts at $50.

BellaVista Lounge

The BellaVista Lounge is another in a long line of Tokyo Disney Resort locales that truly lives up to its name; the "beautiful view" from this elegantly styled lounge is Mediterranean Harbor and Mount Prometheus. Time your meal correctly and you could have the "best seat in the house" for any of the shows on Mediterranean Harbor. The Japanese offerings provide a true Tokyo experience. The restaurant offers Teppan–yaki grill options as well as traditional Kaiseki course menus. The BellaVista Lounge is open for breakfast, lunch and dinner. It also serves snacks and late evening cocktails. Prices start at $31.

Hippocampi

Named for the Greek mythological half–fish, half–horse, this pool bar serves sandwiches, soft drinks, cocktails and snacks throughout the day. It's a great place for a quick snack while enjoying the pool (the milk shakes are great!). Hippocampi is open until the early evening. Attire for the Lounge is "anything goes", as many patrons are taking a quick break from swimming. Guests do not need to pay the daily fee to use the Terme Venezia in order to enjoy Hippocampi. It is open seasonally.

Shops

There are two shops located at the Tokyo DisneySea Hotel MiraCosta.

Minnie Lisa Sundries

Minnie Mouse has been made to look like Mona Lisa and her portrait greets guests as they enter the sundry shop. The offerings are typical, though notably diverse, and include snacks, sundry items, baby food and medicine.

MickeyAngelo Gifts

The marble floors are inset with Mickey ears and the ceilings are adorned with intricately detailed murals. This shop offers Tokyo Disney Resort memorabilia, Disney character souvenirs, toys and clothing, and original merchandise only available in the MiraCosta.

Parking

Parking is $16 per day.

Currency Exchange

Foreign currency exchange is available at the Front Desk for hotel guests only. The exchange rate offered is the same as the rate at Tokyo Disneyland and Tokyo DisneySea's Customer Relations. Utilizing your credit card for charges or ATM card for cash will provide a more favorable rate.

Baggage Storage

The Tokyo DisneySea Hotel MiraCosta's Guest Service Counter will store your baggage prior to check–in and/or after check–out so that you may enjoy the Resort on your day of arrival and day of departure without worrying about your luggage.

Reservations

The Tokyo Disney Reservation Center is open between 9 am and 6 pm Tokyo time and all rates quoted include tax. Remember, you must first dial 011 – so the number as you would dial it from the U.S. is 011–81–45–683–3333 – and it may take several attempts for your call to go through. Listen through the prompts until you can select "English". Reservations may be made up to six months in advance and Saturday nights throughout the year often sell out a full six months ahead of time.

Tokyo Disneyland Hotel
Overview

The Tokyo Disneyland Hotel is the newest of the three Disney hotels. This turn–of–the–century Victorian style hotel is elegant and grand with vibrant colors. The most astonishing, however, is how large this hotel appears. The size is nothing less than stunning. This hotel is the first thing guests see as they arrive to Tokyo Disney Resort via bus; and it is jaw–dropping. The hotel's décor is in line with Disney's Grand Floridian Resort at the Walt Disney World Resort. Similarly, this is what it would look like if Disneyland's Plaza Inn or the Magic Kingdom's Crystal Palace were converted to hotels. Throughout the lobby, you will see hotel employees interacting with children and talking to them about their vacation. This is the only Disney hotel with all non–smoking rooms. In fact, the only place to smoke at the hotel is in a "smoking room" located on the third floor. The Tokyo Disneyland Hotel opened in July 2008 and is owned and operated by the Oriental Land Company.

> **HIDDEN MICKEY ALERT**
> The marble lobby floor is home to several mouse ears.

> **HIDDEN MICKEY ALERT**
> In the Information area in the Disneyland Hotel's lobby is a giant globe. Be sure to take a look at Japan to find a Hidden Mickey.

Contacting

You can reach the hotel directly at +81–47–305–3333 – don't forget to dial 011 first from the U.S. Your call will be answered by someone speaking Japanese. Ask to speak with someone in English and they will politely ask you, in English, to hold while they transfer your call.

Theme

The Tokyo Disneyland Hotel is a turn–of–the century Victorian hotel seemingly pulled right out of Main Street U.S.A. From the Atrium Lobby to the beautiful Gardens, Walt Disney – who loved this time period – is present throughout this hotel. The elegant lobby soars nearly 10 stories and is topped with a beautiful atrium. Oil paintings can be seen behind the front desk and Victorian gardens are abundant. From *Alice's Garden* inspired by Alice In Wonderland to Mickey as the Sorcerer's Apprentice in *Fantasia Court*, Disney characters fill these gardens with pure delight. *Mickey & Friends Square* shows off topiary characters while *Sherwood Garden* is a classical garden with a lovely pond and gazebo. The façade towers above the grounds as the nine–floor hotel culminates with Victorian turrets. Filled with fine craftsmanship, over–stated elegance and subtle Disney references, this hotel feels more like a Ritz Carlton than a Disney hotel and, to us, does not quite capture the grandeur and adventure found in the Tokyo DisneySea Hotel MiraCosta nor the throwback fun of Hollywood's Golden Age at the Disney Ambassador Hotel.

> **HIDDEN MICKEY ALERT**
> There is an area on the lobby floor with a huge art deco rug. Look along the edge toward the center for a purplish gray Hidden Mickey in the circles' center.

Getting to the Parks

The Tokyo Disneyland Hotel is situated directly across from the Main Entrance to Tokyo Disneyland separated only by the tracks of the Disney Resort Line Monorail and ticket booths. Guests of the hotel have a special entrance to Tokyo Disneyland – this entrance is generally available only during opening time when crowds are high. It is available to guests throughout their stay excluding the check–in date. To access Tokyo DisneySea, guests will receive complimentary access to the Disney Resort Line monorail, which has four stops throughout the resort. This provides easy access to Ikspiari and the Tokyo DisneySea Main Entrance. Complementary passes may be picked up at the Tokyo Disney Resort Welcome Center or at the Tokyo Disneyland Hotel.

> **HIDDEN MICKEY ALERT**
> Each white garbage can has the Disneyland Hotel insignia on the side in gold. Look at the top of the design for the famous mouse ears.

Rooms

The Tokyo Disneyland Hotel offers an exhaustive list of room types. The list has been condensed below to focus on the four most common room types and includes an overview of the nine remaining room types plus two suite types. The four most common rooms range in size from 40 sq meters (431 sq ft) to 59 sq meters (635 sq ft) – for reference, the smallest rooms are roughly the size of a standard room at the Grand Floridian at the Walt Disney World Resort and 25% larger than standard rooms at the Disneyland Resort's Grand Californian.

> **HIDDEN MICKEY ALERT**
> The hallways of the hotel have a contemporary art deco carpet. Look closely at the design and you will find some Hidden Mickeys.

The rooms are very nicely appointed and are five–star quality. The light, yet rich colors that reflect the Victorian era permeate through every room. Ceilings feature thick crown molding with recessed insets painted in light pastels. The wallpaper is classic Victorian and Disney characters are tastefully woven into the decor. The richly decorated beds feature a small medallion of Cinderella's Castle on the headboard. The bathrooms are sizeable and the beautiful tubs are surrounded by marble–style tile with a stylish mosaic on the wall. Each room type is decorated in similar fashion. Prices range from $377 to more than $5,500 per night.

In addition to room types, there are two premier view types: Park View and Park Grand View. The latter rooms are located directly in front of Tokyo Disneyland. These views have a significant impact on the price of the room and account for the substantial price fluctuations.

Superior Rooms

These elegant rooms are spacious and include two "regular" beds, a trundle bed, a sofa, two chairs, and moderate sized table. The bathrooms are quite nice and the vanity is located outside the shower and toilet. The rooms have a television, phone, and armoire with drawers. These rooms are available in Standard View, Park View, Park Grand View and Concierge Level (which includes Park Grand View). These rooms generally accommodate up to four guests.

Superior Alcove Rooms

These rooms are exactly the same as the Superior Rooms except that the couch has been replaced with a bed in the alcove of the room. Essentially, this allows a fourth guest to stay in the room for about $40 more per night compared to the Superior Room. These rooms are available in Standard

View, Park View, Park Grand View and Concierge Level (which includes Park Grand View).

Deluxe Rooms

Deluxe Rooms offer two regular beds or one larger bed (a trundle only comes with the rooms with two regular beds). These rooms are very large and feature a living area next to the windows complete with side tables and coffee table. These rooms are available in Standard View only.

Corner Rooms

As the name might suggest, these rooms are located in the corners of the hotel and, like the Deluxe, offer two regular beds or one larger bed. The living area features two arm chairs and a coach that turns into a sofa bed (believe it or not, there is an extra fee to use the sofa bed!). These rooms are available in Standard View and Park View.

TOKYO DISNEYLAND HOTEL ROOM OVERVIEW

Room Type	Size (sq ft)	Beds	Value ($)	Regular ($)	Peak ($)	Top ($)
Superior	431	2+	377-655	455-733	577-855	633-910
Superior Alcove	431	3+	422-699	500-777	622-899	677-955
Deluxe	517	2+	488-522	566-599	688-722	744-777
Corner	635	2+	555-655	633-733	755-855	810-910

+denotes a trundle bed is included in addition to the number of regular beds

Character Rooms

Character Rooms are located above the main entrance to the Tokyo Disneyland Hotel and are Superior, Superior Alcove, Deluxe or Corner Rooms with a twist. Instead of the general variety of Disney characters represented in the room in pictures, wall paper, furniture, etc., the Character Rooms offer a specific group of Disney characters themed to the room. In all other ways, these rooms are identical to their counterparts. All things considered, the cost difference can be as low as $50 per night difference and could be a real treat if these characters mean something special to you or a member of your party.

Disney's Peter Pan Rooms

The Peter Pan Rooms feature photos and wallpaper with Peter, Wendy, Captain Hook, Mr. Smee and the rest of the stars of this 1953 classic film.

The headboards feature a medallion of Captain Hook's ship instead of Cinderella's Castle. These rooms are available in Superior or Superior Alcove and range in price from $433–733 per night.

Disney's Alice in Wonderland Rooms

The Alice Rooms feature photos and wallpaper with Alice, the White Rabbit, and other zany characters from Walt Disney's 1951 movie. The headboards feature the Mad Hatter's Hat instead of Cinderella's Castle. These rooms are available in Superior only and range in price from $433–688 per night.

Disney's Snow White Rooms

The original Disney Masterpiece from 1937 is the headliner in the Snow White Rooms. Here, guests will find all their favorite Dwarfs in wallpaper and décor along with the Princess. These rooms are available in Deluxe only, though a few also have an alcove bed, and range in price from $522–821 per night.

Disney's Cinderella Rooms

Cinderella, her pumpkin coach, animal companions, Prince and evil step relatives from the 1950 feature are abundant throughout these rooms. The headboards retain their Cinderella's Castle inlay and are accented by the icy "Cinderella" blue of the comforters. Available as Corner Rooms only, the Cinderella Rooms range in price from $588–844 per night.

Additional Room Options
Luxury Triple Rooms

Triple Rooms are 61 square meters (657 sq ft) and feature three regular beds and a living area complete with two armchairs, coffee and side tables, lamps and a sofa bed that may be used for a fee. These rooms range from $588–877 and sleep fewer people than the Superior Alcove rooms. Dollar for dollar (or Yen for Yen), we recommend the Superior or Superior Alcove over the Triple. These rooms are available in Standard View only.

Junior Family Rooms

These rooms are 57 square meters (614 sq ft) and are similar to the Triple Rooms, except they feature a trundle bed for the fourth person included in the price. Also, the living area is separated from the bedroom by a door. Prices range from $588–977 per night. These rooms are available in Standard View and Park View.

Family Rooms

Essentially two rooms in one, the Family Rooms are 93 square meters (1,001 sq ft) and feature a bedroom with two regular beds and an alcove bed, and a separate living room with an additional alcove bed and sofa bed (at no additional charge!). These rooms also include two separate bathrooms – the least they could offer to justify the $1,188–1,843 per night price tag. These rooms are available in Park View and Concierge Level which includes Park View. The Concierge Level Family Rooms include two separate entrances and are two rooms connected by a common living room. The ability to close the door to the bedroom offers additional privacy. The window–side bathroom sports a whirlpool style tub.

Turret Rooms

As you probably guessed, these rooms were built into the turrets visible from outside the hotel. These 55 square meter (592 sq ft) rooms are available with two regular beds or one larger bed, a sofa bed (additional fee) and a few include a trundle. Similar in layout to the Corner Rooms, these feature two armchairs, a coffee table and side tables, lamps and a sofa. These rooms range from $688–1,021 per night and are only available on the Concierge Level.

Suites

There are two suites offered at the Tokyo Disneyland Hotel. They are exceptionally appointed from the tile artwork in the bathrooms with separate shower and whirlpool style tub to the canopy style beds and separate living areas. They are exclusively located on the top two floors (eighth and ninth) and have tremendous views of the Tokyo Disney Resort.

> **DID YOU KNOW?**
> Of the 705 rooms at the Tokyo Disneyland Hotel, 65 are concierge rooms and suites.

Disney's Magic Kingdom Suite

This suite has plenty of space to encompass the features listed above at 99 square meters (1,066 sq ft). The shimmering platinum of the décor and bedspreads will make guests feel like royalty. The Magic Kingdom Suite runs $2,775 per night.

Walt Disney Suite

It is only fitting in a hotel inspired by Walt Disney's youth, that the crème de la crème of the Tokyo Disneyland Hotel would be coined the Walt Disney Suite. This exquisite room is a massive 235 square meters (2,530 sq ft) and from the molding and artwork on the ceiling to the deep burgundy of the bedroom carpet, this suite is truly one–of–a–kind. The bathroom is as large as most hotel rooms. The whirlpool tub and walk in shower could each comfortably hold four or five people. The suite boasts a living room and dining room along with pictures of Walt Disney. Statues of Mickey Mouse put the finishing touches on this unmatched space. The Walt Disney Suite is $5,550 per night.

Marceline Salon

The Marceline Salon – owing its name to Walt Disney's childhood town of Marceline, Missouri – is a concierge floor style service and is reserved exclusively for guests staying in Concierge Rooms or Suites. The rich socialite club décor reflects the hotel's Victorian theme complete with antique–style furnishings. The Marceline Salone's services include complimentary beverages and continental breakfast, though the complimentary breakfast is served in the lobby's Dreamers Lounge. Additionally, the staff will handle your check–in and check–out procedures. Given the hefty room price–tags, even the drinks and breakfast may not completely offset the 16–22% premium for the Concierge Floor.

Pool

The Tokyo Disneyland Hotel's pool – Misty Mountains Pool – is hidden among the gardens. Guests who seek it out will find a Peter Pan themed pool complete with Skull Rock and a fountain sporting the crocodile from the 1953 film. The shadow of Captain Hook's ship graces the bottom of the pool and the area is a delightful place to get lost in Neverland. Many of the features and "look" of the Misty Mountain Pool is similar to the Neverland pool at the Disneyland Hotel in California. The pool is open only during the summer. There is no fee to use the Misty Mountain Pool and lockers and towels are available to guests at no additional charge.

Spa

The Tokyo Disneyland Hotel has a spa called Lilac Rose that offers a handful of spa services from massages to facials. Reservations may be made up to three months in advance – and you had better start saving now! A 60 minute massage starts at $200 and a 90 minute facial will cost $283. Our advice? Save your money and get your massage back home *after* the 12 hour plane ride....you may need it.

> **HIDDEN MICKEY ALERT**
> The beautiful marble floor of the spa entrance has a rather large set of mouse ears.

Gardens/Courtyards

There are four gardens and courtyards throughout the Tokyo Disneyland Hotel property. Each is themed to the Victorian style hotel in a very unique way. A walk through these gardens is a must for any guest; even those not staying at this hotel.

Alice's Garden

Alice in Wonderland is a natural movie to build a Victorian garden around. Located on the third floor deck, this sprawling garden featuring the inhabitants of Wonderland is a stroll worth taking.

Fantasia Court

Mickey Mouse as the Sorcerer's Apprentice from the 1940 film Fantasia stands in the fountain that is the centerpiece of this court. The whimsical fountain is surrounded by perfectly manicured topiaries. The Court is located on the third floor and sits on the opposite side of the driveway where guest vehicles and taxis pull into the hotel. While it is worth a look, its location, effectively on a street, leaves something to be desired.

Mickey & Friends Square

Topiaries of Mickey, Minnie and the gang welcome you to the Tokyo Disneyland Hotel. The Square resides between the Disney Resort Line Monorail station and the hotel entrance, effectively extending the ambiance of the World Bazaar from the entrance of Tokyo Disneyland to the entrance of the Tokyo Disneyland Hotel.

> **HIDDEN MICKEY ALERT**
> While standing in Mickey & Friends Square, look up at the balconies of the surrounding hotel rooms. Incorporated into the railing around the balconies are numerous Hidden Mickeys.

Sherwood Gardens

A relaxing stroll through Sherwood Gardens is a must for Tokyo Disneyland Hotel guests after a long day of touring the parks. This Victorian–style garden boasts a spectacular layout that transports guests to the gardens of some of the world's great chateaus. The gazebo, fountains and intricately designed pond combine together to deliver a wonderfully peaceful experience.

Dining

There are three restaurants at the Tokyo Disneyland Hotel. Each maintains very strong ties to the Victorian era embodied by the hotel.

Sherwood Garden Restaurant

This restaurant – a fairly standard, albeit well–done, take on the Victorian theme – offers a breakfast and dinner buffet and doubles as a café for the afternoon. The view from the Sherwood Garden Restaurant faces – you guessed it – Sherwood Garden. Breakfast is highlighted by a waffle station as well as traditional Japanese dishes and salads. Dinner includes intriguing seafood options and changes throughout the year. There is a selection of sandwiches, pastries and the like. A la carte sandwiches can be ordered starting at $7 and lunch buffets start at $35.

> **HIDDEN MICKEY ALERT**
> A beautiful white marble fountain sits against the wall with a marble Hidden Mickey that nearly blends in.

Canna

Canna's décor, like its cuisine, is a fusion of Victorian and Asian styles. The modern Asian setting is augmented by giant flower chandeliers hanging from the ceiling. This chic setting is matched by the fusion menu choices. This is a creative, imaginative and enjoyable restaurant. Canna is open for lunch and dinner and dishes are offered as a course menu or al la carte. Lunch buffets start at $50.

Dreamers Lounge

This lounge, located off the main lobby, is an inspiring work of architecture. From the massive window, to the Victorian columns that tower high above the room, the Dreamers Lounge is an elegant and uplifting setting. Light meals are served for breakfast, lunch and dinner. Guests staying in Concierge Rooms and Suites are served their complimentary continental breakfast in this room. Breakfast buffets start at $21.

Shops

There are two shops and two "studios" housed in the Tokyo Disneyland Hotel.

Looking Glass Gifts

This shop offers a combination of hotel gifts and traditional sundries.

Disney Mercantile

The unimposing doorway to this "quaint" shop looks like a store found on Main Street U.S.A. Disney Mercantile offers Tokyo Disney Resort memorabilia, Disney character souvenirs, toys and clothing, as well as original merchandise only available in the Tokyo Disneyland Hotel.

Bibbidi Bobbidi Boutique

Likes its namesakes at the Walt Disney World and Disneyland Resorts, this boutique will make a Disney Princess out of your little girl. For a Hippity Hoppity price, the fashion experts will help young ones select the right dress, style their hair, and apply makeup until they are near unrecognizable! Every little girl longs for the chance to shop here and Disney magic is everywhere. Be warned – $200 can disappear before the spell is complete.

Magic Memories Photo

Fun for the whole family, Magic Memories Photo will allow your entire group to dress up and step into the magic for one–of–a–kind portraits.

Laundry

Coin operated laundry facilities are available to hotel guests at $1.11 per wash or dry.

Parking

Parking is $16 per day.

Currency Exchange

Foreign currency exchange is available at the Front Desk for hotel guests only. The exchange rate offered is the same as the rate at Tokyo Disneyland and Tokyo DisneySea's Customer Relations. Utilizing your credit card for charges or ATM card for cash will provide a more favorable rate.

Baggage Storage

The Tokyo Disneyland Hotel's Guest Service Counter will store your baggage prior to check–in and after check–out so that you can enjoy the Resort on your day of arrival and day of departure without worrying about your luggage.

Reservations

The Tokyo Disney Reservation Center is open between 9 am and 6 pm Tokyo time and all rates quoted include tax. Remember, you must first dial 011 – so the number as you would dial it from the U.S. is 011–81–45–683–3333 – and it may take several attempts for your call to go through. Listen through the prompts until you can select "English". Reservations may be made up to six months in advance and Saturday nights throughout the year often sell out a full six months ahead of time.

Tokyo Disney Resort Official Hotels
Overview

There are six non–Disney hotels that are "on–property" at the Tokyo Disney Resort. They are called the Tokyo Disney Resort Official Hotels and include: Sunroute Plaza Tokyo, Tokyo Bay Maihama Hotel, Tokyo Bay Hotel Tokyu, Hilton Tokyo Bay, Hotel Okura Tokyo Bay and Sheraton Grande Tokyo Bay Hotel. These hotels are situated around the perimeter of the property, in the above order, moving counterclockwise from Tokyo Disneyland's main entrance. Each of these six hotels is independent of each other and the Tokyo Disney Resort hotels. Because of this, there are different services an amenities including availability of English speaking staff, pricing, amenities, and overall resort quality. What they all offer, however, is excellent proximity to Tokyo Disneyland and Tokyo DisneySea. An overview of these six hotels has been provided below.

> **TRAVEL TIP**
> Not all of Tokyo Disney Resort Official Hotels have English speaking staff available, though the employees will do their best to communicate with you and provide excellent service.

Pricing and Packages

Like the non–Disney owned hotels of the Downtown Disney Resort Area at the Walt Disney World Resort, the Tokyo Disney Resort Official Hotels are traditional hotels. Each hotel has different pricing and package structures. In order to compare and contrast, price them out individually. Unlike the Disney Hotels, each of these six will offer different promotions and special offers. If staying at the Tokyo Disney Resort is important to you, spending some time in front of your computer comparing prices at these hotels can save a significant amount of money and some real bargains may be found. Be sure to shop the traditional travel sites (Expedia, Travelocity, etc.) as they may offer discounted rates at these hotels. Be alert when comparing rates – unless otherwise stated, the rates listed on their web sites *include* service charges and taxes; this may not be the case with the travel sites. Many of these hotels also have a "Contact Us" form that allows you to communicate the hotel staff via email to ask any questions you may have. You can expect to hear back regarding your inquiry within 24–48 hours.

> **TRAVEL TIP**
> When reviewing the Tokyo Disney Resort Official Hotels' web sites, be sure to look for the "special offers" or "promotions" link as they can include steep discounts over the regular rates.

Tokyo Disney Resort Official Hotels Guest Benefits

The Tokyo Disney Resort cites eight "benefits" to guests staying at these six Official hotels. These benefits include complimentary Baggage Delivery Service (they will deliver your bags from the train station to your hotel). Another benefit is that hotel guests will be guaranteed entrance to Tokyo Disneyland and Tokyo DisneySea – even during times of peak attendance when admissions are being restricted. Each of these hotels has a shop called Disney Fantasy that is filled with Disney and Tokyo Disney Resort merchandise. Also, complimentary bus service aboard the Disney Resort Cruiser will transport guests between these hotels and the Bayside Station where guests can access the Disney Resort Line Monorail for a fee. These hotels also offer transportation from the JR Maihama Station (the train station where guests arrive by train from Tokyo) to the hotels via the Disney Resort Cruiser or hotel shuttle.

Reservations

Reservations may be made by contacting these hotels directly, visiting their web sites or through internet travel sites. Additionally, like the Disney Hotels, reservations are available via the Tokyo Disney Resort Reservation Center by calling +81–45–683–3333 between 9 am and 6 pm Tokyo time. We recommend making your reservations online.

Getting to the Parks

Guests of these hotels will have complimentary access to the Disney Resort Cruiser – a bus that provides transportation from the Tokyo Disney

> **HIDDEN MICKEY ALERT**
> Be on the look out for Hidden Mickeys while riding the monorail. At times, you will see that the parking lot attendants have arranged the orange cones into a giant Mickey!

Resort Official Hotels to the Disney Resort Line's Bayside Station. From here, guests board the monorail to Tokyo Disneyland, Tokyo DisneySea or the Resort Gateway Station near Ikspiari and the JR Maihama Station. Fares for the monorail start at $2.60 one way for adults and all–day and multiple day passes are available.

Pools

Like the Disney Hotels, outdoor pools are typically open only in July and August. Many hotels have heated indoor pools. If a swimming pool is important to your trip, be sure to inquire about the pool facilities to ensure they will be open during your trip. Indoor pools are sometimes closed for maintenance during slower times of the year.

Workout Facilities

Every hotel has different workout facilities and/or saunas. Some of these gyms require an extra fee and some are included. If this is important to you, inquire about these facilities when making reservations. At the Hilton Tokyo Bay, for example, Hilton Honors members are given complimentary access. There are some unique cultural aspects to these facilities. Some have traditional Japanese–style communal baths, showers and saunas (generally there are separate facilities for men and women as many bathers will be naked). Some workout facilities offer practice areas for ping pong – it is a unique set–up that consists of a ping pong table with a basket of balls on one side and a suspended square target where the other player would stand on the opposite side to allow the server to practice hitting the target. In some cases, ping pong players can be observed practicing for an hour or more.

Sunroute Plaza Tokyo

Web site: www.sunroute–plaza–tokyo.com
Phone number: +81–47–355–1111

The Sunroute Plaza Tokyo is a contemporary hotel. While pleasing in both design and service, it is not as contemporary as the other Official Hotels. The hotel boasts three restaurants:

Hamakaze – a Japanese restaurant featuring an a la carte menu and sushi bar.

California Coffee House – traditional coffee shop fare with a wide range of food choices.

Carnival Sky Lounge – located on the top floor, this elegant dining area offers beautiful nighttime views of Cinderella's Castle in Tokyo Disneyland and of Tokyo Bay. It's worth a visit for an evening nightcap.

Rooms

Rooms are well appointed with contemporary décor. They can range in size from the very small Cruising Cabin at 16.5 square meters (178 sq ft) – 2/3 the size of a Walt Disney World Value Resort room or ½ the size of a standard room at the Disneyland Hotel – to the very comfortable Elegance Room at 49.8 square meters (536 sq ft). Depending on the room type, time of year and number of guests in your party, rack rates can range from $333–1,102 per night. Be sure to check out their "Offers for special reservations" in the upper right corner of the home page and "Special Offers" under the Reservations tab. Bargain hunters can save HUGE Yen off the rack rates – we have seen some offers that include Tokyo Disneyland/Tokyo DisneySea Passports and represented a savings of more than $420!

Tokyo Bay Maihama Hotel
Web site: www.maihamahotel.jp/en
Phone number: +81–47–355–1222

This circular and fully enclosed hotel (picture an ultra–modern looking Embassy Suites) is quite stunning. The atrium soars up 11 stories to an all glass ceiling that allows natural light to illuminate the entire building. Filled with fountains, streams, trees and plants, it offers a unique and soothing atmosphere. Internet access is available in the rooms free of charge. The Tokyo Bay Maihama Hotel has three eateries:

Restaurant Fine Terrace – a buffet and menu featuring western food.
Hotel Bakery Honey Bee – a bakery offering fresh breads and pastries
Brook – located in the atrium, it offers light meals and drinks.

Rooms

Rooms are sleek and contemporary and comfortable. They are all roughly the same size at 32–35 square meters (344–377 sq ft). Rates can vary dramatically, but deals can be found around $130 per night.

Tokyo Bay Hotel Tokyu
Web site: www.tokyuhotelsjapan.com
Phone number: +81–47–355–2411

The terrific façade of the building looks like Treasure Island in Las Vegas. But the interesting architecture at the hotel's entrance and great views of the parks from the higher rooms are not nearly enough to overcome the outdated decor of this hotel. These rooms are done in brass, mauves and atrocious bedding and are accented by bland and cramped bathrooms. These rooms belong in an outdated motel and not in the heart of the Tokyo Disney Resort. Some of the higher floors have a look that is better than most, but still cannot compensate for the low ceilings and tacky interior. In the center of the enclosed lobby – similar in set–up to an Embassy Suites – is a fun–house style play area for kids where, for a fee, your little ones can burn some energy. With Tokyo Disneyland and Tokyo DisneySea a very short distance away, this "benefit" probably does not warrant a stay in this hotel. One can only imagine that with up to 27 million visitors each year, enough guests must trickle into this hotel to keep occupancy high enough to forgo a severely needed remodel. There are nine dining establishments in the Tokyo Bay Hotel Tokyu:

Farandole –casual dining and fare.
Hana –Teppan–yaki (food cooked on an iron griddle).
Juan – a lounge with park views on the 12th floor.

Kujakucho – Chinese fare.
L'avenue – a coffee shop.
Manyo – a Japanese restaurant and Sushi bar (Mai).
Mimosa Lounge – serves drinks and snacks in the atrium.
Sur La Mer – French cuisine.

Rooms

Rooms are adequately appointed, albeit with outdated colors and furniture that make you feel as if you are your grand mother's house in 1988. Rooms range in size from 28–140 square meters (301–1507 sq ft). Paling in comparison to its eight neighbors, the Tokyo Bay Hotel Tokyu rooms are no less expensive with rack rates ranging from $315–$3,600 per night.

Hilton Tokyo Bay
Web site: www.hilton.com
Phone number: +81–47–355–5000 / 800–HILTONS

The Hilton Tokyo Bay is a contemporary Hilton resort that does not disappoint. This full–service Hilton boasts an enormous outdoor pool, kids' pool, indoor pool, spa and workout facilities. There are multiple "family" floors that are decorated with green grass–colored carpet and painted with trees and birds; these floors match the soft tones of the small play area found in the lobby. Guests will want for nothing in this resort. Seven dining options are present in the Hilton. Three include:
Bay Lounge –light snacks and drinks.
Patisserie –sandwiches and fresh–baked goodies
Starbucks – no explanation required!

The other restaurants combine to make the four sections of *the square*. Each is stylishly decorated and the enjoyable ambiance is enhanced by the lighting throughout these restaurants:
Silva's – a 30 foot wide stone water wall is the highlight of this chic coffee shop by day and bar by night.
Dynasty – offers Chinese cuisine, an award winning chef and shark's fin soup.
Accendo's – an open kitchen features French, Italian and Spanish fare in a Mediterranean setting.
Forest Garden – Pan–Asian delights.

Rooms

Rooms offer contemporary styles, though some décor can appear a bit dated. Sizes include 35, 40 and 80 square meters (377, 430 and 861 sq ft). Rates can fluctuate dramatically, but there are some good deals to be had here. Rooms with Park Views for two adults can be as low as $150 or less and suites can cost as much as $3,400 per night. Be sure to review "Hotel Specials" for discounts and packages. This hotel is an excellent cost–effective alternative to the Disney hotels.

Hotel Okura Tokyo Bay
Web site: www.okura.com/hotels/tokyobay
Phone number: +81–47–355–3333

The Hotel Okura Tokyo Bay's theme revolves around dolphins. Statues are immediately visible on the columns as you approach the resort and are used in and around the hotel's decor. Overall, the Hotel Okura Tokyo Bay is a stylish hotel built around a palatial open–air courtyard featuring a beautiful design, fountain and bistro tables from which to enjoy the respite. This hotel is equipped with an indoor and outdoor pool, workout facilities, spa, salon tennis courts and (gasp!) complimentary parking. There are five restaurants and bars including:
Bar Corner – a small intimate bar with seating for 23.
Fontana –European cuisine and a selection of fine wines.
Hagoromo –Japanese delicacies.
Terrace –light snacks and desserts
Toh–ka–lin – fine Chinese dining.

Rooms

Rooms are well appointed with modern décor. Given the room sizes – the standard Superior Rooms start off at 44 square meters (473 sq ft) and go up in size from there. They feature a small sofa, flat panel TV, and sufficient work space. The highlight of these rooms is the bathroom – decked out with marble floors and walls, these spacious rooms feature a large tub and separate shower. Be sure to review their "Special Offer" area for discounts.

Sheraton Grande Tokyo Bay Hotel
Web site: www.starwoodhotels.com/sheraton
Phone number: +81–47–355–5555 / 800–325–3535

This resort hotel is a delight. Stylish, but not pretentious, this Sheraton features a stunning pool, intricate craftsmanship and whimsical design and décor. Guests need not go further than the lobby to be impressed as its spacious layout, captivating décor. The lighting will make guests feel like they are under a magical evening sky even in broad daylight. There are complimentary video games at a table in the lobby as well as an area where children can watch a Disney movie. A sports and recreation area called Oasis features a small miniature golf course with a mini version of Mount Prometheus. This hotel was designed for families as well as romantic getaways. From the Kid's Land–Treasure Island indoor play area, to the indoor pool, the outdoor pool surrounded by a garden with brick paths and boasting waterfall caverns and a tropical backdrop, to the fairytale wedding chapel and the public bath in the Oasis, the Sheraton Grande Tokyo Bay managed to incorporate near–Disney magic into this hotel. Nearly all if its 802 rooms has a view of the Tokyo Disney Resort or Tokyo Bay. There are five bars and restaurants:

Belvedere Lounge – an elegant bar.
Grand Café –Western and Japanese fare.
Maihama Teppanyaki –Japanese food.
Asuka –Japanese cuisine.
Café Toastina –light meals.

Rooms

The rooms have everything guests need, though they feel a little sparse – like the IKEA decorating team furnished this hotel. Still, the rooms are nice, spacious and range from contemporary design to mildly themed rooms the kids will like. The Treasures Room, for example, looks like an oversized child's room with bedspreads and chairs that look like cartoon characters. Other themes include the Ocean Room and are available in a variety of room types. All themed rooms are located on the Fantasy Floor. More importantly, all rooms have double beds – a rarity for Tokyo and for the Tokyo Disney Resort. Most rooms range from 36–40 square meters (388–431 sq ft). Typically, room rates can run as low as $170 and up to $525+ per night. Take the time to review Special Offers on the Sheraton site. Sheraton's main web site, www.starwoodhotels.com, has a Hotel Offers section that applies to all properties worldwide. For specials specific to this resort, proceed to the Sheraton Tokyo Bay Hotel overview page and look for the Hotel Offers section from this page.

Travelers Series Recommends

We think the Sheraton and Hilton are the best of the six Tokyo Disney Resort Official Hotels. The Sheraton is nicer, but the Hilton offers a better location directly across from Bayside Station (the Sheraton is a five minute walk). You will not be disappointed with either. The location of all the

Official Hotels makes them all worth considering as opposed to staying off–property.

Tokyo Disney Resort Partner Hotels
Overview
There are five Tokyo Disney Resort Partner Hotels located just outside the Tokyo Disney Resort. Each offers complimentary shuttles to and from Tokyo Disneyland and Tokyo DisneySea.

> **TRAVEL TIP**
> Not all of these hotels will have English speaking staff available.

Pricing and Packages
Like the Tokyo Disney Resort Official Hotels, these are typical hotels, each with its own pricing and package structures. In order to compare and contrast, price them out individually. Remember that unlike the Disney Hotels, each of these six hotels will offer different promotions and special offers. Also, be sure to shop the traditional travel sites (Expedia, Travelocity, etc.) as they may offer discounted rates at these hotels. Be alert when comparing rates – unless otherwise stated, the rates listed on their web sites *include* service charges and taxes; this may not be the case with the travel sites. Many of these hotels also

> **TRAVEL TIP**
> When reviewing the Tokyo Disney Partner Hotels' web sites, be sure to look for "special offers" or "promotions" sections that can include steep discounts over the regular rates.

have a "Contact Us" form that allows you to communicate the hotel staff via email to ask any questions you may have. You can expect to hear back regarding your inquiry within 24–48 hours.

Tokyo Disney Resort Partner Hotels Guest Benefits
The Tokyo Disney Resort cites five benefits to staying at these Partner Hotels including baggage delivery to your hotel from the JR Maihama Station for a small fee and complimentary shuttles to and from Tokyo Disneyland and Tokyo DisneySea.

Reservations
Reservations may be made by contacting these hotels directly, visiting their web sites and shopping the internet travel sites. Like other Tokyo Disney Resort Hotels, reservations are available via the Tokyo Disney Resort Reservation Center by calling +81–45–683–3333 between 9 am and

6 pm Tokyo time. We recommend making your reservations online directly with the hotel.

Getting to the Parks

The primary benefit to staying at a Tokyo Disney Resort Partner Hotel is that guests have access to complimentary shuttle service from their hotel to the Tokyo DisneySea Bus & Taxi Terminal and the Tokyo Disneyland Bus & Taxi Terminal. Be sure to check bus schedules and travel time when considering these hotels as it could add a bit of a commute each morning and limit your ability to go back to your room for a nap or a change of clothes.

Contact Information

Below is a list and basic information for the five Tokyo Disney Resort Partner Hotels:

Palm & Fountain Terrace Hotel
   Web site: www.palmandfountainterracehotel.com
   Phone number: +81–47–353–1234

Hotel Emion Tokyo Bay
   Web site: www.hotel–emion.jp/english/index.html
   Phone number: +81–47–304–2727

Oriental Hotel Tokyo Bay
   Web site: www.oriental–hotel.co.jp (Japanese language only)
   Phone number: +81–47–350–8111

Urayasu Brighton Hotel
   Web site: http://brightonhotels.co.jp/urayasu–e/
   Phone number: +81–47–355–7777

Mitsui Garden Hotel Prana Tokyo Bay
   Web site: www.gardenhotels.co.jp/eng/prana.html
   Phone number: +81–47–382–3331

Tokyo Disney Resort Good Neighbor Hotels
Overview

The Tokyo Disney Resort Good Neighbor Hotels are comprised of 15 properties throughout the greater Tokyo Metropolitan area. The Tokyo Disney Resort used a set of criteria in allowing these hotels in the exclusive "Good Neighbor" Club. For the skeptical traveler, this designation seemingly removes the risk of choosing the wrong hotel with no private bathroom or a sketchy neighborhood. In reality, there are no notable differences from this collection of hotels to other hotels in the Tokyo area. There are two very limited benefits: These hotels will provide guests with "up–to–the–minute" Tokyo Disney Resort information and there is direct shuttle service from the hotels to the bus terminals and the two Disney parks. It should be noted that seating is limited on these shuttles are subject to Tokyo traffic, so travel time can range from 25 minutes to 60 minutes or more each way.

Given that the prices at these establishments rival those of the Official Hotels of the Tokyo Disney Resort and, in some cases, the prices of the three Disney hotels, it seems it would be far better to select one of the nine "On Property" resorts for your stay. Add to this the 25–60+ minute travel time from these Good Neighbor hotels and the choice seems pretty clear.

These hotels do represent a good starting point if your travels extend beyond the Tokyo Disney Resort and you want to be in the middle of the Tokyo scene. More extensive options can be found on the myriad of travel sites.

> **TRAVEL TIP**
> English–only speakers beware: onsite English–speaking staff is not a Good Neighbor requirement. Be sure to inquire with any hotel about the availability of English speaking staff.

Pricing and Packages

Each of these hotels, like the Official Hotels of the Tokyo Disney Resort and the Tokyo Disney Resort Partner Hotels, are independently owned and operated. As such, they have their own web sites, their own price points, their own specials and packages. In order to compare and contrast, price them out individually. Be sure to shop the traditional travel sites (Expedia, Travelocity, etc.) as they may offer discounted rates at these hotels. Be alert when comparing rates – unless otherwise stated, the official web rates include service charges and taxes when this may not be the case

> **TRAVEL TIP**
> Don't forget to review the "special offers" or "promotions" sections that can include steep discounts over the regular rates.

with the travel sites. Many of these hotels also have a "Contact Us" form that allows you to communicate the hotel staff via email to ask any questions you may have.

Tokyo Disney Resort Partner Hotels Guest Benefits

These hotels purport to have insight you just can't find anywhere else including detailed information on the Tokyo Disney Resort from park hours to event schedules (the internet is a pretty good tool for this information too!). The best, and in our opinion only "true", benefit is complimentary shuttle service to the Bus & Taxi Terminal at both Tokyo Disneyland and Tokyo DisneySea.

Reservations

Reservations may be made by contacting these hotels directly, visiting their web sites and shopping the internet travel sites. Like other Tokyo Disney Resort Hotels, reservations are available via the Tokyo Disney Resort Reservation Center by calling +81–45–683–3333 between 9 am and 6 pm Tokyo time. We recommend making your reservations online directly with the hotel.

Getting to the Parks

As a benefit to staying at a Good Neighbor hotel, guests have access to complimentary shuttle service from their hotel to the Tokyo DisneySea Bus & Taxi Terminal. This terminal is located very close to the Main Entrance of Tokyo DisneySea. Likewise, shuttle service to the Tokyo Disneyland Bus & Taxi Terminal is also provided, though this terminal is located bit further from the Tokyo Disneyland entrance near the Tokyo Disneyland Hotel. Be sure to check bus schedules and travel time when considering these hotels as the shuttles can take an hour or more each way to the parks.

Other Tokyo Hotels

Overview

For those travelers who want to save significant Yen or who don't want to be tethered to the Tokyo Disney Resort, there are countless options available to throughout Tokyo. With more than 12.5 million residents and scores of tourists visiting every day, Tokyo is a world–class metropolis. The city does a phenomenal job of moving these people through the city on a daily basis by foot, car, bus, train, and subway. What this means to tourists is that access to public transportation – and the Tokyo Disney Resort – is available from nearly every corner of the city and visitors can select from every type and style of hotel.

Selecting a hotel in a foreign country can be tricky business, though over the past decade the internet has alleviated a significant amount of the guess work. Selecting the wrong hotel or the wrong area can irreparably dampen a vacation. While folks may not spend significant waking hours in their hotel, the comfort and security in a foreign land are crucial for peace of mind. Flexibility is the name of the game for foreign travel. Travelers may end up with smaller beds than requested, might be placed in a smoking room even if a non–smoking room was reserved months ago, among other issues. A tourist's ability to enjoy their trip often depends on their flexibility. Expect that things will not go as planned and that it will be impossible to understand how everything works in Tokyo. Look at the trials and tribulations as an adventure. After all, you are on your way to Tokyo Disneyland!

If you do your homework, you should have no problem selecting a reputable hotel. There are a variety of sites that can help you identify, research and book a hotel. Travel sites, hotel association sites and sites dedicated to reviews can assist in all of these areas. Expedia, for example, is a great way to learn about hotels in addition to being a place to book your room. Expedia, like most travel sites, allows travelers to rank and rate their

> **TRAVEL TIP**
> U.S. reservation and travel sites have become increasingly international and are a great place to research and review Tokyo hotels.

experiences with these hotels and this information can provide insight to what may be in store. Association sites, like those listed below, will allow you to identify potential hotels, research information about them and provide access to reviews and reservations.

Japanese Travel Sites

Japan–guide.com – www.japan–guide.com – more than one million online visitors frequent this site each month. Sign up for an account and their newsletter if you are planning to stay offsite.

Rakuten Travel – www.mytrip.net/en/index.html –one of Japan's most frequented online reservation sites. The site operates like Expedia and is easy to use.

Japan Hotel Association – www.j–hotel.or.jp/en/index.html – moderate to high priced hotels comprise most of this association and must be approved by the Minister of Transportation to join. This site will allow you to view member hotels by region and provides an overview of the hotel, pictures of the rooms, room counts and rack rates. It will also provide the official web site of the hotels.

Japan Ryokan Association – www.ryokan.or.jp/index_en.html – traditional Japanese hotels are called Ryokan. Of the 55,000 such establishments in Japan, only 1400+ are members of this elite association. Ryokan must be approved for membership and these member establishments often come with a steep price tag.

Japanese Inn Group – www.jpinn.com – budget to near–moderate inns, the Japanese Inn Group members consist of small traditional inns and take pride in offering reasonable rates and good service.

Trip Advisor – www.tripadvisor.com – this is a hotel review site where people upload pictures and write reviews about their experiences. While many of the reviews of Tokyo establishments are in Japanese, there is an English overview and a "Google Translation" button that provides a good sense of their thoughts. You may also book some hotels directly from this site.

> **TRAVEL TIP**
> However you make your reservations, be cognizant of booking and cancellation fees. Some rooms will require full payment up front with no changes allowed. This is often avoided by booking directly with the hotel.

Select Additional Travel Sites
Expedia – www.expedia.com
Orbitz – www.orbitz.com
Travelocity – www.travelocity.com
Priceline – www.priceline.com – yes, Captain Kirk will even allow you to name your own price in Tokyo!

Once you identify a few hotels that interest you, consider spending some time cross–referencing these hotels. Research them at travel review sites (www.tripadvisor.com) as well as multiple travel sites to compare opinions and ratings. In addition to reviewing the averages, study a few of the lower scores and find out *why* these travelers ranked the hotel so poorly and do the same for the higher scores. This information will provide you with a solid overview from which to narrow your selection.

Finding the right price is an equally important – and quite simple – endeavor. Once you have your final selections, check the price on each of these sites plus the hotel's site (don't forget to review promotions!) and make your selection. All things being equal, we recommend making the reservation directly with the hotel as the cancellation policy is generally more forgiving.

Travelers Series Recommends
There are some very good reasons for staying at the Tokyo Disney Resort. If money is no object, stay at one of the Disney Hotels. For those who are a bit more cost conscious, there are often great deals at the six Official Hotels of the Tokyo Disney Resort. These hotels are all a short walk to the Bayside Station monorail stop and offer quick and easy access

to both parks and Ikspiari. Deals at these six hotels will often result in significant savings versus the Disney Ambassador Hotel, Tokyo DisneySea Hotel MiraCosta or the Tokyo Disneyland Hotel. If your plans demand staying offsite, don't limit yourself to one of the five Tokyo Disney Resort Partner Hotels or one of the fifteen Tokyo Disney Resort Good Neighbor Hotels. While the complimentary shuttle service is nice, it may be faster (and less expensive) to stay at a hotel close to the Metro where you can take the JR Train into the Tokyo Disney Resort.

SECTION 4: Arriving and Departing Tokyo

Welcome to Tokyo! Your rear end is probably tired and you are a bit jetlagged, but no doubt there is a rush of excitement about what lies ahead. First things first. As you depart the plane at Narita International Airport, you will be directed to Passport Control – it's a good thing all of the signs in the airport are in English! Proceed to the Foreign Passports line where you will be invited to a window by an Immigration Official. Provide him/her with the completed form you were given on the airplane (be sure to review both sides) along with your Passport. They

> **TRAVEL TIP**
> Ask your hotel specifically which mode of transportation and which stops offer the most direct access to your hotel.

may ask a couple of questions, but most likely will waive you through. From here, proceed to Baggage Claim to pick up your bags. Once you have all of your items you will head to the Customs checkpoint. Here, you will be greeted by a Customs Inspector wearing a royal blue uniform and you will hand him/her your passport and the completed Customs form you received on the plane. The entire process is very smooth. Waiting for your luggage will likely be the longest part of this journey.

Hotel Transportation Options

Armed with your luggage and your travel companions, you are free to explore Tokyo. So, now what? You are 37 miles outside Tokyo and you need to either get to Tokyo Disneyland ASAP and hit Space Mountain or get to your hotel to unwind. Either way, you need to get into the city.

74

The Tokyo Disney Resort offers a comprehensive, albeit slightly confusing, guide to get to the resort from the airport or other Tokyo areas at www.tokyodisneyresort.co.jp/tdr/english/plan/access/index.html. This will assist you in identifying the right Rail Lines or Bus Routes. Remember you are headed for the JR Maihama Station – the gateway into the Tokyo Disney Resort.

Like any international airport, there are various transportation options to get you into Tokyo. An overview is below.

Trains and Subways

There are several trains that bring passengers from Narita Airport to Tokyo. Several require reservations. They range in price from $10–32 per person one way and take 60–90 minutes to travel to central Tokyo. Though public transportation in Tokyo is quite good, dragging your luggage up and down subway steps makes you dream of a better alternative. If you are determined to travel by train, you have several trains to choose from including:

> **DID YOU KNOW?**
> The "JR" stands for Japan Railways.

JR Narita Express – www.jreast.co.jp/e/nex/ – $32 one way, 60 minute trip, reserved seating only, tickets may be purchased at Narita Airport.

Keisei Skyliner – www.keisei.co.jp/keisei/tetudou/keisei_us/top.html – $21 one way, 60 minute trip, reserved seating only, tickets may be purchased at Narita Airport.

Keisei Limited Express – www.keisei.co.jp/keisei/tetudou/keisei_us/html/o_express.html – $11 one way, 75 minute trip, does not offer reserved seating.

"Reserved seats" mean that you will have a seat assignment on the train instead of "open seating" where you would take any available seat. Reserved seats do not require advance reservations and may be purchased at ticket counters or ticket machines in train stations including Narita Airport.

Limousine Bus

The most common, comfortable and reasonably priced transportation is a Limousine Bus. These very large tour buses are clean and safe and offer door–to–door service. The buses have routes that run throughout the city and the operators have it down to a science. Limousine Bus is the mode of transportation recommended by the Tokyo Disney Resort. Reservations are not needed from NRT to Tokyo, but are highly recommended for the return trip. Airport Limousine Bus Service provides transportation to all major routes and the most updated information is available via their web site. Rates are approximately $27 per person one way and children are half fare.

Airport Limousine Bus Service (+81–33–665–7220) – www.limousinebus.co.jp/en/index.html – $27 one way, 60 minute trip, does not offer reserved seating.

Rental Car

Can we just say "No Way!"? Your sense of adventure is far beyond ours if you attempt a rental car in Tokyo. The steering wheel is on the right, you drive on the left–hand side of the road and many signs are only in Japanese.

> **TRAVEL TIP**
> If you follow our recommendation and plan on taking the Airport Limousine Bus, be sure to check the schedule of the bus against your scheduled arrival time. Plan an alternate route in case your flight is delayed or you miss the bus. While this probably will not happen, it will save you a great deal of stress if you are prepared.

Taxi

A cab ride into central Tokyo will cost you around $200 or more. Because of Narita Airport's location, very few people (especially tourists) take a taxi. Plan on 60–90 minutes for the trip.

Travelers Series Recommends

Limousine Bus is, by far, the easiest, most direct and most cost effective option. The staff at Airport Limousine Bus Service is terrific. The ride is stress–free and you can sit back, relax and take in the scenery en route to your hotel. However, we think it is very important that you plan an alternate route in case your plan is delayed and you miss the final bus of the day. Communicate with your hotel regarding these alternatives and verify the instructions they give you with the online rail and subway maps and this link found on the Tokyo Disney Resort web site: www.tokyodisneyresort.co.jp/tdr/english/plan/access/train.html.

Getting to Tokyo Disney Resort Hotels via Airport Limousine Bus
Overview

Narita International Airport has two terminals: Terminal 1 and Terminal 2. As you exit customs, the Airport Limousine Bus Service kiosks are plentiful and easy to spot with their orange and white colors. Walk up to the counter and tell the English-speaking staff where you are staying. They will sell you a ticket, tell you which bus stop to wait at and what time your bus will arrive. The bus stops are clearly marked with vertical signs with large numbers on them. In addition, each stop has digital signs in English and Japanese. These digital signs show the next two bus routes that will pick up at the stop. The one closest to the street shows the next pick up and the one closest to the airport shows the second pick up. The signs also list the destination and the time of pick up. These are also on your ticket. The Tokyo Disney Resort stop sometimes is abbreviated as "TDR". The buses run very close to scheduled times and when the bus arrives, someone will look at your ticket, give you claim check for your luggage and load your bags while you climb aboard a comfortable climate-controlled bus complete with bathroom. The bus will make several stops at hotels around your destination. When you arrive at your hotel, disembark the bus and collect your luggage. If you are traveling to a hotel not located at the Tokyo Disneyland Resort, follow these same guidelines, but board the bus marked with your destination.

From Terminal 1

Once you clear Customs, grab your luggage and head for the Arrival Lobby on the first floor. Look for the Airport Limousine Ticket Counter to purchase your tickets. From there, go to bus stop section #7 – this is where the buses heading for the Tokyo Disney Resort are stationed. Section #7 is located directly in front of Terminal 1 and to the right as you exit the terminal. If you are headed for central Tokyo, the ticket counter clerk will direct you to the appropriate section.

From Terminal 2

Once you clear Customs, grab your luggage and head for the Arrival Lobby on the first floor. Look for the Airport Limousine Ticket Counter to purchase your tickets. From there, go to bus stop section #11 – this is where the buses heading for the Tokyo Disney Resort are stationed. Section #11 is located directly in front of Terminal 2 between the Central Exit (the middle exit on the first floor) and the South Exit 1. Exit through the Central Exit and veer very slightly to the left. If you are headed for central Tokyo, the ticket counter clerk will direct you to the appropriate section.

Getting to the Airport via Airport Limousine Bus

Getting back to NRT from your hotel is a decidedly easier experience. Speak with your hotel's front desk or concierge and book your seat on the Airport Limousine Bus. The hotel staff will tell you where to wait and what time to arrive. Just as you did when you arrived, keep your ticket handy and provide it to the driver. Your bags will be loaded onto the bus and you will be dropped off near your airline. Collect your belongings and proceed to the check–in counter for your airline. Bon Voyage!

Getting to the Tokyo Disney Resort from Central Tokyo via Metro and Rail

JR Maihama Station is the gateway to the Tokyo Disney Resort. There are two Rail Lines that service this station – JR Keiyo Line and JR Musashino Line. Depending on where in Tokyo your trip begins, you may need to take the Metro to a Rail Station that connects you to the JR Keiyo or JR Musashino Lines. The interactive Rail Line Map on the Tokyo Disney Resort (www.tokyodisneyresort.co.jp/tdr/english/plan/access/train.html) site is incredibly helpful in identifying your exact route and approximating how long it will take to reach the JR Maihama Station. The fare will be $2 per person one way; children 6–11 are half fare and those under 6 are free. The trip will be 15–45 minutes depending on your point of origin and number of transfers.

> **TRAVEL TIP**
> All Metro and rail signs throughout Tokyo are written in both English and Japanese.

Purchasing tickets is quite simple and may be done from any Metro or Rail Station. Tickets are available via vending machines – be sure to have Yen available. Feed money into the machine until the buttons light up and allow you to select the ticket you want. Your ticket and any change due will drop to the slot at the bottom. Machines accept banknotes up to ¥10,000 bills. Fear not – if you purchase the wrong fare, you can pay the difference upon exiting the line via a fare adjustment machine or fare adjustment window. Just slip in your ticket, pay the difference and be on your way. Be sure to hold on to your ticket as you will need it to exit!

When you see the signs for the JR Maihama Station, exit the train and station. You did it! You have arrived. If you are headed to Tokyo DisneySea, exit the station and head left to the Resort Gateway Station. Buy a ticket and board the monorail. You can also use the monorail for Tokyo Disneyland. To do so, turn right as you exit the station and walk past the large suitcase shaped store, called Bon Voyage, and stay on the path to the Tokyo Disneyland main entrance.

If you are checking into a Disney Hotel or Official Hotel of the Tokyo Disney Resort, gather your belongings and exit at the JR Maihama Station. As you leave, the Tokyo Disney Resort Welcome Center is immediately on your left between the JR Maihama Station and Ikspiari. Review the information below based on your hotel accommodations.

Disney Hotel Guests

There are two counters – Disney Hotels Service Counter and Information Counter. The Disney Hotel Services Counter offers several services. If you arrive before 3pm, you can typically take advantage of the Pre–Check–in Service where you will be able to check–in, receive your key and hand over your bags to be delivered directly to your room. Baggage delivery is complimentary. Taking advantage of Pre–Check–in will delay the availability of your room until 4:30 pm (instead of the normal 3:00 pm check–in).

> **HIDDEN MICKEY ALERT**
> The green metal overhangs outside the Tokyo Disney Resort Welcome Center have Hidden Mickeys visible among the circular cutouts.

The Information Counter will not likely be on your itinerary as it focuses on assisting with future vacation plans at the Tokyo Disney Resort and the sale of Annual Passports, Tokyo Disney Resort Gift Cards and Advance sales.

Official Hotels of Tokyo Disney Resort Guests

If you are checking into one of the six Official Hotels of Tokyo Disney Resort, head to the Tokyo Disney Resort Official Hotels Service Counter. It is located on the lower level/street level of the Tokyo Disney Resort Welcome Center. Here, you will be able to leave your luggage in order to take advantage of the complimentary baggage delivery service.

> **HIDDEN MICKEY ALERT**
> The Disney Resort Line monorail stations have posters welcoming guests. On the upper left, just below the word "Tokyo" are bubbles in the shape of a Hidden Mickey.

The Welcome Center is also a great place to purchase Passports to Tokyo Disneyland and Tokyo DisneySea as well as Disney Resort Line monorail passes. Operating hours are 7:30 am to 5:00 pm and Pre–Check–in is available until 4:00pm. Free of your luggage, you are now free to explore!

SECTION 5: Understanding the Tokyo Disney Resort

<u>Ikspiari</u>

Once you have finished at the Tokyo Disney Resort Welcome Center, the first thing you'll see is Ikspiari. Ikspiari opened July 7, 2000 and this complex – spanning an impressive 29 acres – is a super–sized version of anything you have seen at the Disneyland Resort or Walt Disney World Resort's Downtown Disney areas. Whereas Disneyland Resort's Downtown Disney District houses roughly 40 shops and restaurants and the Walt Disney World Resort's version is home to 70, Ikspiari boasts a jaw–dropping 140 shops and restaurants plus the 16–screen movie theater *Cinema Ikspiari*. This area is so large that it is separated into nine themed "zones" encompassing four levels.

> **TOKYO DISNEY FUN FACT**
> It is a Japanese custom to bring gifts upon retuning from vacation. This likely contributes to Ikspiari offering more shops and restaurants than the combined totals of the Disneyland Resort's Downtown Disney District, Walt Disney World Resort's Downtown Disney, and Disneyland Resort Paris' Disney Village.

Ikspiari is a great place to take a walk on your first day. The tour can be as short as a 20-minute stroll or an all day shopping adventure. In either scenario, it will help you acclimate to your surroundings and immediately immerse you into Japanese culture. It is a great place to people watch and notice some of the subtle and not–so–subtle differences between Tokyo and home. It's an easy walk to the Disney Ambassador Hotel from Ikspiari and the entire complex is great to see and explore.

English maps and store lists are available throughout Ikspiari or you can download them at www.ikspiari.com.

Bon Voyage

Located next to the JR Maihama Station on the opposite side of Ikspiari is Bon Voyage. This store offers the largest selection of Disney merchandise in Japan. The façade of this behemoth shop is Disney architecture at it's finest. Shaped like a giant suitcase and hat box, this massive store is a great place to start your Disney vacation. You will find a vast array of Tokyo Disneyland and Tokyo DisneySea merchandise – a selection so large that you could complete your birthday and Christmas shopping for the next three years and not duplicate any gifts! If you are an early riser, you'll be happy to know that Bon Voyage opens as early as 7:30 am (and to think – it's impossible to get a churro at Disneyland in California before 11 am).

> **HIDDEN MICKEY ALERT**
> Mickey is seemingly everywhere in Bon Voyage. Take a gander at the ceilings and the semi-Hidden Mickeys placed throughout. Then check out the mural with Mickey as the Sorcerer's Apprentice with a young mouse looking at the base of the statue. Hidden Mickeys are visible around the base at eye level from this little mouse.

Cirque du Soleil Theatre Tokyo

Zed arrived at the Tokyo Disney Resort in October 2008. As with any Cirque du Soleil show, Zed is a whimsical journey into the imagination. It is a fable with beautiful visuals and sound and features superb acrobatic talent. This show is fun for the entire family and is worth the Yen. The program is described on the official Zed web site as follows; *"The show follows the journey of a character who ultimately brings two completely opposing worlds, heaven and earth, together in reconciliation and harmony. This dramatic production [features] a colourful array of unique and lively characters in vibrant costumes for a truly dynamic performance."* Whatever your interpretation of the show's meaning, you are bound to agree that this high energy show is a treat.

Following the hugely successful La Nouba (the Cirque du Soleil show at Disney World featuring the first permanent theater built exclusively for Cirque) this 2,170 seat theater was designed and built specifically for

Cirque du Soleil's Zed. The stage design fits perfectly into the Tokyo DisneySea and Tokyo DisneySea Hotel MiraCosta's nautical adventure theme.

Zed actually begins with a pre–show as guests watch clowns interact with the audience. As the lights dim and show kicks into high gear, guests are treated to heart–stopping acrobatics and a moving soundtrack. The show is a great addition to the Tokyo Disney Resort. There is not a bad seat in the house; guests are sure to enjoy themselves from any vantage point in this theater.

> **DID YOU KNOW?**
> There are two parking lots for guests visiting the parks and combined they can hold more than 20,000 vehicles combined.

Ticket prices range from $82–190 per person. Tickets may be purchased in person at the box office or at the Tokyo Disney Reservation Center at +81–45–683–3333. The official online Zed box office is available in Japanese only, but visit http://nippon.his.co.jp/entertainment/zed/top_en.htm to make reservations in English. We recommend booking your tickets ahead of time, but tickets are often available the day of the show.

Dining at the Tokyo Disney Resort

There are well over 100 places to eat at the three Disney Hotels, Tokyo Disneyland, Tokyo DisneySea and Ikspiari. Eateries come in all designs, themes, and price ranges. Some serve food on a stick, some serve food to be eaten by hand, and some serve food to be eaten by chopstick; some foods are to go while more is meant to be slowly enjoyed. With seemingly limitless options, it's hard to decide where to eat and whether dining should take precedence over exploring the parks. While you and your party must decide that age–old question, this guide endeavors to make the choices a bit more clear. Ultimately, Disney dining can be broken into five main categories of restaurants.

Buffet

Buffets are restaurants that offer all–you–can–eat for a set price. Guests may have as many helpings as they like and the food offerings are generally varied.

Buffeteria

Buffeterias are restaurants where guests get in line, grab a tray, and slide it along the tray counter selecting prepared dishes that interest them. At the end of the counter, guests pay based on which items they have selected.

Counter Service

Counter service restaurants require guests to wait in line, place their order and wait at the counter for their meal to be prepared. Once the order is completed, the meal is handed to the guest on a tray and they find a place to sit.

Kiosk

Kiosks are eateries that are small, often mobile eateries. Generally, kiosks offer a very narrow selection or only sell one item. Kiosks are often referred to as Wagons.

Table Service

Table Service restaurants are those where guests are seated at a table and are given a menu to review their options. A waiter or waitress then takes their order and brings their food directly to the table.

With the exception of some kiosks, all eateries sell water and soft drinks; sometimes in cups and sometimes in a plastic bottle. Overall, the quality of food at the Tokyo Disney Resort is good and is very good relative to traditional "theme park" food. There are many interesting options here and kiosks offer an excellent way for the less adventurous to sample some of the local fare without committing to a large or expensive portion.

Hidden Mickeys

Hidden Mickeys are a unique game of hide-and-go-seek that the Imagineers play with Disney park guests and Tokyo Disneyland and Tokyo DisneySea provide an excellent backdrop for this game. A Hidden Mickey is often defined as the famous mark of Mickey Mouse (generally represented by three circles – a large one for the head and two smaller circles for the ears) being subtly placed in the park's décor. Hidden Mickeys occur on building designs, within building paint patterns, on walls, in attractions, on attraction vehicles, within moldings – just about anywhere an Imagineer could place them. Some are obvious once they are spotted and some are debatable and exist only in the eye of the beholder. Some are "not–so" Hidden Mickeys. Hidden Mickey Alerts have been placed throughout this guidebook, however, this is not a comprehensive list and new Hidden Mickeys are continuously popping up – so keep your eyes open during your travels and you may just spot a new Hidden Mickey.

Pin Trading

A favorite pastime for many Disney park fans is Pin Trading. This phenomenon is a sub–culture unto itself and contains a myriad of rules that are meticulously followed by those who participate. While Pin Trading was present at the Tokyo Disney Resort in the late 90s and early 2000s, Pin Trading is not currently practiced. However, many unique pins are available for purchase or as prizes from games of skill.

SECTION 6: Understanding the Tokyo Disney Resort Parks

Tokyo Disneyland and Tokyo DisneySea offer an impressive collection of Disney attractions that represent some of the best of the other parks and some that are exclusive to the Tokyo Disney Resort. Fans of the Disney parks will no doubt spend time comparing attractions to their "home" park just as people traveling between Disneyland and Walt Disney World's Magic Kingdom do. While foreign guests will feel right at home in the Disney parks, there are some very intriguing differences that make a visit here a truly unique experience. No doubt you will be impressed by what you find.

One of the first things Disney park fans will notice is that there are a relatively small number of pre–teen children at the parks; less than 20% of the park's guests are between 4 and 11 years old while nearly the same percentage are over 40 years old. Japan's declining birth rate helps explain this; a government report released in 2009 noted that children younger than 15 make up just 13% of the population, compared to 20% in the U.S., and it is falling. People 65 and older make up 22.5% of the population and is rising. In 2008, Japan's population decreased by a record 51,000 people. Foreign guests will notice an extremely high number of teenage children in school uniforms as well as a much higher ratio of female guests; and it seems every one of them is wearing Disney paraphernalia. Interestingly,

71% of the Tokyo Disney Resort visitors in 2009 were female. Also in 2009, more than 97% of Tokyo Disney Resort guests were Japanese.

The attractions throughout Tokyo Disneyland and Tokyo DisneySea are enhanced by the Cast Members. Each Cast Member really gets into their role; they take a tremendous amount of pride in the role they play in guest entertainment. Every time a ride departs, the Cast Members will wave and every time it returns, the Cast Members wave. This is very effective in keeping a smile on your face throughout your visit. We found it quite funny on carousel rides where the Cast Members wave to all the riders every time they make a revolution. Be sure to be participative – smile and wave back. Overall, the service at the Tokyo Disneyland Resort is amazing. One morning, we were standing in line outside Tokyo DisneySea about 10 minutes before opening and a member of our party asked a Cast Member if she had an English language map. The older cast member apologized profusely for not having one, asked us to wait and literally ran to get us an English map, apologizing again upon her return. Cultural differences like these truly make a trip to the Tokyo Disney Resort special.

One large cultural difference you are sure to notice is the applause during shows – or the lack of it. Applause tends to be very subdued, even in the largest shows where the guests are clearly enjoying themselves. Cast Members are often positioned by the front of the stage and will clap loudly in an effort to encourage applause from the audience.

One of the most interesting spectacles you will witness is the friendly chaos that ensues at park opening. While the Japanese are often thought to be subdued or low–key, the spectacle that occurs as the parks open begs to differ. Long lines will form at the entrances to both parks, though we use the term "line" loosely. The Japanese guests line up, but if there is not a clear queue, they will crowd – not pushing or shoving, but in the absence of rope lines, they will stand in a large crowd and fill in available space. Once a queue or turnstile is in sight, they tend to line up orderly in order to get through. It is important you take crowding or the American perception of "cutting" with a grain of salt and just let the scene unfold before you. Follow the lead of those around you and don't worry if you lose a couple places in line. The best part of park opening is what happens once the guests are through the turnstile – it becomes a dead sprint to the first attraction. You are not likely see people running throughout the day, but the first 15 minutes of the day are an experience! Guests literally spin through the turnstiles and run as fast as they can through World Bazaar at Tokyo Disneyland and Mediterranean Harbor at Tokyo DisneySea. Meanwhile, Cast Members smile and wave as droves of guests run throughout the park.

Don't try this at Disneyland or the Magic Kingdom as it is distinctly against the rules. The U.S. parks have tried varied methods during opening, but none of them include allowing guests to run. The goal of these early morning sprinters is two–fold. Typically, some members of the party sprint to the day's first major attraction where long lines will quickly form. Meanwhile, the other members of the party will sprint to get a FASTPASS for another major attraction. These FASTPASS lines can become crowded immediately after opening, though they move quickly. Keep in mind that the lines at the FASTPASS kiosks tend to be less defined than the queue for the attraction and the "crowd" mentality will be much more evident in these FASTPASS lines. Hold your ground and walk with the crowd...and don't worry if a few people get in front of you. Instead, look around and enjoy the people watching! With FASTPASS tickets in hand, the cell phones start going like crazy as guests text or call their parties to find out where they are in line. This will be the one time you are likely to notice a number of people joining their groups in the middle of a queue. Aside from this being a fantastic people watching experience, we believe this to be the exact strategy you should follow when you arrive to the park. Develop a plan with your party prior to entering through the turnstile. Decide which of the most popular attractions you will experience first and which FASTPASS (Hint – pick one fairly nearby) you will send members of your party to before rejoining the group. This strategy will save you substantial time because you will not only have a FASTPASS to enjoy later in the day, but you will be able to get a second FASTPASS that much sooner (see The FASTPASS Factor below for more details).

Other than the signs describing the attraction and wait times located near the entrance, all of the signs, posters and props used for attractions are in English. While the majority of the dialogue in the attractions is Japanese, be prepared for some Japanenglish. Like Spanglish in the United States, words like "hello", "goodbye", and "okay" are spoken in English in between the Japanese dialogue.

The FASTPASS Factor

FASTPASS is a free service offered at the Tokyo Disney Resort and operates in exactly the same manner as the Disneyland Resort and the Walt Disney World Resort. Essentially, the FASTPASS system will electronically hold your place in line so that you can enjoy other attractions, eat or shop instead of standing in line for certain attractions. FASTPASS is available for seven Tokyo Disneyland attractions and eight Tokyo DisneySea Attractions.

FASTPASS Attractions by Park	
TOKYO DISNEYLAND (1):	TOKYO DISNEYSEA (3):
Big Thunder Mountain	StormRider
Splash Mountain	Journey to the Center of the Earth
Pooh's Hunny Hunt	20,000 Leagues Under the Sea
Space Mountain	Mermaid Lagoon Theater
Buzz Lightyear's Astro Blasters	The Magic Lamp Theater
Haunted Mansion	Raging Spirits
Monsters, Inc. Ride & Go Seek!	Tower of Terror
	Indiana Jones Adventure: Temple of the Crystal Skull

Using the FASTPASS is quite simple. Find the FASTPASS Ticketing Machines; they are located near the entrance to the attractions that offer FASTPASS. Follow the instructions pictured on the machine and insert your park ticket (Passport) one at a time for each person who will be experiencing the attraction. The FASTPASS Ticketing Machine will dispense one FASTPASS at a time. There will be two times listed on the ticket. Guests can return to the attraction during this time period and utilize the special FASTPASS entrance to bypass the majority of the Standby line (guests waiting in line for the attraction). Typically, the wait for the FASTPASS line is between 5 and 15 minutes and this can be a dramatic timesaver, especially on days with high attendance.

TRAVEL TIP
The only time that really matters on your FASTPASS is the first one. Tokyo Disney Resort policy allows FASTPASS holders to return anytime after the initial time. Therefore, if your pass shows that you can return between 10:45 and 11:45, you can actually return anytime after 10:45 until the park closes. Therefore, there is no need to rush to get to the attraction before the timeslot ends.

The bottom of the FASTPASS is stamped with a time. After this time, you may obtain an additional FASTPASS, even if you have not used your current FASTPASS. There is a limited supply of FASTPASS tickets each day and the most popular rides will often dispense all of their FASTPASS tickets by noon or earlier, especially on days of high attendance.

The FASTPASS is a great way to ensure your party can experience many of the premier attractions in one day. When you arrive at an attraction's entrance, check out the Standby time. If the wait is reasonable, get in line to experience the attraction. If it seems too long, get a FASTPASS and come back later. Our philosophy is to make sure you *always* have a FASTPASS; you do not have to use it. Likewise, if you were issued FASTPASS tickets and you return to the attraction to find a very short line, don't waste your FASTPASS if it is an attraction you might want to experience more than once. Get in the short Standby line and experience the attraction. Then, use your FASTPASS to experience the attraction at a later time that day.

On days of lower attendance, some of the attractions that normally offer a FASTPASS may not offer the service.

Single Riders

In addition to the FASTPASS system, Tokyo Disneyland and Tokyo DisneySea offer Single Rider options. Guests who elect this option will be placed in any open seat on an attraction, often next to a stranger and separate from their group. However, this often provides a minimal wait time. Guests interested in this service should follow the Single Rider route at designated attractions.

Single Riders Attractions by Park	
TOKYO DISNEYLAND (1):	TOKYO DISNEYSEA (3):
Splash Mountain	Raging Spirits
	20,000 Leagues Under the Sea
	Indiana Jones Adventure: Temple of the Crystal Skull

Experience the Difference

If you are wearing a backpack or shoulder bag, you will have to remove it before getting on the rides. Be prepared that you will be reminded multiple times on every attraction unless your bag is off your shoulders. On some attractions you will be reminded by Cast Member four or five times that you will need to remove your backpack. Expect to be reminded when you enter the attraction, when you are asked how many in your party and immediately prior to boarding. As always, the Disney Cast Members are extremely polite and have a smile on their face, though you will have to watch your own level of annoyance and recognize they are doing their best to communicate the procedure to you.

One of the rare frustrating things about Tokyo Disney Resort (and Japan overall) is that there is never a trash can around when you need one. There are far fewer trash cans throughout these parks as compared to their U.S. counterparts and yet there is virtually no litter. People are very conscientious about their trash and the Disney Cast Members are on top of it. However, the reason for the small number of trash cans and litter is a direct result of Japanese culture. It is extremely rare (although less taboo at the parks) to see Japanese people eating or drinking while walking. They almost always sit down or stand at a counter to eat or drink and immediately throw away their trash. Vending machines, especially those throughout Tokyo, typically have a small trash can integrated into the machine or next to the machine and it is common to see someone buy a drink and chug it while standing next to the machine, throw away their trash and move on.

DID YOU KNOW?
Medallion Maker machines, similar to pressed coin machines in the U.S. parks, cost $1.11 and take a ¥100 coin. The medallions offered change quite often and with the seasons. These machines can be found throughout the parks and resort hotels.

Eating Your Way Through the Parks

The menus for Tokyo Disney Resort eateries change fairly often. While we did our best to include an overview of what each place serves, there will no doubt be some substantial differences during your trip. Also, buffets are common throughout the Tokyo Disney Resort. One common way to save a significant amount of money is to visit buffets for lunch because they typically cost 50–100%+ more at dinnertime. Many eateries offer items a la carte or in "sets", which are value meals that generally consist of an entrée, french fries and a beverage.

TRAVEL TIP
All restaurants in Tokyo Disneyland and Tokyo DisneySea are non-smoking.

Food carts, kiosks and counters throughout the Tokyo Disney Resort offer a wide variety of snacks, treats and drinks. Interestingly, most of them take their specialization very seriously and serve just one thing. Be prepared to wait in line at multiple stands if your party is looking for variety. In many instances drinks are not served at the snack kiosks and you may find yourself waiting in one line for popcorn and another line for a drink. The stands offer the smallest assortment, kiosks offer a little more and counters offer a wider selection of food items.

TRAVEL TIP
There are many pricey places to eat throughout the Tokyo Disney Resort, however, standard dress codes are not in effect. The vast majority of people will be in theme park attire (jeans, khakis, or slacks).

At most counter service eateries, it is appropriate to leave your tray on the table and a Cast member will pick it up. If a Cast Member is nearby as you begin to clean up, they almost always come by and clean it up for you. If you are unsure whether or not to clear your own tray, watch the other people around you and do what they do!

Staying hydrated at the Tokyo Disney resort is much more complicated than one might think. Drinks are often difficult to find and lines can be quite long when you find them. Likewise, many kiosks sell food (often VERY salty) and do not provide the option to buy drinks. When drinks can be purchased – whether a water, soda or milkshake – the cups are much smaller than in the U.S. (which may explain the slim Japanese figures everywhere around you) and are only filled about 80–90%. As a result, purchasing drinks can be an expensive and often unsatisfying endeavor.

> **TRAVEL TIP**
> If you are having a food emergency and just need something that doesn't require a sense of adventure, Kua 'Aina in Ikspiari is your place. This burger shop sells hamburgers and cheeseburgers in a Hawaiian setting. The burgers are outstanding! Grilled to perfection and served with fries in an atmosphere where the term "no mayonnaise" translates very well, Kua 'Aina can be a welcome respite for many American travelers. As expected, it will not come cheap – a burger, fries and soda will cost $14.

Popcorn is an extremely popular snack at the Tokyo Disneyland Resort. However, finding buttered and salted popcorn is much more difficult than you might think. Flavored popcorn is widely sold throughout Tokyo Disneyland and Tokyo DisneySea. While there are some seemingly "normal" flavors like Salted popcorn, the choices get much more interesting from there. During your trip to the Tokyo Disney Resort you will find popcorn kiosks offering selections including Black Pepper, Strawberry, Milk Tea, Butter and Soy Sauce, Curry, Carmel, Chocolate, and Honey. Some of these flavors are good and some are horrible, though trial and error is the only way for you to know! The smell of some of the more exotic flavors is strong enough to make you gag every time you pass by.

> **TRAVEL TIP**
> Bottled sodas are a much better deal than their cup and ice counterparts. Typically, a bottled soda will cost $2.22 and provide a larger volume versus the $3.19 for a counter–service drink.

Guests with Disabilities

Tokyo Disneyland offers a unique solution for guests who require the use of a wheelchair and/or are unable to stand in line. Guests can obtain a "Guest Assistance Card" from the Stroller and Wheelchair Rentals kiosk when renting a wheelchair or from Guest Relations. The Cast Members will do their best to help you try to understand how to utilize the card, though there tend to be some communication gaps. Essentially, you "wheel" to the entrance of the attraction you wish to experience and present the Guest Assistance Card. The Cast Member will write the current time on the card and, after assessing the wait time, will also indicate at what time you can experience the attraction. This allows your party's place to be held in line and return (like a FASTPASS) anytime after the time indicated on the card. You can only do this for one attraction at a time, meaning while you are "waiting" to experience the attraction, you may not use your Guest Assistance Card to experience or wait for any other attractions.

Mickey Mouse and Friends

Disney Characters are abundant throughout the parks and exceedingly popular. While you will see excitement and long lines for Mickey Mouse and Minnie Mouse the lines will often be longer for Chip N' Dale. These chipmunks are much more popular in Japan than the United States. Although photos with them are highly sought after, none can compare with what we like to call....the Duffy Factor.

> **HIDDEN MICKEY ALERT**
> Hidden Mickeys can be found on Duffy bears and accompanying merchandise. You will no doubt notice the not-so Hidden Mickey sewn onto the bottom of Duffy's feet. But, look closely at his face and the light beige color used to distinguish Duffy's face from the fur – this beige "skin" is shaped like Mickey.

According to Disney lore, Minnie Mouse made a teddy bear for Mickey so that he would not become lonely. When Mickey placed the bear in a duffel bag in preparation for a trip, the bear became known as Duffy. Duffy was launched several years ago and has become an increasingly popular character with the Tokyo Disney crowd. The American Waterfront's Cape Cod section at Tokyo DisneySea has slowly been transforming into a mini Duffyland. Aunt Peg's Village store is a Duffy emporium where guests – having spent $40 or more on the moderate sized version of the teddy bear – line up in droves to buy Duffy merchandise and accessories. Even during non–peak season, the line to Aunt Peg's can be 100–200 people deep just to get into the store to purchase pricey outfits for Duffy. Throughout the American Waterfront, guests will find a Duffy cookie shop, Duffy kiosks to buy one of the many sizes of bears, the My Friend Duffy show at the Cape Cod Cook–Off eatery, Duffy popcorn holders (nearly double the price of other popcorn holders) and a queue to line up and pose for pictures with Duffy! Given the amount of merchandise themed to Duffy, the number of guests you will see wearing or holding Duffy booty and the lines to shop for Duffy accessories and pose with Duffy, this bear is arguably the most popular character in the park.

Rated and Reviewed

In the following chapters, this guide book provides detailed information on attractions, shops and eateries throughout Tokyo Disneyland and Tokyo DisneySea. The attractions include the TRAVELERS SERIES RATES IT feature which is intended to help prioritize which attractions to experience. These ratings include Yuunaru (Outstanding! Disney at its best); Yoshi (Good – make this a priority); Abere–ji (Average – experience this attraction if time allows); Nakaguri (Boring – this attraction is not worth the time); and Osanai (Young – experience if traveling with young children). Additionally, each attraction review contains a HOW IT COMPARES section to draw on your knowledge of the U.S. parks to better understand the Japanese parks. Attractions from Disneyland and Disney's California Adventure at the Disneyland Resort in California as well as the Magic Kingdom, Epcot, Disney's Hollywood Studio and Disney's Animal Kingdom at the Walt Disney World Resort in Florida are constantly referenced for comparison. Providing these comparisons is the best way to draw a mental picture of the Tokyo Disney Resort. Plus, Disney park fans are notorious for comparing the differences between the parks!

TRAVEL TIP
Celebrating a wedding, birthday or anniversary at Disney parks is not just an American tradition. Be sure to stop by Guest Relations if you have something to celebrate and pick up a sticker announcing your reason for celebrating (they do not provide pins like Disneyland Resort or Walt Disney World Resort).

Shopping Around

Souvenirs are a very important part of Japanese culture. It is expected that those going on a trip will bring gifts back for their family and friends. Because of this, expect to receive multiple bags whenever you purchase something at the Tokyo Disney Resort or any other store where people regularly purchase souvenirs. You will receive a bag to carry your purchases, plus an additional bag for each item you purchase will be folded and placed in the bag you will carry. This will make it easy for guests to "wrap" souvenirs to give to family and friends.

Subtitles

Even the most seasoned Disney theme park veteran should spend some time studying the maps for both Tokyo Disneyland and Tokyo DisneySea. There is a lot of information contained within these maps including the fact that a handful of attractions in both parks are offered with English, Chinese or Japanese subtitles. This can dramatically add to your enjoyment and understanding of the attraction. On the official park maps, these attractions have a pink box underneath them advising guests to ask Cast Members about viewing the attractions in another language (on our initial trip, we didn't notice these boxes until our third day and had to go back to experience some attractions a second time with significantly improved understanding. If you are interested in viewing English, Chinese, or Japanese subtitles, ask any Cast Member at the entrance or while in line. It generally takes them a minute or two for them to retrieve the wireless handheld devices. The unit has a display screen that shows the dialogue in the selected language. They are programmed to automatically follow along with the attraction. If this service is unavailable, the Cast Members at the entrance to the attraction will provide you with any alternative material that is available, like a one-sheet handout that provides an overview of the storyline in English.

Section 7: Tokyo Disneyland

Overview

Tokyo Disneyland opened in 1983 and was dedicated by Card Walker, then Chairman of Walt Disney Productions (before the name change to the Walt Disney Company) and Takahashi–san, then President of the Oriental Land Company. This dedication represented Disney's first foray into international theme parks. To date, four additional international parks have followed including Disneyland Paris, Tokyo DisneySea, Walt Disney Studios (Paris) and Hong Kong Disneyland.

> **HIDDEN MICKEY ALERT**
> There is a courtyard with a small fountain in the middle to the far left of the main entrance to Tokyo Disneyland behind the East Gate Guest Reception area. There are four paved areas around the fountain and each is shaped like a Mickey. It is easy to spot these with the help of a Tokyo Disneyland map.

Tokyo Disneyland occupies 126 acres – nearly 50% larger than Disneyland – and has grown to include 46 attractions, 47 shops, and 48 eateries. The park is spread over seven themed lands, five of them located directly off the Plaza in the center of the park. These lands include: World Bazaar, Adventureland, Westernland, Critter Country, Fantasyland, Toontown and Tomorrowland.

Tours of Tokyo Disneyland are available and can be arranged through Guest Relations. The cost of the tour is $39 per person. Private tours can be arranged for $233 for up to 6 people.

ATTRACTIONS, RESTAURANTS AND SHOPS BY LAND

World Bazaar:

Attractions (3)
Penny Arcade
The Disney Gallery
Omnibus

Restaurants (7)
Eastside Café
Center Street Coffeehouse
Restaurant Hokusai
Ice Cream Cones
Sweetheart Café
Refreshment Corner
Great American Waffle Company

Shops (14)
World Bazaar Confectionary
Grand Emporium
Main Street Daily
Camera Center
Town Center Fashions
Harrington's Jewelry & Watches
Pastry Palace
Toy Station
Magic Shop
House of Greetings
Silhouette Studio
The Disney Gallery
Disney & Co.
The Home Store

Adventureland:

Attractions (8)
Pirates of the Caribbean
Jungle Cruise
Western River Railroad
Swiss Family Treehouse
The Enchanted Tiki Room: *Stitch*
   Presents "Aloha E Komo Mai!"
"Lilo's Luau & Fun"
"Mickey and Minnie's
   Polynesian Parade"
"Minnie Oh! Minnie"

Shops (10)
The Golden Galleon
Pirate Treasure
Cristal Arts
La Petite Parfumerie
Party Gras Gifts
Chiba Traders – Arts and Crafts
Safari Trading Company
Tiki Tropic Shop
Adventureland Bazaar
Candy Wagon

Restaurants (12)
Royal Street Veranda
Blue Bayou Restaurant
Café Orleans
The Gazebo
Crystal Palace Restaurant
Polynesian Terrace Restaurant

Parkside Wagon
Boiler Room Bites
China Voyager
Squeezer's Tropical Juice Bar
Fresh Fruit Oasis
The Skipper's Galley

Westernland:

Attractions (8)
Westernland Shootin' Gallery
Country Bear Theater
Mark Twain Riverboat
Big Thunder Mountain
Tom Sawyer Island Rafts
"Horseshoe Roundup"
"Pecos Goofy's Frontier Revue"
"Super–Duper Jumpin' Time"

Shops (6)
Frontier Woodcraft
Western Wear
General Store
Westernland Picture Parlour
Trading Post
Country Bear Bandwagon

Restaurants (7)
Plaza Pavilion Restaurant
Pecos Bill Café
Slue Foot Sue's Diamond Horseshoe
Hungry Bear Restaurant

Luck Nugget Café
The Canteen
Chuck Wagon

Critter Country:

Attractions (2)
Splash Mountain
Beaver Brothers Explorer Canoes
Restaurants (2)
Grandma Sara's Kitchen

Shops (2)
Hoot & Holler Hideout
Splashdown Photos

Rackety's Raccoon Saloon

Fantasyland:

Attractions (9)
Peter Pan's Flight
Snow White's Adventures
Pinocchio's Daring Journey
Dumbo The Flying Elephant
Castle Carousel
Haunted Mansion
It's a Small World
Alice's Tea Party
Pooh's Hunny Hunt

Shops (7)
Fantasy Gifts
The AristoCats
The Glass Slipper
Baby Mine
Pleasure Island Candies
Stromboli's Wagon
Pooh Corner

Restaurants (5)
Troubadour Tavern
Captain Hook's Galley
Queen of Hearts Banquet Hall

Cleo's
Village Pastry

Toontown:
Attractions (8)
Roger Rabbit's Car Toon Spin
Minnie's House
Mickey's House and Meet Mickey
Chip 'n Dale's Treehouse
Gadget's Go Coaster
Donald's Boat
Goofy's Bounce House
Toon Park

Shops (2)
Toontown Delivery Company

Restaurants (8)
Dinghy Drinks
Toon Pop
Out of Bounds Ice Cream
Huey, Dewey and Louie's
    Good Time Café
Daisy's Snack Wagon
Mickey's Trailer
Goofy's Drink Stand
Pop–A–Lot Popcorn

Gag Factory/Toontown
    Five & Dime

Tomorrowland:
Attractions (8)
Star Tours
Space Mountain
Captain EO
StarJets
Grand Circuit Raceway
Buzz Lightyear's Astro Blasters
Monsters, Inc. "Ride & Go Seek!"
"One Man's Dream II –
    The Magic Lives On"

Shops (6)
Cosmic Encounter
Planet M
ImageWorks
Stellar Sweets
Solar Ray's Light Supplies
Monsters, Inc. Company Store

Restaurants (7)
Plaza Restaurant
Soft Landing
Pan Galactic Pizza Port
Tomorrowland Terrace

Space Place FoodPort
Lite Bite Satellite
The Popping Pod

Shows and Parades

Tokyo Disneyland, like other Disney parks, provides ever–changing shows and parades. Some are permanent fixtures of the park while others change annually or with the season. Be sure to review the latest entertainment options before you depart on your trip so that you may plan any additional "must sees". Check the daily schedule for specific times and locations for these events.

Tokyo Disneyland parades are spectacles. They are high energy and high quality. The parade route begins next to the Haunted Mansion and winds through Fantasyland to the central hub (located between the castle and World Bazaar), partially circles the hub and heads back through Tomorrowland, into Toontown and ends next to Roger Rabbit's Car Toon Spin.

Tokyo Disneyland is constantly experimenting to find ways to improve the guest experience. Due to the popularity of some Tokyo Disneyland shows, the park has decided that instead of watching guests line up earlier and earlier for shows (1–2 hours during high attendance days), they instituted a lottery system. This distribution systems allows guests to know early in the day whether or not they will be able to attend a show and, if so, what time. With tickets to the show in hand, guests can arrive at shows a knowing that their party has reserved seats together. Tomorrowland Hall has been converted into the lottery distribution center. We found the set–up a little confusing at first, but if you know what to expect, it's a breeze. There are two entrances to Tomorrowland Hall. The right–hand side entrance is for people who are attempting to get tickets to one show and the left–hand entrance is for people attempting to see a different show. Prioritize the show that is most important to you and head for those lottery machines first. After waiting in a short line, proceed to an available machine. Select English on the monitor, select the show time you want, scan the passports of everyone who wants a ticket (i.e. if there are six people in your party, scan all six tickets before proceeding to the next step). Select "okay". The lottery machines will tell you whether or not you were awarded tickets to your selected show. Win or lose, you can only attempt to get tickets one time for each show and you can only win tickets to one show. If you are issued tickets on

> **TRAVEL TIP**
> We highly recommend you stake out a spot in front of the Haunted Mansion 15 minutes before the parade (30-45 minutes on days of heavy attendance) and then experience the Haunted Mansion after the parade passes. It is important you are immediately in front of the Haunted Mansion as you will not be able to cross through the parade route for quite some time. Because the entrance to the Haunted Mansion becomes isolated, the line to the attraction decreases significantly during the parade, often allowing guests who are positioned appropriately to walk on as the parade passes by.

> **DID YOU KNOW?**
> Tokyo Disneyland opened in April 1983 and only four months later, the park broke the single day attendance record of Disneyland in California. On August 13, 1983, 94,378 guests visited Tokyo Disneyland and broke the 28-year old California record.

your first attempt, gather your tickets, exit the building and report to the show when indicated. You may not attempt to win additional tickets for the other show. If you were not lucky enough to be issued tickets for the first show, exit the building and enter the line for the other show and follow the same process. Shows held in places like Tomorrowland's Showbase issue reserved seating while shows held in open venues like the Castle Forecourt Stage issue tickets for reserved standing room only.

> **TRAVEL TIP**
> Take a moment to review the location of the shows as you decide which show to attempt first – you can only get tickets to one show per day. Some of the most popular shows are held at the Castle Forecourt Stage directly in front of Cinderella's Castle. While the Reserved Standing Area encompasses the space closest to the stage, guests without tickets can easily enjoy the show from numerous vantage points around the central hub. Conversely, shows held in Tomorrowland's Showbase venue cannot be seen without a ticket.

Stroller and Wheelchair Rental

Strollers and wheelchairs (regular and motorized) are available to rent at Tokyo Disneyland. The rental kiosk is located near the far right of the entrance plaza before you move into the covered streets of World Bazaar. The daily rental fee is substantially lower than in the U.S. Strollers are $7.75, wheelchairs $3.30 and motorized wheelchairs $22.20. If you plan to visit both parks in the same day, keep your receipt and you will be issued the same item in the other park at no additional cost.

Main Entrance

The Main Entrance to Tokyo Disneyland boasts an enormous amount of open space – truly unique in Tokyo – between the transportation area and the ticket booths. Off in the not–so–far distance, you will see the spires of Cinderella's Castle and the glass canopy above World Bazaar. In the spirit of Disney, souvenir shops are open at both ends of the entrance – Promenade Gifts East and Promenade Gifts West. Two sets of ticket booths, with covered queues for inclement weather, flank a shrub-lined flowerbed sporting the latest creation by the

> **HIDDEN MICKEY ALERT**
> The metal support bars under the ticket window counters offer an early peak at the many Hidden Mickeys within Tokyo Disneyland.

Disney garden staff. Beyond the ticket booths are the security bag check and turnstiles for entrance to the Happiest Place in Japan. Once inside, it's time for the requisite picture in front of the Mickey Mouse face created from flowers – the layout of this stand–alone Mickey's flowerbed appears to have been "borrowed" by Disneyland Paris (the Mickey flowerbed at Disneyland and the Magic Kingdom is in front of the Main Street train station). The courtyard is very large and the Victorian buildings decadent as you feel you could get lost before you even get started. If you did not do so when you purchased your tickets, grab an English–language map for your day's adventure and head for the streets of World Bazaar.

World Bazaar
Overview

World Bazaar is a turn–of–the century Victorian style shopping and eating area complete with 14 shops, seven restaurants and three attractions. Names on the widows of these faux businesses give you a sense that you are in a nostalgic American town in the early 1900s. This area is fashioned after Walt

> **NOT SO HIDDEN MICKEY ALERT**
> Check out the weather vane at the top of the Tokyo Disneyland sign above the entrance gate.

Disney's recollection of his boyhood home of Marceline, Missouri. World Bazaar helps transition guests from the "real world" into a world of fantasy and fun. Cast Members are dressed the part and the subtle music and smells help transport you.

World Bazaar:	
Attractions (3)	*Shops (14)*
Penny Arcade	World Bazaar Confectionary
The Disney Gallery	Grand Emporium
Omnibus	Main Street Daily
	Camera Center
Restaurants (7)	Town Center Fashions
Eastside Café	Harrington's Jewelry & Watches
Center Street Coffeehouse	Pastry Palace
Restaurant Hokusai	Toy Station
Ice Cream Cones	Magic Shop
Sweetheart Café	House of Greetings
Refreshment Corner	Silhouette Studio
Great American Waffle Company	The Disney Gallery
	Disney & Co.
	The Home Store

There are two streets – Main Street, which runs from the Main Entrance to the central Plaza and Cinderella's Castle, and Center Street, which runs perpendicular to Main Street about halfway down and provides access to Adventureland and Tomorrowland. The entire complex is covered with a glass canopy to offer respite from inclement weather and to make sure that if guests cannot enjoy the attractions, at least they can spend some Yen. Given the crowds and the enclosed structure, it can get quite loud in World Bazaar. The entire area is impeccably clean and upkeep is top notch.

> **TRAVEL TIP**
> World Bazaar stays open at least 30 minutes after the attractions close. You may want to save some shopping for the end of the day to provide maximum time to enjoy the attractions.

How it Compares

Just as its predecessors in Disneyland and the Magic Kingdom, World Bazaar was clearly inspired by Walt Disney's hometown of Marceline, Missouri. The look of the buildings is the same, but the ambiance and layout is quite different. The canopy, with all its natural light, still gives you the surreal sensation that you are outside, especially at night. Where Main Street U.S.A. funnels guests to the central hub, World Bazaar empties into the central Plaza and is also cross–sectioned by Center Street. Center Street provides additional shopping and food for guests and allows them direct access to Tomorrowland on the right and Adventureland on the left. This helps disperse crowds and provides a multitude of paths through the park. There is no train station, trolley cars, horse–drawn carriages, curbs (though curbs and sidewalks are painted into the walk area) or tracks in the middle of the road to wreak havoc on strollers. Some of Main Street's charm is missing from World Bazaar, but it is very unique and themed extremely well.

> **HIDDEN MICKEY ALERT**
> As you enter the main gates and walk into World Bazaar, turn around and look at the windows separating World Bazaar from the main entrance. The window perimeters are decorated in fanciful Victorian painting and at the bottom center of the border you will find a Hidden Mickey.

If you are familiar with Disneyland or the Magic Kingdom, one of the first things you will notice as you leave World Bazaar heading toward the Cinderella's Castle is the immense amount of real estate covering that area. The distance is two to three times that of the same area in other parks and sets the tone for the size and scope of Tokyo Disneyland.

Tips

Japanese and Americans have significantly different views of "personal space". Be forewarned that should it rain – and it's quite likely you will experience some rain – World Bazaar can fill up quickly to the point that it is difficult to move. We recommend you find a different area to take cover from the rain, or better yet take advantage of the smaller crowds by grabbing a parka and hitting the rides!

Attractions

Penny Arcade

TRAVELERS SERIES RATES IT – Nakaguri (boring – not worth the time)
ATTRACTION SNAPSHOT – Antique arcade
QUEUE – There is no wait to enter the storefront.
ATTRACTION LENGTH – Self–directed.

DESCRIPTION AND REVIEW – Designed to replicate the 19th and 20th century theme of World Bazaar, the Penny Arcade is a room with about twenty authentic mechanical arcade games. Examples of these antiques range include pinball, Strength Meters, and kinetoscopes that allow the operator to view "moving pictures" with this early motion picture technology. Each game is a throw-back to a simpler time when these machines were state of the art technology. There are also Medallion Maker machines that, like the Pressed Penny machines at the U.S. parks, sell a coin souvenir with a Disney or Tokyo Disneyland picture embossed on it. These coin operated machines range from $0.10 – $1.10 and only accept Japanese Yen.

TRAVEL TIP
Tokyo Disneyland stores that sell umbrellas and ponchos:
World Bazaar: Grand Emporium, The Home Store (umbrellas only), Disney & Co.
Adventureland: The Golden Galleon (umbrellas only), Tiki Tropic Shop, Adventureland Bazaar
Westernland: Western Wear, Trading Post
Critter Country: Hoot & Holler Hideout (umbrellas only)
Fantasyland: AristoCats (umbrellas only), Baby Mine (umbrellas only), Pooh Corner (umbrellas only)
Toontown: Gag Factory/Toontown Five & Dime
Tomorrowland: Cosmic Encounter (umbrellas only), ImageWorks (umbrellas only)

HOW IT COMPARES – There is nothing really different about this "attraction" compared to those at other Disney parks. If anything, the World Bazaar arcade looks a little sparse compared to its Disneyland and Magic Kingdom counterparts. This is not a result of fewer games, but rather the slow conversion of the U.S. arcades to become retails space (they are stuffed with merchandise and candy with a few games off to the side). You will often see a line at the Medallion Maker machine with tourists lining up for an inexpensive souvenir.

TIPS – World Bazaar is open thirty minutes or more after the rest of the park closes. This would be a good time for this attraction, if you choose to visit.

The Disney Gallery

TRAVELERS SERIES RATES IT – Abere–ji (Average – experience this attraction if time allows)

ENTERTAINMENT SNAPSHOT – Museum of Disney attractions, drawing class, and shop

QUEUE – There is rarely any wait to view the Gallery. The Drawing Class accepts same day reservations.

ATTRACTION LENGTH – The Gallery is self–directed. Drawing classes are offered in 20 or 60 minute intervals.

DESCRIPTION AND REVIEW – The Disney Gallery is an attraction combining a museum, drawing class and store all in one. The museum portion of the Disney Gallery is a delightful and interesting experience. The rotating exhibits include art work, models and mock–ups of Disney attractions, movies, characters, hotels and resorts. This non–descript shop in the World Bazaar sends guests up a flight of stairs to the second floor where they can peek into the minds of the Imagineers and view how attractions and characters came to be, how they changed from concept to construction and other ideas that never materialized. Set in a richly appointed gallery, The Disney Gallery pays homage to the Imagineers in an elegant setting. We highly recommend the Gallery for any Disney fan. If you are big enough fan to make the trek to Tokyo, you are sure to enjoy this exhibition.

The Disney Drawing Class offers guests the opportunity to go to Animation School and learn to draw a Disney character. The classroom features a Gepetto's workshop style room complete with Mickey Mouse chairs. Two courses are offered: Standard, which lasts 20 minutes and costs $5.50, and the Advanced Course, which lasts 60 minutes and costs $11. Reservations may be made at the entrance to the Disney Gallery.

> **TOKYO DISNEY FUN FACT**
> Tokyo Disneyland is approximately 126 acres. Here's how it stacks up to the other "Disneyland" parks:
> Disneyland – 85 acres
> Hong Kong Disneyland – 55 acres
> Magic Kingdom (Disney World) – 142 acres
> Disneyland Paris – 126 acres

Behind the cashier, there are pictures of the characters that will be taught that day and the times for each course. The courses are only available in Japanese. If this is important to you and you are adventurous enough, the overhead used by the artist will easily allow you to keep up with the class and learn to draw the character, though you'll be left out of the inside jokes as the other 30 people in the class laugh.

HOW IT COMPARES – The Disney Gallery "museum" is unique since the artwork includes originals and rotating exhibits. It is similar in concept and execution to Disneyland's version. The Disney Gallery "classroom" is similar to The Magic of Disney Animation at the Disney Hollywood Studios in Florida and Animation Academy at Disney's California Adventure where guests can learn to draw a Disney character. The major difference is Tokyo Disneyland's intimate setting with a capacity of only 30 people per class. Also, guests have to pay an extra for the class.

TIPS – Tour the museum during a break in your day or in the 30 minutes after the park closes. If you are going to attempt the Drawing Class, make reservations early to ensure your seat.

Omnibus
TRAVELERS SERIES RATES IT – Nakaguri (Boring – this attraction is not worth the time)
ENTERTAINMENT SNAPSHOT – Early 1900s replica bus drives in a circle around the Plaza.
QUEUE – guests line up by a pole on the sidewalk and can see the entire attraction while standing in line.
ATTRACTION LENGTH – Six minutes.

DESCRIPTION AND REVIEW – Take a ride on a turn–of–the–century double–decker bus. The Omnibus is an excellent replica of these 20th century vehicles. The "tour" takes you around the Plaza in a complete circle. The driver provides an overview of the sights in Japanese. This attraction runs a limited schedule to avoid crowds and parades.

HOW IT COMPARES – This attraction is sub–par to its predecessors in every way. The vehicle itself is an excellent replica of an Omnibus, but the limited route and lack of Main Street intimacy surrounding it highlights why this attraction is not worth the wait (or even the six minute ride).

TIPS – Skip this one and just take a walk around the Plaza.

Dining
Eastside Cafe
EATERY SNAPSHOT –Table–service restaurant offering pasta dishes, steak and fish

PRICES – $22 to $32 per person; kids' meals are $14.
CAPACITY – 240
PRIORITY SEATING AVAILABILITY – Yes
DESCRIPTION AND REVIEW – This Victorian–style "sit–down" restaurant offers a two prix fixe menu options. All include a starter, pasta, dessert and beverage. The Entrée Course also includes grilled beef tenderloin or grilled fish.

Center Street Coffee House
EATERY SNAPSHOT – Table–service coffee shop
PRICES – Entrees range from $8.50 to $21, kids' meals are $9.75.
CAPACITY – 230
PRIORITY SEATING AVAILABILITY – No
DESCRIPTION AND REVIEW – This is a 1930s style art deco coffee shop. This sit–down restaurant offers meals ranging from deep fried shrimp to cream of corn soup to spaghetti. Breakfast options include a large Mickey Mouse pancake!

> **DID YOU KNOW?**
> There are a number of vendors selling balloons throughout World Bazaar and the rest of the park. The balloons, however, are not mylar. Instead they are thick latex/plastic material.

TIPS – Breakfast is served until 10 am. Center Street Coffee House is not open for breakfast on days when the park opens at 10 am.

Restaurant Hokusai
OVERVIEW – Japanese fare in a table–service setting
PRICES – Sets range from $18 to 26; kids' meals are $13.
CAPACITY – 270
PRIORITY SEATING AVAILABILITY – Yes
DESCRIPTION AND REVIEW – Named for a famous Japanese artist, Restaurant Hokusai is Tokyo Disneyland's only sit–down establishment featuring Japanese food. Delicacies include tempura, sushi and other traditional Japanese fare. Offering a wonderful opportunity to enjoy Japanese cuisine, Hokusai should make your short list of restaurants.
TIPS – Request a seat by the window so you can enjoy people watching and a view of Cinderella's Castle.

Ice Cream Cones
EATERY SNAPSHOT – Counter–service Ice cream parlor
PRICES – $3 for a single scoop; $5 for a sundae.
CAPACITY – 160
PRIORITY SEATING AVAILABILITY – No

DESCRIPTION AND REVIEW – This eatery offers ice cream cups, cones or sundaes plus a few other sweet treats. Indoor and outdoor seating is available.

TIPS – Grab a seat outside with a beautiful view of Cinderella Castle.

Sweetheart Cafe

EATERY SNAPSHOT – Counter–service bakery
PRICES – $2 to $5 for pastries and drinks
CAPACITY –90
PRIORITY SEATING AVAILABILITY – No
DESCRIPTION AND REVIEW – You will smell the fresh–baked goodies inside as you walk by the Sweetheart Café. Offering quick–order and freshly made breads, pastries and desserts. This is a great place to grab a latte on your way into the park…especially on cold mornings.

TIPS – Tables outside enjoy a view of Cinderella Castle.

Refreshment Corner

EATERY SNAPSHOT – Counter service hot dogs and soda
PRICES – $4.20 for a hot dog and $10 for a set meal
CAPACITY – 170
PRIORITY SEATING AVAILABILITY – No
DESCRIPTION AND REVIEW – Refreshment Corner is a brighter and better–lit version of the Disneyland eatery of the same name. It is located in almost the exact same location as its Disneyland counterpart. The Victorian–themed hot dog stand is a great place to grab a quick bite and Coke.

TIPS – Cinderella Castle provides a beautiful backdrop when eating outside. You may also hear the music of the bicycle pianist as he rides his "piano bike" and stops to play a tune.

Great American Waffle Company

EATERY SNAPSHOT – Counter–service waffles
PRICES – $4.50 to $5.30
CAPACITY – 120
PRIORITY SEATING AVAILABILITY – No
DESCRIPTION AND REVIEW – This waffle house offers quick–service waffles with a variety of toppings including maple, chocolate, strawberry custard, and brown sugar sauces as well as green tea mousse and red beans (eeww!). The Great American waffle Company offers an interesting motif as you can begin to see the subtle changes occurring to transition from World Bazaar to Adventureland.

TIPS – Mini–waffles ($5) to go offer a unique snack option.

Shopping
World Bazaar Confectionary
RETAIL SNAPSHOT – Cookie and candy shop

> **HIDDEN MICKEY ALERT**
> Check out the display windows of World Bazaar Confectionary and pay close attention to the designs in the border of the paper doilies....see the Hidden Mickey? HINT: Look for pink and yellow doilies.

DESCRIPTION AND REVIEW – If you have a sweet tooth, it's difficult not to be excited when you walk into this store and see Sugarman Bank! This shop includes well–lit shopping areas and a richly colored "chocolate room" as well as some spectacular Disney/Pixar murals on the ceiling. You need look no further than unusually large cashier area to realize that the World Bazaar Confectionary is an extremely popular shop. It is located in the center of World Bazaar at the cross–section of Main Street and Center Street – no doubt to maximize exposure. From the tempting window displays that lure you in to a statue of Mickey wearing a

> **TOKYO DISNEY FUN FACT**
> Before its expansion, the World Bazaar Confectionary was a 2,000 square foot store generating annual sales near $100 million.

"candy suit", this oversized candy shop offers both fresh and packaged delights. Cookies, chocolate covered pretzels, licorice, candy, chocolate bars, jaw breakers and lollipops are just the beginning. Countless chocolates may be found in a separate room painted in a rich, seemingly edible, chocolate brown. As it stands today, the World Bazaar Confectionary is nearly three times its original size.

> **HIDDEN MICKEY ALERT**
> Just above the World Bazaar Confectionary sign is a pink lollipop Hidden Mickey.

TIPS – This shop gets extremely crowded at the end of the day as Japanese guests finalize their souvenir purchases. Take a slow walk through the shop, or at least poke your head in, to witness the crowds.

Grand Emporium
RETAIL SNAPSHOT – Large store stuffed with Disney merchandise
DESCRIPTION AND REVIEW – Like its Disneyland and Magic Kingdom counterparts, the Emporium is the World Bazaar's marquee shop. Offering more than 3,000 items ranging from t–shirts, polo shirts, sweatshirts, dresses, stuffed animals, and stationery to umbrellas, ponchos, film, batteries, diapers and a selection of tissue paper, this super shop will provide you with an overview of nearly all Tokyo Disneyland souvenir options.

TIPS – This shop can get so crowded that it is very difficult to get past the front door, especially after the attractions close for the evening. Our recommendation is to take a stroll through here if you must, but save your shopping for Bon Voyage.

Main Street Daily

RETAIL SNAPSHOT – Newsstand style kiosk offering packaged sweets

DESCRIPTION AND REVIEW – Disney Imagineers are never satisfied with the "typical". Main Street Daily is another example of the attention to detail Disney gives to its projects. This kiosk is designed to look like a newsstand of old and offers lollipops, packaged cookies and candy.

> **TOKYO DISNEY FUN FACT**
> Due to overwhelming popularity, the original Emporium that opened in Tokyo Disneyland in 1983 was expanded to double its size in 2002 and re-christened the Grand Emporium.

Camera Center

RETAIL SNAPSHOT – Shop offering everything for your camera

DESCRIPTION AND REVIEW – The murals at the front of the store depict early 1900s guests admiring Cinderella Castle and an Automobile Club parade. The murals showcase photographers who are set to capture the special moment. As you walk in the door, you find yourself in an era when photographs were a relatively new technology. Don't be fooled by the early 20th century reporter's desk, this is a state–of–the–art shop. This World Bazaar outlet is sponsored by Fuji Film (you probably guessed that) and offers everything guests may need (or have forgotten) for their camera including film, batteries and an assortment of accessories and disposable cameras. Camera Corner also allows guests to develop and print film as well as print digital camera pictures complete with a Disney "frame" – a border printed directly on your picture. These digital kiosks are easy to use and make a one–of–a–kind souvenir.

Town Center Fashions

RETAIL SNAPSHOT – Largest clothing store in Tokyo Disneyland

DESCRIPTION AND REVIEW – Town Center Fashions sports the largest selection of apparel within the park. The store is purported to be owned by Minnie and Daisy and, as such, the vast majority of the goods are for women and girls.

TIPS – Fashion Alert! Sizes in Japan run much smaller than those in the United States. A "large" (L) in Japan is roughly equivalent to a medium, if not a bit smaller. Guests who wear large or extra–large shirts in the U.S. may have a very difficult time finding clothes that fit. It is essential that you try clothes on before making a purchase. If buying souvenirs for people back home, buy them at least one size larger than you would in the U.S. We recommend you play it safe and opt for souvenirs that do not have a "size" requirement.

Harrington's Jewelry & Watches
RETAIL SNAPSHOT – Store featuring Disney character jewelry and watches
DESCRIPTION AND REVIEW – The rectangular glass display case that encompasses most of the interior showcases many of the unique jewelry pieces and watches for sale. A large selection of timepieces, rings, earrings, necklaces and bracelets may be found at this shop. Items range from casual to elegant and encompass every price point. A variety of wall clocks are also sold here and the most interesting include Disney cuckoo clocks.

Pastry Palace
RETAIL SNAPSHOT – Packaged pastry shop
DESCRIPTION AND REVIEW – Originally designed to look like your great-great-grandmother's kitchen, Pastry Palace has been redesigned in the light–pink Victorian style that reflects the look of World Bazaar. This shop offers Disney "tins" of prepared goods and mixes to take home. Other treats include packaged cookies, cakes and other baked goods.

Toy Station
RETAIL SNAPSHOT – Toy store
DESCRIPTION AND REVIEW – Toys, toys, toys! The word "toy" at the entrance will lure children and adults alike. Inside, guests will find toys of all shapes and sizes. Statues of Disney characters "toying around" are on display throughout the shop. There is also memorabilia themed to special events.
TIPS –Toys make for unique souvenirs with the Japanese–language packaging. Be aware that many instruction manuals are only available in Japanese.

Magic Shop
RETAIL SNAPSHOT – Magic shop
DESCRIPTION AND REVIEW – A larger version of its Disneyland predecessor, the Magic Shop offers a variety of tricks, puzzles and souvenirs. Here, aspiring magicians will find Disney-themed and traditional magic tricks for all ages. The Cast Members regularly perform demonstrations of the in–stock "illusions" both inside the store and directly in front of the store. It is fun to watch both the magicians and the reactions of their audience.
TIPS – Buyer beware! Some products include English instructions, though many are only available in Japanese.

House of Greetings

RETAIL SNAPSHOT – Stationery and postcard shop

DESCRIPTION AND REVIEW – This might be the largest "writing room" you ever enter. Stocked with greeting cards, stationary, pens, pencils, markers, postcards, stamps and just about anything you would need to remind the people back home that you are on vacation, the House of Greetings is dedicated to written communication. This considerate shop provides writing desks should you be inclined to spend time writing postcards while actually at Tokyo Disneyland (we think the hotel in the evening would be just as good).

TIPS – The House of Greetings is a great place for inexpensive souvenirs for the folks back home!

Silhouette Studio

RETAIL SNAPSHOT – Portrait studio creating custom silhouettes

DESCRIPTION AND REVIEW – Located inside a tucked–away corner of the Disney Gallery, this tiny studio's artists will capture your visit with a silhouette containing up to four people. Like its Disneyland counterpart, Cast Members use special scissors to cut out instantly recognizable profiles of you and your group on black paper and place it on a cream background. You can even have your silhouette alongside Mickey or Minnie.

TIPS – Most of these Silhouette Artists are English–speaking and can provide some insight about the park.

The Disney Gallery

RETAIL SNAPSHOT – Disney Art for sale

DESCRIPTION AND REVIEW – The Disney Gallery is a combination attraction infusing a museum, drawing class and store all in one. Items on sale include books, posters and animation art.

Disney & Co.

RETAIL SNAPSHOT – Store featuring Disney character merchandise

DESCRIPTION AND REVIEW – The Disney characters in the shop window appear to be having a lot of fun riding turn–of–the century bicycles and going for a stroll. You will undoubtedly want to take a peek inside, where you will find a very large – and almost overwhelming – assortment of character merchandise.

TIPS – Although smaller than the Grand Emporium, you will find many of the same items here and much smaller crowds.

The Home Store

RETAIL SNAPSHOT – Household goods with a Disney flare

DESCRIPTION AND REVIEW – Need a Mickey Mouse waffle iron? It's here! How about Disney salt and pepper shakers? They got 'em! Offering both the normal and unique, this store carries a wide selection of goods for your home. While browsing through this store, it can be fun to imagine your home with these items or to wonder, "Who would have that in their house?".

Adventureland
Overview
As you move from Center Street or the central Plaza toward Adventureland, you will slowly transition from the Victorian pastels and crown molding of World Bazaar into the exotic paradise that is Adventureland. You will quickly become immersed in this realm of adventure-filled lands from across the globe. Adventureland is part Africa, part tropical jungle, part Pacific Rim and part Louisiana bayou. Here, you will combat pirates, tour the Amazon, sing with tropical birds and explore a ship–wrecked tree house.

Adventureland:	
Attractions (8)	*Shops (10)*
Pirates of the Caribbean	The Golden Galleon
Jungle Cruise	Pirate Treasure
Western River Railroad	Cristal Arts
Swiss Family Treehouse	La Petite Parfumerie
The Enchanted Tiki Room: *Stitch Presents "Aloha E Komo Mai!"*	Party Gras Gifts
"Lilo's Luau & Fun"	Chiba Traders – Arts and Crafts
"Mickey and Minnie's Polynesian Parade"	Safari Trading Company
"Minnie Oh! Minnie"	Tiki Tropic Shop
	Adventureland Bazaar
	Candy Wagon
Restaurants (12)	
Royal Street Veranda	Parkside Wagon
Blue Bayou Restaurant	Boiler Room Bites
Café Orleans	China Voyager
The Gazebo	Squeezer's Tropical Juice Bar
Crystal Palace Restaurant	Fresh Fruit Oasis
Polynesian Terrace Restaurant	The Skipper's Galley

Whether you enter this tropical locale by road or by bridge, you are sure to be impressed as you walk through Caribbean–style buildings worn by the sun, through lush landscapes or down the streets of New Orleans.

Adventureland is home to 12 restaurants, 10 shops and seven attractions – including two Disney classics.

How it Compares

Adventureland is a combination of the Magic Kingdom's Adventureland with its Caribbean buildings and Polynesian–style theater and lush tropics, Adventureland at Disneyland with it's African tribal props and dense forest and Disneyland's New Orleans Square with the architecture and charming intimate streets of this Louisiana city. Adventureland is a wonderful collection of the best parts of the Magic Kingdom and Disneyland including the classic attractions Pirates of the Caribbean and the Jungle Cruise.

Attractions
Pirates of the Caribbean

TRAVELERS SERIES RATES IT – Yuunaru (Outstanding! Disney at its best)
ENTERTAINMENT SNAPSHOT – Slow boat ride through the Caribbean.
QUEUE – The adventure begins at the front of a Louisiana–style mansion. Guests wind their way through dimly lit corridors as they are transitioned into the bayou under the evening stars.
ATTRACTION LENGTH – 15 minutes

DESCRIPTION AND REVIEW – A true Disney classic. As you board the 20–person boat and "set sail" through this attraction, you will already feel like a part of the scene. Beginning in the deep bayous of Louisiana, the ride transports guests to the islands of the Caribbean. This is an inspired ride filled with audio–animatronic pirates singing, fighting, yelling and chasing. Every detail is carefully considered and the superbly crafted scenes range from ships exchanging cannon fire with a fort to a pillaged town and the classic jailed pirates trying to coax the key from the obstinate pooch. Most of the scenes are pretty funny. The attraction moves relatively slow, but there is one drop which may splash you with just a few drops. The props are in English and the soundtrack is in both Japanese and English, though the story is easy enough to follow regardless of the soundtrack. Characters from the blockbuster Disney trilogy (the three Pirates of the Caribbean movies have grossed more than $2.6 billion) are interwoven into the scenes, including Jack Sparrow himself. Pirates of the Caribbean is always a good attraction for resting in the cool darkness –save this ride for the mid to late part of the day. As you disembark, you'll be glad you dropped anchor in this port of call.

HOW IT COMPARES – Most of these scenes were pulled directly from its Disneyland and Magic Kingdom predecessors – if it ain't broke, don't fix it ya scurvy scoundrel. The attraction more closely resembles Disneyland primarily because of the Blue Bayou restaurant's placement and accompanying scenery at the beginning of the attraction. The largest difference, of course, is that some of the audio is in Japanese – though we think this makes for a fun change!

TIPS – Look for Jack Sparrow – Johnny Depp's much acclaimed character from the Pirates of the Caribbean movies – as he appears several times throughout this attraction.

Jungle Cruise

TRAVELERS SERIES RATES IT – Yuunaru (Outstanding! Disney at its best)
ENTERTAINMENT SNAPSHOT – A boat ride through tropical jungles.
QUEUE – Guests enter a tropical boat station and see tools that will be used on the exploration. Posters on the walls provide insight as to what can be expected on the journey. The queue is mostly covered and the beginning of the attraction can be seen from most places in line.
ATTRACTION LENGTH – 10 minutes

DESCRIPTION AND REVIEW – Once aboard the ship, the skipper immediately starts making wise cracks. At least, that's what you will think since the narration is in Japanese. The trek begins through the jungles of Asia and quickly moves to the Nile in Africa and the perilous Amazon in South America. "Wild" audio–animatronic animals are all around including a tiger staring from ancient ruins and African bull elephants roaming the jungle. On the African plains, you will encounter lions, zebras, rhinos and more than a few humorous scenes of safari–goers and their camps. As your boat enters the treacherous hippopotamus-infested waters and is about to be attacked – you'll be forewarned when the animal blow bubbles and wiggle their ears – the skipper grabs a toy gun and the "gunshot" blasts over the speakers. The skippers are extremely energetic and enthusiastic. They speak very quickly, very loudly and with a great deal of inflection. While the guests will laugh at the jokes occasionally, they are far more subdued than the skipper. This is a fun ride that guests big and small and English–speaking and Japanese–speaking will enjoy.

HOW IT COMPARES – Compared to the Disneyland and Magic Kingdom versions of this classic, the humor level is actually not that different. If you have ridden this ride in the IS, you can almost imagine the skippers telling the same jokes – almost verbatim – at the same time and laugh along with the rest of the crowd. This ride looks and feels like its U.S. counterparts as

114

the elephants are still bathing, the lions still hovering over the "sleeping" zebra, and the rhinos are still attacking as the African safari guides scale a totem pole. The ride more closely resembles the Jungle Cruise in the Magic Kingdom primarily because of the mystic cave the cruise passes through. The skippers at Tokyo Disneyland are extremely high energy compared with the dry sarcasm of Disneyland and the Magic Kingdom. You'll also notice the skipper uses a toy gun without blanks as guns are illegal in Japan – even those with blanks. The most notable differences are that the boats travel counter–clockwise through the attraction and the presence of Japanese warrior statues in the cave.

Western River Railroad

TRAVELERS SERIES RATES IT – Yoshi (Good – make this a priority)

ENTERTAINMENT SNAPSHOT – A train ride through jungles, American Indian villages, and Primeval World.

QUEUE – Guests climb the stairs to board the steam locomotive through a remote outpost train station. While portions of the queue are covered, even moderate lines extend outside to the area in front of the entrance.

ATTRACTION LENGTH – 15 minutes

> **NOT SO HIDDEN MICKEY ALERT**
> As the train passes the Indian Village, the famous mouse can be seen in the dirt in front of the fire.

DESCRIPTION AND REVIEW – The Western River Railroad allows guests the opportunity to board a colorful steam locomotive and travel through the jungles of Adventureland and on to the frontier of Westernland. During the journey, guests will be treated to lush greenery, views of the wild, and a prehistoric trip back in time to Primeval World. The Western River Railroad begins its round–trip in the jungles of Adventureland alongside the waters of the Jungle Cruise. The first several minutes are relaxing and confined to dense greenery with nothing more than trees to look at. From there, the train passes an Indian Village, and then guests are treated to terrific views as the train steams through Splash Mountain and Critter Country en route to a lap around the Rivers of America . There, guests can see the Mark Twain Riverboat and Beaver Brothers Explorer Canoes (the people paddling on those are working a lot harder than the guests relaxing on the train!). From there, it's on to the mountains of Big Thunder, and into Primeval World – a diorama depicting dinosaurs and other prehistoric creatures – before returning to the station. The Western River Railroad is enjoyable for the entire family and is a very relaxing ride.

HOW IT COMPARES – The most significant difference between the Western River Railroad and the comparable attraction in Disneyland and the Magic Kingdom is that this trip amounts to a round–trip ride with no stops where

115

the U.S. versions are used widely for transportation as well as entertainment. The Disneyland and Magic Kingdom railroads roll over tracks that span the perimeter of their respective parks, whereas the Tokyo Disneyland version is confined to Adventureland, Westernland and Critter Country. Also, the Tokyo Disneyland steam train is closer in color schemes to the Little Engine That Could with candy–apple red and royal blue and appears more whimsical as opposed to the muted tones of the authentic locomotives in California and Florida.

Swiss Family Treehouse

TRAVELERS SERIES RATES IT – Abere–ji (Average – experience this attraction if time allows)

ENTERTAINMENT SNAPSHOT – Walk-through exploration of a giant treehouse.

QUEUE – There is rarely a wait to enter the attraction. The queue and the attraction are essentially one and the same, so there will be times when the attraction bottlenecks as guests walk through.

ATTRACTION LENGTH – This attraction is self–directed and depends on your speed and the number of people in front of you. Typically, this attraction takes about 8 minutes.

> **TOKYO DISNEY FUN FACT**
> The Swiss Family Treehouse is a part of the rare species Disneyodendrron eximus...or "Out–of–the–Ordinary Disney Tree".

DESCRIPTION AND REVIEW – The Swiss Family Treehouse is a walk–through exhibit placing guests in the center of the 1960 Disney film's interpretation of Johann Wyss' 1812 novel, *The Swiss Family Robinson*. Here, guests will climb stairs through this enormous "tree" and see first–hand how the Robinson family utilized furniture and wreckage from their stranded ship to build spectacular living quarters. While this is a very well done attraction, it is not worth seeing if you have limited time.

HOW IT COMPARES – The Swiss Family Treehouse is, for all intents and purposes, the same as the Magic Kingdom's Swiss Family Treehouse and Disneyland Paris' La Cabana des Robinson. The props and some elements of the attraction differ quite a bit from Disneyland since it was converted to Tarzan's Treehouse in 1999.

The Enchanted Tiki Room: *Stitch Presents "Aloha E Komo Mai!"*

TRAVELERS SERIES RATES IT – Yoshi (Good – make this a priority)

ENTERTAINMENT SNAPSHOT – Stitch and a large flock of Audio–animatronic birds stage a musical show.

116

QUEUE – The covered queuing area is set in the courtyard of the Polynesian building that houses the attraction. Guests sit or stand in a semi–circle to look at the fountain and a few audio–animatronic birds that make an occasional appearance.

ATTRACTION LENGTH – 13 minutes; shows start every 20 minutes

DESCRIPTION AND REVIEW – The Enchanted Tiki Room welcomes guests form the courtyard into a Polynesian themed room decorated with tiki statues, flowers and birds from the Hawaiian Islands. The show starts and the audio–animatronic birds come alive. There are four "host" birds and each has a Hawaiian name – Hau'Oli, WahaNui, Manu, and Mahina – and one has a French accent. Guests are treated to Hawaiian music as the birds begin talking and singing until the show is interrupted by the arrival of Stitch, who makes his presence known by drawing on the windows around the room when the lights are off. He then proceeds to joke with the audience as his arm occasionally appears in a flower bed playing instruments. Stitch then appears front and center rocking a ukulele and entertaining the crowd. This attraction is very well done and allows guests to sit in a climate–controlled room for 13 minutes with minimal crowds!

HOW IT COMPARES – Disney has taken care to differentiate its three Tiki Rooms. Disneyland still sports the "original" Tiki Room while the Magic Kingdom's show has been overtaken by Iago and Zazu, the birds from Aladdin and Lion King, respectively. As a result, each experience is unique. The addition of recent movie characters adds an updated and humorous element while the original remains a tribute to Walt Disney and the Disney parks. The Tokyo Disneyland version is themed the same way, but the music and show are very different from the other two parks. An original soundtrack was produced for the Tokyo version featuring Hawaiian music and Stitch, whose movies take place in Hawaii.

TIPS – This theater holds 344 people and there are rarely long lines. Typically, you will wait for no more than one complete show to cycle (20 minute cycles). This attraction is perfect during the middle of the day when the park is at its busiest or for a climate controlled rest in the afternoon.

"Lilo's Luau & Fun" / "Mickey & Minnie's Polynesian Parade"

TRAVELERS SERIES RATES IT – Abere–ji (Average – experience this attraction if time allows)

ENTERTAINMENT SNAPSHOT – Meal with a musical show

QUEUE – Guests may wait a short time to be seated. Since reservations are required, there is no "line".

ATTRACTION LENGTH – 65–75 minutes

DESCRIPTION AND REVIEW – Tokyo Disneyland categorizes Lilo's Luau & Fun and Mickey & Minnie's Polynesian Parade as attractions. In reality, they are lunch or dinner theater. Both are held at the Polynesian Terrace Restaurant and Lilo entertains at lunch while Mickey performs at dinner.

> **HIDDEN MICKEY ALERT**
> There is a popcorn cart near The Enchanted Tiki Room and the cart itself is painted with corn cobs and popped corn. Several of the popped kernels show more than a traditional Hidden Mickey, they show the actual face of Mickey Mouse!

Lilo's Luau is a Polynesian themed musical. Lilo, Stitch, Mickey, Minnie and a few others – complete with Hawaiian shirts – perform several musical and dance numbers. Kids are invited to the stage to learn how to hula and parents pushing their little tykes to go join in the fun can be seen throughout the theater. The characters travel to each table to greet the guests, take pictures and give hugs to the kids. This is an excellent spin on the traditional character dining experience as it combines character dining with a show.

Mickey and Minnie's dinner show features Polynesian dancers wearing traditional and colorful grass skirts and leis. With the rhythmic beat of the Tahitian drums, the fast–paced hip–shaking hula dancing and the songs of the Polynesian islands, Mickey & Minnie's Polynesian Parade feels more like a traditional Hawaiian Luau than Lilo's lunch party. In traditional luau style, guests of various ages are selected from the crowd to participate in the festivities.

There are multiple shows daily. Guests must make reservations in advance on a Japanese–language only web site.

TIPS – Seating is limited and will likely sell out. If attending this show is important to you, you must find someone who can read Japanese to assist with the online reservations.

"Minnie Oh! Minnie"
TRAVELERS SERIES RATES IT – Abere–ji (Average – experience this attraction if time allows)
ENTERTAINMENT SNAPSHOT – Outdoor musical stage show
QUEUE – Guests line up outside the small outdoor amphitheater.
ATTRACTION LENGTH – 30 minutes

DESCRIPTION AND REVIEW – The rhythm is gonna get you in this Latin American musical stage show featuring Minnie, Mickey, Donald, Goofy and Chip 'n Dale. The show begins as Donald, Goofy, Chip and Dale hit the stage in bright orange Latin outfits (Donald looks like he just left the set of the Three Caballeros) and try to keep up with the beat. Minnie then takes the stage and performs a couple of numbers before being joined by Mickey. Guests are invited to participate on stage and dance with the group and the finale is filled with bright colors, energetic dancers and the entire character cast of this show. Dancing and music are top–notch. Most of the songs performed are in English.

Dining
Royal Street Veranda
EATERY SNAPSHOT – Counter–service offering drinks
PRICES – $2.50 to $3.20
CAPACITY – 20
PRIORITY SEATING AVAILABILITY – No
DESCRIPTION AND REVIEW – Fitting in perfectly with its Cajun surroundings, this tiny corner "snack shack" is located next to Pirates of the Caribbean. Options include apple tea soda, mixed orange drink, green milk tea and hot cocoa.

Blue Bayou Restaurant
EATERY SNAPSHOT – Table service offering deluxe fare *inside* the Pirates of the Caribbean attraction
PRICES – Entrees range from $17.25 to $30; kids' meals are $16
CAPACITY – 210
PRIORITY SEATING AVAILABILITY – Yes
DESCRIPTION AND REVIEW – The Blue Bayou Restaurant offers the Tokyo Disney Resort's only dining option *inside* an attraction. As they are seated, guests will find themselves in the middle of the Louisiana bayou circa 1850. It is nighttime, the moon is out, fireflies are in the air and the sounds of the swamp are all around. Every few moments, boats carrying passengers through the bayou en route to view the raucous characters in Pirates of the Caribbean pass by. This restaurant is both elegant and magical. The wrought iron chairs and lanterns hanging above provide the New Orleans atmosphere. The food is delicious and the service is excellent. Menu options include grilled beef tenderloin on white sorghum pilaf, Creole chicken and shrimp gumbo over buttered rice, sautéed veal escalope and a variety of seafood dishes. The wait staff is close at hand and extremely responsive. This is a wonderful experience and is highly recommended. Be sure to make a priority seating reservation for this popular restaurant.
HOW IT COMPARES – Themed after Disneyland's restaurant of the same name, theme and setting, there are very few stylistic differences between

the two. The menus are slightly different though both change constantly and offer Cajun dishes. The main difference is the level of service. As service levels have diminished over the years at Disneyland, Tokyo Disneyland has continued to provide extremely friendly Japanese wait staff who are on hand and eager to ensure guests enjoy their experience giving it a distinctive edge over its California predecessor.

TIPS – Request a seat by the water as the best way to enjoy the Blue Bayou is with unobstructed views of the attraction and the riders.

Café Orleans

EATERY SNAPSHOT – Counter–service offering crepes
PRICES – $4.60 to $5.30
CAPACITY – 170
PRIORITY SEATING AVAILABILITY – No
DESCRIPTION AND REVIEW – This creperie, accented in rich woods against a brick backdrop, specializes in a variety of crepes. For guests looking for a light meal or a hearty snack, chicken patty and vegetables, chicken salad, and Cajun shrimp salad crepes are available. For those seeking their afternoon sweet treat, banana and chocolate, strawberry and mango crepes may do the trick. The crepes are prepared near the counter, so take advantage of the view and watch the talented crepe chef perform some magic. Café Orleans' menu (crepe toppings) changes periodically.

The Gazebo

EATERY SNAPSHOT – Soups and beverages served counter–style
PRICES – $4.50 to $6.00
CAPACITY – 110
PRIORITY SEATING AVAILABILITY – No
DESCRIPTION AND REVIEW – This counter–service café specializes in soups complete with French rolls. Soup varieties include spicy beef and egg soup, cream of corn soup, seafood gumbo soup, and curried meatball soup, among others. There is generally a variety of soup and other options including shaved ice in the summer.

TIPS – There is rarely a long line at The Gazebo, though you will notice a severe uptick at times before, during and after parades and shows in the central Plaza. If you are going to eat here, plan to avoid these times.

Crystal Palace Restaurant

EATERY SNAPSHOT – Buffet for lunch and dinner and a character breakfast
PRICES – $28 adults, $18 children ages 7–12, $10.50 children ages 4–6
CAPACITY – 450
PRIORITY SEATING AVAILABILITY – No

DESCRIPTION AND REVIEW – Owing it's theming much more to World Bazaar than its Adventureland home, this elegant Victorian style building that hosts the Crystal Palace Restaurant faces the central Plaza. The building itself is decadent featuring three glass domes, countless windows and exquisite iron work and offers excellent views of the Plaza. Food is served buffet style and there are plenty of selections for Westerners and Japanese alike. When the park opens before 10 am, the buffet is a Disney Character Breakfast where Mickey and the gang visit each table to take pictures and give hugs. The food is quite good, especially for a buffet.

HOW IT COMPARES – The Crystal Palace Restaurant looks very similar to its namesake at the Magic Kingdom. Both are elegantly crafted and styled Victorian splendors, from the glass domes to the intricate design. If you've seen one, you've seen them both.

Polynesian Terrace Restaurant

EATERY SNAPSHOT – Table service Polynesian with a show

PRICES – Lunch ranges from $40 to $49 for adults and $29 to $38 for children 4–8 years old depending on the seats selected; Dinner ranges from $44 to $53 for adults and $30 to $39 for children depending on the seats.

CAPACITY – 230

PRIORITY SEATING AVAILABILITY – Reservations are required. No Priority Seating.

DESCRIPTION AND REVIEW – The Polynesian Terrace Restaurant is home to "Lilo's Luau & Fun" and "Mickey & Minnie's Polynesian Parade" – Lilo hulas at lunch while Mickey & Minnie dance at dinner. In keeping with the authenticity of a Hawaiian luau, food options are relatively limited at both meals.

Lilo's Luau is a Polynesian themed musical. Lilo, Stitch, Mickey, Minnie and a few others – complete with Hawaiian shirts – perform several musical and dance numbers. Kids are invited to the stage to learn how to hula and parents pushing their little tykes to go join in the fun can be seen throughout the theater. The characters travel to each table to greet the guests, take pictures and give hugs to the kids. This is an excellent spin on the traditional character dining experience as it combines character dining with a show.

Mickey and Minnie's dinner show features Polynesian dancers wearing traditional and colorful grass skirts and leis. With the rhythmic beat of the Tahitian drums, the fast–paced hip–shaking hula dancing and the songs of the Polynesian islands, Mickey & Minnie's Polynesian Parade feels more like a traditional Hawaiian Luau than Lilo's lunch party. In traditional luau style, guests of various ages are selected from the crowd to participate in the festivities.

There are multiple shows daily. Guests must make reservations in advance and the only way to make reservations is on a Japanese–language only web site.

The entertainment is top–notch in typical Disney style. However, there are better much better meal options – even for character dining – in the park that take much less time.

TIPS – Seating is limited and will likely sell out. If attending this show is important to you, you must find someone who can read Japanese to assist with the reservations.

Parkside Wagon
EATERY SNAPSHOT – Counter–service churros and drinks
PRICES – $2.75 churros; $2.50 to $3.20 drinks
CAPACITY – 0
PRIORITY SEATING AVAILABILITY – No
DESCRIPTION AND REVIEW – This early 1900s style delivery truck turned–snack shack, sits at the entrance to Adventureland near World Bazaar's Center Street. Options are limited to churros, coffee and soda.
TIPS – Lines can be pretty long here. Unless you are dying for a churro, drinks are available with a shorter wait elsewhere. Likewise, other stands sell churros (typically with shorter lines).

Boiler Room Bites
EATERY SNAPSHOT – Counter–service steam buns and tortilla sandwiches
PRICES – $4.50 to $5.50 snacks; $2.50 to $4.20 drinks
CAPACITY – 170
PRIORITY SEATING AVAILABILITY – No
DESCRIPTION AND REVIEW – When an old explorer ship wrecked on this area, those thoughtful and ingenious Imagineers decided to salvage the wreckage and turn it into a restaurant. The boiler from the ship is used to heat Mickey-shaped pork steam buns. The rest of the ship was assembled to provide shade, tables and chairs, and the building. Options are limited and include Mickey Mouse-shaped pork steam buns and pork tortilla sandwiches with sweet miso sauce. Beverages include sodas and "Jungle Tea" made with black tapioca and mango jelly in milk tea. Boiler Room Bites shares its seating area with China Voyager.
TIPS – The seating areas around Boiler Room Bites are wonderful places to enjoy a meal, snack or just to rest.

China Voyager

EATERY SNAPSHOT – Noodles served counter–style

PRICES – Entrees start at $11; kids' sets are $8.60

CAPACITY – 260

PRIORITY SEATING AVAILABILITY – No

DESCRIPTION AND REVIEW – The shores of Adventureland are dangerous and many ships were destroyed while navigating its waters. After completing Boiler Room Bites, the Disney folks were clearly in the mood to salvage more wreckage and build another eatery. The China Voyager is fashioned from the wreckage of an old clipper ship. Here, the food choices include a variety of soup noodle dishes as well as a few sides and desserts. Varieties of soup noodles include minced pork and shrimp in spicy miso soup and shrimp and vegetables in pork soup while toppings like a soy–simmered egg can be added for $1.11. China Voyager shares its outdoor seating area with Boiler Room Bites.

> **HIDDEN MICKEY ALERT**
> The sign displaying China Voyager has three circular Chinese signs below it. The middle sign has a couple of ears.

Squeezer's Tropical Juice Bar

EATERY SNAPSHOT – Counter service featuring fruit beverages and sherbet

PRICES – $2.30 to $4.50

CAPACITY – 0

DESCRIPTION AND REVIEW – Squeezer's Tropical Juice Bar offers fruit juice, Italian ice and soft serve sherbet. One if its most popular items is the soft serve sherbet available in green apple, grape or swirl. Both options are very refreshing. Drinks include a tapioca mango drink or a guava drink.

PRIORITY SEATING AVAILABILITY – No

> **HIDDEN MICKEY ALERT**
> This *very* Hidden Mickey requires a little investigative work. There is a bench behind Squeezer's Tropical Juice Bar near the restrooms. Check out the wall at the base of the bench and see if you can find the three rocks that create this camouflaged Hidden Mickey.

Fresh Fruit Oasis

EATERY SNAPSHOT – Kiosk offering fresh fruit

PRICES – $1.30 to $4.50

CAPACITY – 0

PRIORITY SEATING AVAILABILITY – No

DESCRIPTION AND REVIEW – At this small fruit stand, guests will find a variety of fresh fruit and bottled drinks. Choices include bananas, apples, oranges and other healthy snacks. It might be a good idea to work at least one natural and healthy option for the day!

The Skipper's Galley
EATERY SNAPSHOT – Teriyaki chicken legs served over the counter
PRICES – $4.65
CAPACITY – 0
DESCRIPTION AND REVIEW – This kiosk offers tasty teriyaki chicken legs. If you are eating here, grab your food and a few napkins, and find a table near Boiler Bites or China Voyage.
PRIORITY SEATING AVAILABILITY – No

Shopping
The Golden Galleon
RETAIL SNAPSHOT – Pirate merchandise
DESCRIPTION AND REVIEW – If the Pirates of the Caribbean were real, they would want to spend their galleons here. The pirate ship themed cashier stand and skull and cross–bone décor will make any pirate feel at home. Nearly everything in this store is themed to the swashbuckling profession and there is tremendous variety. Whether you need a toy sword, eye patch or a shirt, The Golden Galleon is the place. In addition to traditional souvenirs, the Galleon offers many unique "non–Disney" items relevant to its pirate heritage including model ships.

Pirate Treasure
RETAIL SNAPSHOT – Souvenir shop featuring trading pins
DESCRIPTION AND REVIEW – Collectible pins have caught on in Tokyo. While still not at the fever pitch of Disney collectors in California and Florida, pins and collectible souvenirs are gaining steam here. This trove will provide options for the pin collector and many are exclusive to Tokyo Disneyland. Pin Trading is not a part of the Tokyo Disney experience, but it will be fun to trade some Japanese pins on your next Trip to the Magic Kingdom or Disneyland!

Cristal Arts
RETAIL SNAPSHOT – Glassworks shop
DESCRIPTION AND REVIEW – This quaint shop seems more European than French Quarter in theme and matches the elegance of the merchandise. Hand crafted glassworks are available and range from Disney characters and castles to shot glasses, mugs and picture frames. Engraving is available for many of these items. Guests have an opportunity to watch how these fragile items are created by glassblowers. Behind their protective work

bench, these artisans mold, torch and shape a variety of unique items. The merchandise is similar to that available at the Glass Slipper in Fantasyland.

La Petite Parfumerie

RETAIL SNAPSHOT – Perfumes and soaps

DESCRIPTION AND REVIEW –The beauty of this shop's interior, with intricate moldings, design and pastels reserved for French royalty, is only matched by the decadence of its offerings. La Petite Parfumerie specializes in smelling good. It offers a wide variety of perfumes, lotions and soaps from various regions of the world. Products range wildly in aroma and price including Tokyo Disneyland branded perfumes, which are an exclusive line available only to park guests.

Party Gras Gifts

RETAIL SNAPSHOT – Mardi Gras accessories

DESCRIPTION AND REVIEW – Typical of many stores in Louisiana's real French Quarter, this New Orleans style shop features a wealth of Mardi Gras items. From feathered masks, beaded necklaces and souvenirs both Disney and non–Disney, there is plenty to peruse at Party Gras Gifts.

Chiba Traders – Arts and Crafts

RETAIL SNAPSHOT – Authentic Japanese gifts

DESCRIPTION AND REVIEW – If the Tokyo Disney Resort is your primary destination in Japan, Chiba Traders, along with a few stores in Ikspiari – is definitely worth a visit. Here, guests will find trinkets and crafts from Chiba and around Japan. Ranging from the small and standard (dolls and hand–crafted wooden toys), to large and unique, you are sure to be able to find a terrific Japanese souvenir.

> **DID YOU KNOW?**
> The Tokyo Disney Resort is technically located in Chiba and not in Tokyo. Then again, Disneyland Paris isn't located in Paris….

Safari Trading Company

RETAIL SNAPSHOT – African Safari merchandise

DESCRIPTION AND REVIEW – This small shop is decorated in sand-colored tile and dark rich woods. The items offered at the Safari Trading Company fit in with the African scenery throughout Adventureland. This rustic looking shop is filled with animal, jungle and tribal merchandise. Whether your souvenir list calls for an authentic tribal mask or a stuffed animal of a non–Disney elephant, you will find it here.

Tiki Tropic Shop
RETAIL SNAPSHOT – Polynesian gifts
DESCRIPTION AND REVIEW – Guests inspired by the décor and theme of the Enchanted Tiki Room will find a myriad of Hawaiian and Polynesian gifts here. From clothing and jewelry and hand–made crafts to hula dancer clocks, ukuleles and loud Hawaiian shirts, there is a wide variety of merchandise here. The sheer tackiness of some of these items makes the Tiki Tropic Shop worth a quick browse.
TIPS – Additional merchandise can usually be found in the kiosk just outside near the stone courtyard fountain and Adventureland Bazaar.

Adventureland Bazaar
RETAIL SNAPSHOT – Handmade crafts
DESCRIPTION AND REVIEW –Adventureland Bazaar depicts a colonial shop set in Africa. Its wares include woven baskets, a variety of musical instruments like maracas and bongo drums, and other "handmade" goods. This shop is set near a stone courtyard fountain.

Candy Wagon
RETAIL SNAPSHOT – Candy–toting kiosk
DESCRIPTION AND REVIEW – This stationary cart – borrowing its Victorian look from World Bazaar – offers a variety of sweet treats. Candy Wagon offers both souvenir treats as well as snack-size bags to be enjoyed while touring the park.

Westernland
Overview
Westernland is accessible by bridge from the central Plaza and by footpath from Adventureland and Fantasyland. America's Old West lives on in Japan as guests enjoy the peaks and canyons of Big Thunder Mountain and the Mark Twain Riverboat's paddlewheel churning the Rivers of America. This rustic 19th century town is complete with General Store and Trading Post and it would only seem natural to see a cowboy of the Wild West stroll down the street atop his steed. Each building portrays the simplicity of this time in the Old West. Westernland sports eight restaurants, six shops and eight attractions including an infamous Disney Mountain. And folks, "hang on to them hats and glasses, 'cuz this here's the wildest ride in the wilderness."

How it Compares
Westernland is Frontierland by another name. The look and feel of this area is very similar to its California and Florida cousins. The core walking

area within Westernland is witness to some of the prime differences. Where Frontierland's shops and restaurants at Disneyland are located in a relatively small area, Westernland's buildings are bigger and guests have the sensation they are on the "streets" of an Old Western town. The Magic Kingdom differs from Westernland in that guests typically walk down the narrow "street" with the water on one side and the buildings on the other, where Westernland feels more like a mining town.

Westernland:	
Attractions (8)	*Shops (6)*
Westernland Shootin' Gallery	Frontier Woodcraft
Country Bear Theater	Western Wear
Mark Twain Riverboat	General Store
Big Thunder Mountain	Westernland Picture Parlour
Tom Sawyer Island Rafts	Trading Post
"Horseshoe Roundup"	Country Bear Bandwagon
"Pecos Goofy's Frontier Revue"	
"Super–Duper Jumpin' Time"	
Restaurants (7)	
Plaza Pavilion Restaurant	Luck Nugget Café
Pecos Bill Café	The Canteen
Slue Foot Sue's Diamond Horseshoe	Chuck Wagon
Hungry Bear Restaurant	

Attractions
Westernland Shootin' Gallery
TRAVELERS SERIES RATES IT – Nakaguri (Boring – this attraction is not worth the time)
ENTERTAINMENT SNAPSHOT – Coin operated shooting gallery
QUEUE – There is rarely a wait to play this game.
ATTRACTION LENGTH – about 2 minutes

DESCRIPTION AND REVIEW – The Westernland Shootin' Gallery provides guests the opportunity to "shoot" at targets staged in an Old West saloon. Targets are located on or next to various "people" including the objects like a bartender, piano player, guitar, lanterns and bottles. When the shooter hits the targets with the infrared light of the gun, the items spill, spin, jump, fall, explode, or play music. The scene and results from well–aimed shots are humorous and light–hearted. The cost is $2.20 for 10 shots and each player receives a scorecard complete with note from Pecos Goofy.

HOW IT COMPARES – While the scene and props differ from the outdoor Old West graveyard scenes found in both the Magic Kingdom's Frontierland Shootin' Arcade and Disneyland's Frontierland Shootin' Exposition, the attraction is effectively the same save for the message from Pecos Goofy. The major difference is in the pricing and the number of shots. At Disneyland, the cost is $0.50 for 20 shots and at the Magic Kingdom, it is $1.00 for 35 shots; both offer two to three times the number of shots for a fraction of the price.

TIPS – If you hit 10 out of 10 targets, you will be given a Sherriff's badge!

Country Bear Theater

TRAVELERS SERIES RATES IT – Abere–ji (Average – experience this attraction if time allows)

ENTERTAINMENT SNAPSHOT – Musical review starring audio–animatronic bears

QUEUE – The queue is indoors and climate–controlled. Guests will have time to look at myriad of pictures, posters and other props while waiting. It is also an opportunity just to sit and relax. There is rarely a wait as the theater holds more than 300 guests. The longest you will likely wait is for the show to cycle.

ATTRACTION LENGTH – 15 minutes

DID YOU KNOW?
One day Walt Disney stopped by Imagineer Marc Davis' work area and noticed an early sketch for what would become the Country Bears. Walt was said to have noticed one particular bear playing a tuba and began laughing hysterically and praising Marc for the idea. Disney lore has it that this was the last time Walt Disney ever had a good laugh; he died a few days later.

DESCRIPTION AND REVIEW – Once seated in the theater, guests know they are in for a silly treat when the mounted heads of a moose, buffalo and deer (Melvin, Buff and Max, respectively) start talking in Japanese! So begins the zany show featuring a number of extremely talented talking and singing bears. The "performers" play instruments, sing songs and dance. The set's scenes changes several times throughout the show to introduce new characters and new songs. These characters communicate as much with their looks and body language as they do with their words and the show is good old fashioned down home country fun. Three different versions of the Country Bears grace the stage throughout the year including the original "Country Bear Jamboree", "Vacation Jamboree" and Christmas themed "Jingle Bell Jamboree". The dialogue is in Japanese and most of the songs are in English save for a Japanese rendition of *Davey Crocket*!

HOW IT COMPARES – The Tokyo Disneyland version of the Country Bears includes the same scenes and gags as the Magic Kingdom's Country Bear Jamboree right down to crowd favorite, Big Al. If nothing else, the Japanese dialogue adds to the humor of the show.

Mark Twain Riverboat

TRAVELERS SERIES RATES IT – Abere–ji (Average – experience this attraction if time allows)
ENTERTAINMENT SNAPSHOT – Paddlewheel boat ride
QUEUE – The waiting area for the Mark Twain Riverboat looks like an elegant riverfront train depot. Themed to colonial America, this queue welcomes guests into the 1800s.
ATTRACTION LENGTH – 12 minutes

DESCRIPTION AND REVIEW – Board the Mark Twain Riverboat and set a course for a round–trip excursion through the Rivers of America. The Mark Twain is a large white sternwheeler with towering twin black stacks on the top deck. It holds about 475 guests. Travelers aboard this boat will travel the rivers of America with views of Westernland and Big Thunder Mountain, Critter Country and Splash Mountain. Tom Sawyer Island, a western-themed playground for kids, is always on the right hand side. Among the scenes guests will view from the deck are an Indian Village and some other poor guests who decided to sweat it out by powering themselves around the Rivers of America in the Beaver Brothers Explorer Canoes. The trip is relaxing and allows guests to see these lands from a different vantage point. The Westernland River Railroad provides many of the same views and is, in our estimation, a much better choice. Not only does it offer more diverse scenery, there is seating available for all guests and every seat has a great view.

HOW IT COMPARES – The Mark Twain Riverboat is similar to the Magic Kingdom's Liberty Square Riverboat and Disneyland's Mark Twain Riverboat. Similarities include it circling Tom Sawyer Island, cruising by an Indian Village, and providing views of multiple lands within the park. It looks nearly identical to the 1955 Disneyland original. It's different because it's Tokyo Disneyland. The view is different, the attractions and lands you will see are different and it provides a unique perspective of this amazing park. Lastly, it's different because it is far more popular than its two counterparts in Florida and California.

TIPS – The top desk is the most popular because it offers the best views.

Big Thunder Mountain (FASTPASS)
TRAVELERS SERIES RATES IT – Yuunaru (Outstanding! Disney at its best)
ENTERTAINMENT SNAPSHOT – Runaway mine train roller coaster
QUEUE – You will hear the screams of passengers as you wait in a rustic outpost full of tools from the mine. This Old West covered queue is designed to alert future riders to the rickety instability of Big Thunder Mountain.
ATTRACTION LENGTH – 4 minutes

DESCRIPTION AND REVIEW – "Hang on to them hats and glasses", it's Big Thunder Mountain! This wild and crazy roller coaster ride through the canyons and shafts of an Old West mine is among the best of what Disney has to offer. This ever–popular attraction is exciting and fun and offers plenty of corny gags throughout the journey. Guests board what is soon to be a runaway mine train. The adventure begins in a mine shaft and as the track curves into the dark recesses of the mine, guests are treated to rainbow caverns with mineral pools and stalactites and stalagmites. As the mine train climbs out of the cave and into the light, it takes guests through a waterfall and then the fun really begins. Through twists, turns, and falls up and down the canyon, guests hang on and enjoy the ride. Next, the train comes to another mine shaft following an explosion – rocks are shaking and the track is unstable. Just as the train appears to be climbing out of the collapsing mine, it approaches a broken track. The train cannot continue its climb to safety and races out of the mountain. The ride is a blast for all ages and kids over 102cm/40 in.

HOW IT COMPARES – Tokyo Disneyland's Big Thunder Mountain more closely resembles it's Magic Kingdom compadre from the look as you enter the line and the larger covered queuing area to the ride itself. Similarities between the two include the ride starting in a mine shaft and the outdoor mineral pools off to the side. One notable item missing from the Tokyo version is that you will not hear the prospector remind you to "hold on to them hats and glasses". The only time you will hear the famous announcer is when the attraction is temporarily stopped. Even without him, the ride is a lot of fun and a must see!

Tom Sawyer Island Rafts & Tom Sawyer Island
TRAVELERS SERIES RATES IT – Abere–ji (Average – experience this attraction if time allows)
ENTERTAINMENT SNAPSHOT – Raft ride to Tom Sawyer Island and play area

QUEUE – Guests enter the covered awning of the shabby Langhorne Landing to catch a raft to Tom Sawyer Island. From this outdoor line, guests have a view of the Rivers of America, Tom Sawyer Island and the incoming rafts.

ATTRACTION LENGTH – 2–3 minutes

DESCRIPTION AND REVIEW – Mark Twain would be proud of the style of these rafts. Guests board log rafts and head straight for Tom Sawyer Island. The Cast Members are dressed in straw hats, plaid and patched shirts, and a piece of rope for a belt. The purpose of these rafts is to transport guests to and from Tom Sawyer Island and effectively serve as the pre–show entertainment for the island. The rafts help transition guests into "Tom Sawyer" mode as they leave civilization behind for the simplicity of the Mississippi and the dusty playground of Tom Sawyer Island.

> **DID YOU KNOW?**
> Fort Sam Clemens is named after Mark Twain, the author of the 1876 novel *The Adventures Tom Sawyer*. His real name is Samuel Clemens.

Tom Sawyer Island is located in the middle of the Rivers of America. Once guests disembark, they find themselves on a seemingly uninhabited island and right in the middle of a Mark Twain novel. The island can keep guests busy for 30–40 minutes or more while they explore Smuggler's Cove, Indian Camp, Fort Sam Clemens, Injun Joe's Cave, Castle Rock Ridge, Harper's Mill and Tom Sawyer's Treehouse. There are barrel and suspension bridges, caves and interactive props.

For those guests who work up an appetite, there is a snack bar in the middle of Tom Sawyer Island called The Canteen that serves snacks, drinks and milkshakes!

HOW IT COMPARES – Tokyo Disneyland's Tom Sawyer Island has more features than the Disneyland version though it is very similar its Magic Kingdom cousin. The rafts and raft ride look and feel the same and the island is very similar. The most notable difference is the existence of The Canteen – a snack bar in the middle of Fort Sam Clemens.

TIPS – Free souvenirs! An Explorer's Map of the Island is available for all guests. It's a terrific tool to guide you through Tom Sawyer Island and makes a unique souvenir as the map is printed in both English and Japanese.

The Diamond Horseshoe: "Horseshoe Roundup" and "Pecos Goofy's Frontier Revue"

TRAVELERS SERIES RATES IT – Abere–ji (Average – experience this attraction if time allows)

ENTERTAINMENT SNAPSHOT – Stage show with table–service

QUEUE – Guests may wait a short time to be seated. Since reservations are required, there is no "line".

ATTRACTION LENGTH – about 50 minutes

DESCRIPTION AND REVIEW – The Diamond Horseshoe is a vaudeville style stage show performed in a 19th century playhouse. The theater has two floors – each with tables and chairs throughout. Each table has a view of the stage. The theater is well–designed and ornately decorated to reflect the times. Table–service food is offered during the performances.

There are two shows playing at The Diamond Horseshoe – "Horseshoe Roundup" and "Pecos Goofy's Frontier Revue". "Horseshoe Roundup" is a lunch show featuring Jessie, Woody, and Bullseye from Toy Story 2. There is plenty of singing and dancing during the show. Dinner features Goofy starring as Pecos Goofy in "Pecos Goofy's Frontier Revue". Guests will be treated to Goofy performing the Can–Can! Vaudeville dancing and singing, along with a Mickey Mouse guest appearance, rule the stage during the show. Both shows are quite entertaining and both have multiple performances daily. Guests must make reservations in advance on a Japanese–language only web site.

HOW IT COMPARES – The theming and look of The Diamond Horseshoe is very similar to the Golden Horseshoe in Disneyland, though the shows are quite different. Where Disneyland's version is a comedy and musical show starring Billy Hill & The Hillbillies, the Tokyo Disneyland version is much more of a dance and musical revue. The shows are good, but The Diamond Horseshoe's entertainment is similar to most stage shows at the park and lacks the unique and original qualities present in California. Additionally, the service here is table–service versus counter–service at the Golden Horseshoe.

TIPS – Seating is limited and will likely sell out. If attending this show is important to you, you must find someone who can read Japanese to assist with the online reservations.

Super–Duper Jumpin' Time

TRAVELERS SERIES RATES IT – Osanai (Young – experience if traveling with young children)

ENTERTAINMENT SNAPSHOT – Disney character stage show

QUEUE – Guests line up directly in front of the Plaza Pavilion Bandstand stage.

ATTRACTION LENGTH – 25 minutes

DESCRIPTION AND REVIEW – This show is designed for children. Set to the beat of several classic Disney songs, Mickey, Minnie, Donald, Pluto and the gang put on a puppet show, dance numbers and corny gags. The costumes are retro 1980s with rainbows of bright colors. The dialogue is in Japanese, though the Disney songs are the original English versions. Unless you are traveling with children, this show is not worth the time.

Dining

Plaza Pavilion

EATERY SNAPSHOT – Counter–service restaurant offering hearty Western dishes

PRICES – Entrees start at $12; kids' meals are $10

CAPACITY – 400

PRIORITY SEATING AVAILABILITY – No

DESCRIPTION AND REVIEW – Like the Crystal Palace Restaurant, the land to which Plaza Pavilion Restaurant is assigned is a bit of an anomaly. It is located directly off the Plaza and sports Victorian craftsmanship both inside and out. So why it is a part of Westernland and not the World Bazaar is a bit of an unknown. This restaurant serves a range of fare including Salisbury steak, grilled chicken, and fried prawns. Overall, the Plaza Pavilion looks very similar to the Disneyland Plaza Inn. The outdoor plaza is a great place to eat and the tiled tables feature a beautiful circular pattern and design.

TIPS – Grab a table outside near the Plaza Bandstand Stage. If you time your meal right, you can watch Super–Duper Jumpin' Time while you enjoy your meal. The show times are posted at the Plaza Bandstand Stage.

Pecos Bill Cafe

EATERY SNAPSHOT – Counter–service offering Old West morsels

PRICES – $2.60 to $3.30

CAPACITY – 60

PRIORITY SEATING AVAILABILITY – No

DESCRIPTION AND REVIEW – Located in a small but quaint building in Westernland, Pecos Bill Café offers a small selection including meat pies, apple pies, maple churros and nachos.

Slue Foot Sue's Diamond Horseshoe

EATERY SNAPSHOT – Table service and a vaudeville character show

PRICES – Lunch ranges from $35.50 to $44.50 for adults and $24.50 to $33.50 for children 4–8 years old depending on the seats selected; dinner ranges from $44 to $53 for adults and $30 to $39 for children depending on the seats.

CAPACITY – 220

PRIORITY SEATING AVAILABILITY – Reservations are required. No Priority Seating.

DESCRIPTION AND REVIEW – Slue Foot Sue's Diamond Horseshoe is a vaudeville theater that offers table service for lunch and dinner shows. The décor resembles a two–story 19th century playhouse – each with tables and chairs throughout and each table has a view of the stage. The theater is well–designed and ornately decorated to reflect the times. Table–service food is offered during the performances. The food is Western American including smoked chicken, Cajun shrimp, and coleslaw.

There are two shows playing at The Diamond Horseshoe – "Horseshoe Roundup" and "Pecos Goofy's Frontier Revue". "Horseshoe Roundup" is a lunch show featuring Jessie, Woody, and Bullseye from Toy Story 2. There is plenty of singing and dancing during the show. Dinner features Goofy starring as Pecos Goofy in "Pecos Goofy's Frontier Revue". Guests will be treated to Goofy performing the Can–Can! Vaudeville dancing and singing along with a Mickey Mouse guest appearance, rule the stage during the show. Both shows are quite entertaining and both have multiple performances daily. Guests must make reservations in advance on a Japanese–language only web site.

TIPS – Seating is limited and will likely sell out. If attending this show is important to you, you must find someone who can read Japanese to assist with the online reservations.

Hungry Bear Restaurant

EATERY SNAPSHOT – Counter–service with hearty fare and hearty portions

PRICES – Entrees start at $9

CAPACITY – 520

PRIORITY SEATING AVAILABILITY – No

DESCRIPTION AND REVIEW – You had better be Hungry when you hit the Hungry Bear. This restaurant, complete with frontier style wooden chairs, serves up an unusual variety of food. Vittles include a variety of curry dishes, rice dishes and beef hash. The fact that this restaurant shares its name with a Disneyland eatery is where the similarities end – the food, ambience and décor are completely Western instead of the Critter Country theme in California.

TIPS – The courtyard offers outside seating and is surrounded by a variety of Old West buildings. The ambience is Western and is a charming place to enjoy your meal.

Lucky Nugget Cafe

EATERY SNAPSHOT – Fried chicken and sides offered counter–service style
PRICES – Chicken starts at $5.50; up to $14 for a set.
CAPACITY – 400
PRIORITY SEATING AVAILABILITY – No
DESCRIPTION AND REVIEW – The Lucky Nugget Café is sandwiched between Big Thunder Mountain and the Rivers of America. The exterior is worn and rustic and this eatery serves up some traditional and unhealthy American fare served here in the way of fried chicken and french fries. Other sides include smoked turkey legs, coleslaw, fresh fruit cup, cinnamon churro and the ever–present cream of corn soup. Outdoor seating offers views of the Mark twain Riverboat on the Rivers of America and the screams of those riding Big Thunder.

TIPS – This restaurant is a bit hidden and generally is less crowded than many other eateries. Also, if you are dying for some traditional greasy U.S. theme park food, you will not be disappointed.

The Canteen

EATERY SNAPSHOT – Counter–service snacks and milkshakes
PRICES – Snacks and drinks start at $2.50; milkshakes are $4.75.
CAPACITY – 0
PRIORITY SEATING AVAILABILITY – No
DESCRIPTION AND REVIEW – Safely secured within the barricades of Fort Sam Clemens on Tom Sawyer Island, The Canteen offers guests access to snacks and some *very* good milkshakes (try the tropical fruit, if available – it's a Japanese favorite). It's a treat – figuratively and literally. The Canteen serves soft pretzels and a variety of drinks. Milkshake flavors include vanilla, tropical fruit and choco–banana. Be prepared to receive the smallest $4.75 shake of your life. The cup is tiny and the straw is enormous, but the milkshake is very good.

TIPS – Grab your snack (hopefully you choose a milkshake) and find a semi–secluded place on Tom Sawyer Island to sit, relax and enjoy.

Chuck Wagon

EATERY SNAPSHOT – Cart selling smoked turkey legs
PRICES – $4.50
CAPACITY – N/A
PRIORITY SEATING AVAILABILITY – No
DESCRIPTION AND REVIEW – Not one, but two Westernland covered wagons specialize in selling one thing – smoked turkey legs. Due to the location of these carts it is not unusual to see a line winding endlessly in both directions.
TIPS – Lucky Nugget Café also sells smoked turkey legs and its line is a fraction of the length of the Chuck Wagon.

Shopping
Frontier Woodcraft

RETAIL SNAPSHOT – Handmade and engraved wood and leather
DESCRIPTION AND REVIEW – A small shack with large queuing capacity, the Frontier Woodcraft sells a variety of wood and leather crafts. Wares range from wooden signs to leather bracelets to luggage tags. Most items can be personalized with your name.
TIPS – This shop is extremely popular there is almost always a line of tourists waiting to shell out some Yen for a personalized item. The line, especially late in the day, can be very long even on days of low park attendance.

Western Wear

RETAIL SNAPSHOT – Western Apparel
DESCRIPTION AND REVIEW – The Tokyo Disneyland version of the US-based Boot Barn stores, Western Wear features leather jackets with tassels, cowboy boots, cowboy hats, jeans, belt buckles and a variety of other apparel for the tourist trying to blend in with the Westernland motif.
TIPS – This store's wares may be unique to the Japanese, but we recommend you save your Yen and visit a store in the states for a broader selection and significant cost savings.

General Store

RETAIL SNAPSHOT – Grocery store offering snacks, candy and coffee
DESCRIPTION AND REVIEW – The General Store sells packaged goods like coffee, beef jerky, an assortment of candy, snacks and other tasty treats. The ambience is on target for Westernland from the cabinets to the hardwood floors.

Westernland Picture Parlour
RETAIL SNAPSHOT – Old West portrait studio
DESCRIPTION AND REVIEW – Guests can choose from a variety of 19th and early 20th Western costumes and props and then pose for a souvenir picture. This studio reflects the intense Japanese interest in America and the Old West. It's debatable whether a studio like this would make it at Disneyland or the Magic Kingdom.

Trading Post
RETAIL SNAPSHOT – Western crafts
DESCRIPTION AND REVIEW – The Trading Post features Western and Native American arts and crafts. There is nothing very unique here for the U.S. traveler as the wares are those regularly available at home.

Country Bear Bandwagon
RETAIL SNAPSHOT – Kiosk selling Disneyland souvenirs
DESCRIPTION AND REVIEW – The Country Bear Bandwagon sells a variety of traditional souvenirs from stuffed animals to giant Mickey Mouse gloves and the ever–popular Mickey ears.

Critter Country
Overview
    Critter Country lies on the other side of the Rivers of America opposite Westernland. Critter Country is the smallest land within Tokyo Disneyland and is home to a famous Disneyland Mountain – Splash Mountain.

Critter Country:	
Attractions (2)	*Shops (2)*
Splash Mountain	Hoot & Holler Hideout
Beaver Brothers Explorer Canoes	Splashdown Photos
Restaurants (2)	
Grandma Sara's Kitchen	Rackety's Raccoon Saloon

    Accessible only by footpath from Fantasyland, Critter Country sports a lot of open space for having so few attractions, restaurants and shops – a total of two in each category. However, a surprising number of people are always present in this area due to the immense popularity of Splash Mountain and the lines can snake throughout this land. The top of Splash Mountain towers above Critter Country and is incorporated into the lush greenery of its surroundings. The bright pink of the briar patch can be spotted from a distance and adds color to this charming land.

How it Compares

Critter Country is, effectively, Splash Mountain Land. Like Tokyo's version, Disneyland's Critter Country is tucked away in the back corner of the park, but it offers more than just Splash Mountain including a popular restaurant and The Many Adventures of Winnie the Pooh ride. At the same time, Tokyo Disneyland's Critter Country offers a bit of a respite because it is a "dead–end" and guests are not passing through. Where Disneyland's version is rustic and almost Frontierland–like, Tokyo Disneyland's creators engineered a whimsical, colorful and delightful area. Overall, the whimsical elements of Splash Mountain land are a treat. The colorful mountains and accents, statues of Br'er Rabbit, Fox and Bear along with a small cottage by the water for other critters that "live" in this land bring the fantastical world to life.

Attractions

Splash Mountain (FASTPASS / SINGLE RIDER)

TRAVELERS SERIES RATES IT – Yuunaru (Outstanding! Disney at its best)
ENTERTAINMENT SNAPSHOT – Flume ride through Disney's 1946 Song of the South
QUEUE – After weaving through the lengthy outdoor queue, guests enter an underground "critter" hole and begin to see things from the perspective of rabbits and other underground dwellers. Guests can catch small glimpses attraction while line, but the fun begins once you board a hollowed out log.
ATTRACTION LENGTH – 10 minutes

DESCRIPTION AND REVIEW – Splash Mountain is one of the most popular rides in Tokyo Disneyland's arsenal and it lives up to the hype. Once guests step into their log, they embark on a journey through the trials and tribulations of Br'er Rabbit, Br'er Fox and Br'er Bear. Having seen the outside of these characters' homes, guests fall down a water slide deep underground. Music, including the classic Zip–A–Dee–Doo–Dah, and singing animals are everywhere. These crooning creatures include frogs, chickens, alligators, rabbits, bees, opossums, porcupines, blue birds and many others. None of them, however, is caught in quite the predicaments of the three main characters. The scenes follow Br'er Fox and Br'er Bear in all sorts of predicaments in their unsuccessful attempts to catch Br'er Rabbit. Many of the animals warn Br'er rabbit, in song, not to follow Br'er Fox to the Laughin' Place just as the log begins a long climb up. Filled with numerous slides and opportunities to get wet, Splash Mountain culminates in one of the longest and steepest flume rides in the world – right into the Briar Patch to escape Br'er Fox and Br'er Bear. During this massive drop, Splashdown Photos snaps your picture so that you can see your own face frozen in terror. The old Splash Mountain slogan "You will get wet, you may get soaked" absolutely applies here. Some guests disembark with barely a drop of water on their clothes while others come out soaking wet. Either way, the ride is one of Disney's finest and is a must for any Tokyo Disneyland visit.

HOW IT COMPARES – Tokyo Disneyland's Splash Mountain is very similar to its Disneyland and Magic Kingdom cousins. Although the surrounding scenery in Critter Country is themed much more to Splash Mountain than the other parks, the ride itself offers little differences.

> **HIDDEN MICKEY ALERT**
> From the attraction loading area, look at the rock formations just above the tiny bridge connecting two tree houses. You'll see one large and two smaller boulders forming a Hidden Mickey.

TIPS – The lines for this ride get long and stay long! Most guests do not want to get wet first thing in the morning; however, the trade off is very long lines for the remainder of the day. Splash Mountain should be one of your first stops, even if only to get a FASTPASS and experience some of the other popular rides while the day heats up a bit. Lines here can be well over 60 minutes on cold or rainy days and can exceed 3 hours in hot weather.

Beaver Brothers Explorer Canoes

TRAVELERS SERIES RATES IT – Nakaguri (Boring – this attraction is not worth the time)
ENTERTAINMENT SNAPSHOT – Guest–powered canoe tour
QUEUE – Traditional outdoor rope line in full view of the Rivers of America.
ATTRACTION LENGTH – 10 minutes

DESCRIPTION AND REVIEW – With two guides to lead the way and to keep the canoe from running in circles, guests board a canoe in Critter Country and paddle around the Rivers of America. While the drawback is the effort of paddling, the payoff is a unique perspective of Tokyo Disneyland. On the waters of the Rivers of America, guests will find quiet – a rarity in this otherwise crowded park. To be sure, the screams of Big Thunder Mountain and Splash Mountain will be heard as will the splash of the Mark Twain Riverboat – but most of these and other sounds are off in the distance. The journey provides some spectacular views and a moment with nature before heading back to the technological wonders of the park. Cross your fingers that the canoe is near its 16 person capacity, or you are going to work a bit harder to get your boat moving!

HOW IT COMPARES – Tokyo Disneyland's Beaver Brothers Explorer Canoes is virtually identical to its Disneyland cousin – the Davy Crocket Explorer Canoes. The attraction itself is the same, but the location and overall experience is a bit different. We're still not sure how to say "row, row, row" in Japanese.

TIPS – If seeing Tokyo Disneyland from the water is important to you, take a ride on the Mark Twain Riverboat. We maintain that similar views and a far more comfortable and relaxing ride can be had on the Western River Railroad in Adventureland.

Dining

Grandma Sara's Kitchen
EATERY SNAPSHOT – Counter service and home–style cookin'
PRICES – Sets start at $13.50; kids' meals are $8.30
CAPACITY – 530
PRIORITY SEATING AVAILABILITY – No
DESCRIPTION AND REVIEW – Nestled into the base of Splash Mountain is a cute and whimsical door to Grandma Sara's Kitchen. Once inside, guests are sure to feel like a "critter" in this seemingly endless cave turned restaurant. The theming and ambiance are top–notch in this eatery. Fare includes spicy chicken and seafood pilaf, beef tomato stew with seasoned rice, and chicken and rice au gratin.
TIPS – Given its location, tucked–away from the rest of the park, Grandma Sara's Kitchen is rarely crowded. With plenty of indoor seating and a great theme, this is a good place for a meal.

Rackety's Raccoon Saloon
EATERY SNAPSHOT – Counter–service ice cream and snacks
PRICES – $3.50 to $4.20 for hot dogs; $2 to $3.30 for treats
CAPACITY – 0
PRIORITY SEATING AVAILABILITY – No
DESCRIPTION AND REVIEW – This little log cabin offers some big tastes and serves tortilla wrapped hot dogs (with or without cheese), soft serve ice cream, cookies and maple churros. Located in a park like setting, Rackety's Raccoon Saloon is a must for anyone with a sweet tooth.
TIPS – If you find yourself in a long line for Splash Mountain, send someone from your party to grab some snacks for the group. Just be sure they can find their way back to you!

Shopping
Hoot & Holler Hideout
RETAIL SNAPSHOT – Critter clothes and souvenirs
DESCRIPTION AND REVIEW – Hoot & Holler Hideout is buried in a cave and is sure to make you feel like you are "squirreling" away your goods. With roots coming down from the ceiling and lights made of acorns, this is one of the best themed shops in the Disney arsenal and completely at home in this well themed land. Wares include t–shirts, stuffed animals, stickers and stationary – many of the items with the Song of South Characters emblazoned on them.

Splashdown Photos
RETAIL SNAPSHOT – Personalized photos of your party on Splash Mountain
DESCRIPTION AND REVIEW – Just as the name suggests, this is the shop where guests can purchase pictures of themselves smiling, screaming, or laughing as they head down the Splash Mountain's largest flume and into the briar patch. Pictures are printed in with a customized Splash Mountain border.

Fantasyland
Overview

At the heart of Tokyo Disneyland – and Disney fans the world over – is Fantasyland. This area of the park embodies all that is Disney. It is a magical and wondrous area. While Fantasyland may be accessed by foot via Westernland or Tomorrowland, the best way to first see this domain is directly from the Plaza across the drawbridge and through Cinderella Castle. The castle – with it's royal blue turrets and golden spires stretching up to the Tokyo sky – is surrounded by a "moat" that is among the most peaceful areas of the Disney parks. Once inside the castle walls, guests will find a charming mix of a royal fair complete with large "tents" covering the attractions. There is an old European charm to the design and structure of many of the "cottages" that give shelter to attractions, shops and restaurants. Guests pass a statue of Walt and Mickey in the central Plaza en route to Cinderella Castle and are treated to another statue of Mickey as the Sorcerer's Apprentice once inside. The cottage streets are sprinkled with numerous trees and flowerbeds surrounded by benches. Fantasyland has a wide variety of offerings with nine attractions, five restaurants and seven shops.

How it Compares
Every Fantasyland is different, though some constants always remain such as the castle with a carousel just beyond the entrance. The layout and

feel of each is unique. Tokyo Disneyland's Cinderella Castle is a near replica of the Cinderella Castle of Walt Disney World Resort's Magic Kingdom, including a stage in front near the Plaza. However, one noticeable difference is the number of trees and accompanying benches at Tokyo Disneyland. Trees, benches and shade are abundant, as compared to the other parks, throughout Fantasyland. Dumbo is situated through the castle and past the carousel and to the left, whereas it is on the right in Disneyland and the Magic Kingdom. The inclusion of the Haunted Mansion in Fantasyland is unique to Disney parks, though the rest of the attractions reflect a combination of California and Florida's Fantasylands.

Fantasyland:

Attractions (9)	Shops (7)
Peter Pan's Flight	Fantasy Gifts
Snow White's Adventures	The AristoCats
Pinocchio's Daring Journey	The Glass Slipper
Dumbo The Flying Elephant	Baby Mine
Castle Carousel	Pleasure Island Candies
Haunted Mansion	Stromboli's Wagon
It's a Small World	Pooh Corner
Alice's Tea Party	
Pooh's Hunny Hunt	

Restaurants (5)	
Troubadour Tavern	Cleo's
Captain Hook's Galley	Village Pastry
Queen of Hearts Banquet Hall	

Tips

Fantasyland is the heart and soul of Tokyo Disneyland and this is never more apparent than at night. The entire area lights up in colorful splendor with Cinderella's Castle as the highlight. Fantasyland at night is a must see!

Attractions

Peter Pan's Flight

TRAVELERS SERIES RATES IT – Yuunaru (Outstanding! Disney at its best)
ENTERTAINMENT SNAPSHOT – Indoor "flying" dark ride through Disney's animated Peter Pan (1957)
QUEUE – The queue for Peter Pan's Flight is covered and winds inside the interior of the inner curtain of the castle. While there is no pre–show

entertainment, guests can watch as ships fly in and out dropping off and picking up riders.

ATTRACTION Length – 2 ½ minutes

DESCRIPTION AND REVIEW – Guests board a flying pirate ship and head for Wendy, John and Michael Darling's bedroom where they meet Peter Pan and fly out of the window to take a nighttime tour of London's sites including Big Ben. With a little bit of pixie dust and a track strategically placed on top of the ships, guests have the sensation they are flying high into the night sky as London with its lights and moving cars grow tiny below. From London, it's off toward the moon and Neverland. Here, the ships will encounter an Indian Village, help rescue Tiger Lily (the Indian princess), and watch Peter Pan take on the villainous Captain Hook. All dialogue is in Japanese as guests and Peter fly from scene to scene. The colors of this dark ride are bright and fanciful and when the pixie dust lights up Peter's pirate ship and guests see Captain Hook trying to escape from Tic–Toc Croc, the attraction is at its best. The flight ends at the Mermaid Lagoon and guests disembark.

> **DID YOU KNOW?**
> If you see Captain Hook walking around the park, get near his backside and say "tick–tock, tick–tock" – he will think Tic–Toc Croc with the clock in his belly is chasing him and Captain Hook will run away!

HOW IT COMPARES – Peter Pan's Flight is a combination of the Disneyland and Magic Kingdom versions. The queuing area, location and façade looks like the Magic Kingdom version. There are royal tents set up against the inner curtain of the castle where guests wait (Disneyland and Disneyland Paris' version queues through a cottage). The loading, unfortunately, is "Disneyland style" where the ships are loaded individually and one at a time versus the Magic Kingdom's much faster continuous loading system with moving walkway. The actual layout and appearance of the attraction's scenes are virtually the same in each park.

TIPS – Peter Pan's Flight is a very popular attraction and loads slowly. Each ship only has enough room for two adults versus other Fantasyland attractions like Snow White or Pinocchio that hold four. Ride this attraction early in the morning for the shortest lines – it should be one of the first handful of attractions you experience. Otherwise, attempt to visit this attraction during a parade or right before closing time.

Snow White's Adventure

TRAVELERS SERIES RATES IT – Yoshi (Good – make this a priority)

ENTERTAINMENT SNAPSHOT – Indoor dark ride depicting scenes from Disney's 1937 <u>Snow White and the Seven Dwarfs</u> classic

QUEUE – This covered queuing area is the standard Fantasyland design. The queue winds back and forth and there is no pre–show entertainment other than guests' ability to view guests loading and unloading from the dwarf's mine cars.

ATTRACTION LENGTH – 2 ½ minutes

DESCRIPTION AND REVIEW – Guests are invited to board wooden mine cars – each bearing "hand–crafted" animals and the name of one of the seven dwarfs – on the outskirts of a lovely forest to explore the three–dimensional world of this 1937 Disney classic. After a small trip around the castle courtyard with Snow White singing beautifully in Japanese, the attraction takes guests into the dwarf's house where Snow White has just arrived and finished cleaning. The merry group is throws a party to celebrate their new friendship, though unbeknownst to them, they are being watched by the Queen. Guests continue their journey through the colorful dwarf's mine and into the interior of the Queen's castle where she transforms herself into a witch and creates a wicked potion to poison the apple. The witch then finds Snow White and offers her the apple. The scene quickly moves to the climax where the dwarfs have cornered the witch on top of the mountain on a stormy night. As the witch attempts to crush the seven protagonists, she slips and the rock follows to her death. The attraction is very well themed and the props are ornate and crafted with amazing detail. The dialogue, of course, is in Japanese and this ride can be a little scary for very small children especially in the forest scene where the trees look like monsters.

> **HIDDEN MICKEY ALERT**
> In the middle of the ride, there is a scene where the Evil Queen, now an old hag, is dipping the apple into a cauldron to complete her spell. Look at the way the green poison has formed around the red apple.

HOW IT COMPARES – It's all in the name. Tokyo Disneyland's Snow White's Adventure somehow lost the word "scary", which appears in the title at both the Magic Kingdom and Disneyland. However, the ride is no less intense in Tokyo. The trees in the forest scene are much more animated (and a bit scarier) and the bats have giant eyes. Additionally, scenes such as the dwarf's mine are more vibrant and colorful than the other versions of this attraction. The queuing area and façade resemble the Magic Kingdom as the ride is located under a royal tent in the inner curtain of the castle. Snow White's Adventure also offers scenes very similar to those in California and Florida, though, like the Magic Kingdom, more scenes are present as additional space allowed the Imagineers to allow the story to unfold a bit more instead of coming to the abrupt end at Disneyland. Disneyland's queue offers much more charm with the golden apple at the entrance, the Queen occasionally looking down at those entering and the view of the Queen's dungeon just inside.

Pinocchio's Daring Journey

TRAVELERS SERIES RATES IT – Abere–ji (Average – experience this attraction if time allows)

ENTERTAINMENT SNAPSHOT – Indoor dark ride through the 1940 Disney classic

QUEUE – Guests line–up in a covered area waiting to board a hand–carved cart through Pinocchio's Daring Journey. There is no pre–show entertainment and guests waiting in line can see others both beginning and ending their adventure.

ATTRACTION LENGTH – 2 minutes

DESCRIPTION AND REVIEW – Guests board intricately carved carts and are treated to an intimate view of Pinocchio's story. From an early run–in with Stromboli, the mine car twists and turns through the fun and perils of Pleasure Island, Pinocchio's escape from the Salt Mines and ultimate rescue of Gepetto from Monstro. Disney magic is present when the Blue Fairy magically appears and makes Pinocchio a real boy. The dialogue for this attraction is in Japanese and parts of the attraction, especially the scene with Monstro, can be frightening for small children.

> **TOKYO DISNEY FUN FACT**
> Pinocchio's Daring Journey was originally designed and built for Disneyland in California in 1976. It was then put into storage and then dusted off and installed for Tokyo Disneyland's grand opening in 1983. Disneyland's version of the attraction opened a year later as part of the new Fantasyland.

HOW IT COMPARES – Having opened one year apart, this Tokyo Disneyland version is nearly identical to Disneyland's version. Both are located in charming cottages, both have short lines and the ride – from the name down to the scenes and the track layout – for this 1940 Disney movie is nearly the same. The most discriminating guests will be able to make out small differences like the ability to see the people in the Treasure Island scene brawling in the Rough House instead of an indistinguishable mass of figures fighting. Of course, hearing Jiminy Cricket trying to be Pinocchio's conscience in Japanese adds a twist!

TIPS – This attraction is likely the least visited in Fantasyland and, as a result, often has little or no line. If you pass by when there appears to be a long line, try again later.

Dumbo the Flying Elephant

TRAVELERS SERIES RATES IT – Osanai (Young – experience if traveling with young children)
ENTERTAINMENT SNAPSHOT – Outdoor circular ride aboard the star of the Disney's 1941 animated feature, Dumbo
QUEUE – The queue is a standard covered outdoor rope chain line with clear visibility of the entire ride.
ATTRACTION LENGTH – 1 ½ minutes

DESCRIPTION AND REVIEW – Ten Dumbo elephant vehicles form a circle waiting for guests to board. Once situated inside Dumbo, guests control this famous pachyderm with a lever commanding him up or down as he flies in a circle. Timothy Mouse directs the flight perched on a disco ball in the center of the attraction. Although it represents basic technologically, Dumbo is a favorite albeit slow–loading ride. While children will demand a ride, adults will have excellent views of Fantasyland from Dumbo's top heights. What you see is what you get with this attraction. With only 10 elephants, the line moves at a snail's pace even with two or three guests in each pachyderm. If the line is very short, take a ride.

HOW IT COMPARES – Tokyo Disneyland's Dumbo the Flying Elephant really differs in only three ways. One, the outside queuing area is permanently covered (Disneyland uses a series of umbrellas when necessary). Two, there are only 10 elephants – Disneyland and Magic Kingdom's version sport 16 beasts and, by definition, offer 60% shorter waits. Three, the design of the attraction's centerpiece is much more intricately designed in California and Florida following the re–work of the attraction. Tokyo Disneyland's Dumbo looks like an outdated basic circus– themed version compared to its ornate stateside counterparts.

Castle Carrousel

TRAVELERS SERIES RATES IT – Osanai (Young – experience if traveling with young children)
ENTERTAINMENT SNAPSHOT – Merry–go–round featuring scenes from 1950's Cinderella
QUEUE – Covered outdoor standard queue providing views of the entire ride.
ATTRACTION LENGTH – 2 minutes

DESCRIPTION AND REVIEW – Sitting under a large royal tent, Castle Carousel stables 90 white horses and each is intricately designed with ornate saddles. Guests step aboard this carousel, and mount the steed of their choosing. At the center of the carousel are 18 hand–painted scenes from Disney's Cinderella.

HOW IT COMPARES – Other than minor stylistic differences – including the covered queuing area – the only difference is that Tokyo Disneyland, like Magic Kingdom, features vignettes of Cinderella whereas Disneyland's King Arthur Carousel showcases scenes from Sleeping Beauty.

TIPS – With its lights and polished brass, be sure you get a look at this stunning carousel at night when it is lit up.

Haunted Mansion (FASTPASS)

TRAVELERS SERIES RATES IT – Yuunaru (Outstanding! Disney at its best)
ENTERTAINMENT SNAPSHOT – Indoor dark ride featuring scenes of ghosts
QUEUE – The queue and pre–show to the Haunted Mansion are integral parts of this Disney masterpiece. The creative genius of this ride incorporates every possible element. From the moment guests step past the gargoyles at the gate and onto the Haunted Mansion's property and begin the long winding path up to the front door, they are immersed in the attraction. The walk through the graveyard sets the mood as guests approach the mansion – be sure to read the tombstones. Once they are invited in by a Cast Member, guests are directed to the ante chamber, a parlor of sorts. Here, the ghosts begin to take over as a creepy Japanese "ghost" voice begins to narrate the adventure and strange things begin to happen –

> **TOKYO DISNEY FUN FACT**
> There is a cawing crow located throughout the ride. This crow was originally designed to serve as the "host" of the attraction until Imagineers settled on the "ghost host" who speaks in your ear throughout the attraction.

especially to the fireplace. Guests are moved into another room that stretches before their very eyes depicting some wickedly humorous scenes of the Haunted Mansion's residents. Guests exit this "stretching room" into a second queuing area. In these haunted halls, guests are treated to a variety of spooky artifacts including pictures that transform from death to life and back again as guests pass by en route to their "doom buggy".
ATTRACTION LENGTH – 7 ½ minutes

DESCRIPTION AND REVIEW – The Haunted Mansion is a true Disney classic that masters that art of incorporating sets, lighting, music and dialogue to set the mood – just as one might expect from a movie production. In fact,

147

the enormous and towering mansion looks very similar to the layout of the home in the 2003 Eddie Murphy movie, The Haunted Mansion, complete with attached atrium. Guests are invited to board a "doom buggy" for a supernatural trip through this spirited house. Candles float, knockers knock, and doors stretch throughout the mansion. No trip to the Haunted Mansion is complete without conducting a séance with Madame Liota, being invited to a witness a ghost dance in the ballroom, a peek in the attic and a stroll through the graveyard. The ghosts appear to be active participants and the detail, down to the carved doorknockers and wallpaper, is stunning. Far from scary, the scenes are whimsical and the singing and music ensures a fun journey for all ages. The scariest part for the younger set tends to be the stretching room and the screaming that occurs as the lights momentarily go dark. This attraction is absolutely not to be missed. Much of the singing and some of the dialogue are in English, though the narration is in Japanese.

The Haunted Mansion sports a continuous loading system and can handle significant capacity – making even long lines very manageable.

HOW IT COMPARES – Tokyo Disneyland's Haunted Mansion is virtually identical, both inside and out, to the Magic Kingdom's Haunted Mansion located in Liberty Square. Both facades are the same Dutch Gothic design and, unlike Disneyland, the "stretching" room's ceiling actually rises to give the illusion of stretching. Here, guests exit the room on the same level they entered (in Disneyland, guests are lowered 15 feet into a corridor below the façade). The logistical reason for this difference is that space is much more of a premium at Disneyland and Imagineers needed a creative way to get guests on the opposite side of

> **TOKYO DISNEY FUN FACT**
> The effect of having the eyes on the busts "follow" guests as their doom buggy goes by was something the Imagineers discovered by accident. It is created by developing a hollowed bust, facing it away from the ride and providing backlight.

the railroad tracks and into the "show building", technically located outside the park. The largest difference between the Florida and Tokyo versions is that two griffin–like gargoyles sit atop brick columns as guests enter the queuing area to Tokyo Disneyland's Mansion. These gargoyles were added to give a more fantasy–esque feel to the Haunted Mansion and help it blend with its surroundings. The Imagineers felt that the Magic Kingdom's Haunted Mansion looked so natural against the backdrop of the Rivers of America and Frontierland, that they specifically selected its location in the Tokyo park to be the transition point of Fantasyland to Westernland. In contrast to both Tokyo Disneyland and the Magic Kingdom, Disneyland's Haunted Mansion façade is themed to an old Southern Antebellum–style mansion.

TIPS – Although FASTPASS is available for the haunted mansion, other attractions tend to have much longer wait times. Plus, if you time your visit to the Haunted Mansion around the parade, you can practically walk on the ride. The parade route begins directly in front of the Haunted Mansion and you should stake out a spot for the parade about 15 minutes prior to the start (30+ minutes on crowded days) and then experience the Haunted Mansion as soon as the parade passes. It is important you are immediately in front of the Haunted Mansion (the closer to the entrance, the better) as you will not be able to cross through the parade route for quite some time. The entrance to the Haunted Mansion becomes isolated and the line to the attraction decreases significantly during the parade, allowing you to practically walk on the attraction.

> **TOKYO DISNEY FUN FACT**
> Imagineers initially struggled with where to place the Haunted Mansion at Tokyo Disneyland. Original ideas had the mansion being built in World Bazaar or Westernland, but neither seemed to make sense. As the development team researched Japanese culture, they learned that ghost stories are categorized as fables or fairy tales. Thus, the natural home for the Haunted Mansion became Fantasyland! The griffin–like gargoyles at the entrance were placed there to give the Haunted Mansion a more fantasy–like feel.

It's a Small World

TRAVELERS SERIES RATES IT – Osanai (Young – experience if traveling with young children)

ENTERTAINMENT SNAPSHOT – Indoor boat ride depicting children from countries around the world

QUEUE – It's a Small World has a traditional indoor queue where, like many places in Fantasyland, guests have a clear view as others board and disembark the attraction.

ATTRACTION LENGTH – 10 minutes

DESCRIPTION AND REVIEW – Originally conceived for the 1964 World's Fair in New York, It's a Small World quickly became a Disney classic, though it is set to a song so repetitive that it makes adults want to jump overboard. The attraction takes guests on a boat ride through many areas of the globe and shows children (in the form of dolls) dancing to the same song as scenes depict different parts of the world. The primary version of the theme song is in Japanese, though the song will be heard in several languages throughout the attraction. The ride is charming and the message upbeat. However, unless you are traveling with children or have never been on this ride at another Disneyland park, it is not necessary to experience this attraction.

HOW IT COMPARES – Tokyo Disneyland's It's a Small World is a combination of the Disneyland and Magic Kingdom versions. The façade of the attraction is very similar to Disneyland, patterned after the stylings of Mary Blair (credited with setting the tone, colors and design of the original It's a Small World) complete with pastel spires, well–manicured topiaries and a clock at it's center – though it is not surrounded by the water filled flumes like Disneyland. The queuing and loading area is very similar to the Magic Kingdom as it is all indoors. Disneyland incorporated many Disney characters into the Small World countries that matched their setting (i.e. Stitch in Hawaii, Mulan in China, Alice in England, etc.) whereas these are not yet a part of the Tokyo version. Aside from these few differences, the ride is a clone of its predecessors.

Alice's Tea Party

TRAVELERS SERIES RATES IT – Abere–ji (Average – experience this attraction if time allows)
ENTERTAINMENT SNAPSHOT – Covered outdoor tilt–a–whirl style ride themed to 1951's Alice in Wonderland
QUEUE – A traditional covered queuing area where the entire attraction is in full view.
ATTRACTION LENGTH – 1 ½ minutes

DESCRIPTION AND REVIEW – Guests board giant teacups situated on a large turntable with a giant tea pot in the center. As the entire table turns, a mouse occasionally appears from the teapot in the center. Guest's individual teacups spin while they turn the wheel inside their cup to determine how much (or little) spinning occurs. This ride can be dizzying fun, though the limited capacity and long loading and unloading times can cause the line to move slowly.

HOW IT COMPARES – Alice's Tea Party at Tokyo Disneyland is a carbon copy of the Magic Kingdom's Mad Tea Party. It differs from Disneyland's Mad Tea Party in that it is covered by a royal tent. Overall, the outdoor feel of the Disneyland version is far more charming, but the ride is the same.

Pooh's Hunny Hunt (FASTPASS)

TRAVELERS SERIES RATES IT – Yuunaru (Outstanding! Disney at its best)
ENTERTAINMENT SNAPSHOT – Indoor dark ride featuring the classic Disney residents of the Hundred Acre Wood

150

QUEUE – A giant Winnie the Pooh book greets guests as they enter the woodsy queuing area. Guests wind their way outside among the leaves and trees before making their way under a quaint awning near a peaceful pond. As guests step into the interior queuing area, the scene changes and they are suddenly among the pages of The Many Adventures of Winnie the Pooh. The queue turns and twists until guests finally arrive at the loading area where guests climb aboard "hunny" pots.

ATTRACTION LENGTH – 4 ½ minutes

DESCRIPTION AND REVIEW – Guests enter hunny pots for a trip through the Hundred Acre Wood. While Pooh's Hunny Hunt is a dark ride, the detail and technology far surpass the earlier rides installed in Fantasyland. The scenes are taken right out of the 1966 classic and guests have the opportunity to see all their favorite characters as they travel through a blustery day, a rain storm and Pooh's dreams. The technological feat of this attraction is that no visible tracks are used. Instead, the hunny pots seem to be on automatic pilot as they travel straight, in reverse and spin around through the scenes. The unpredictability of these hunny pots is never more evident than at the beginning of the attraction. Three hunny pots start out together like a normal train and it would seem they will stay together throughout the ride; but this theory is to be short–lived. No sooner do guests begin their journey than the hunny pots begin traveling next to each other, changing order, heading in different directions and then back in a straight line allowing guests to see the attraction from a variety of angles and vantage points.

The ride begins with a short video of Pooh Bear and Christopher Robin talking before the adventure kicks into gear. Guests begin by following Winnie the Pooh as he hangs onto a balloon and begins floating away. The hunny pots split up and begin to move around randomly as guests move from scene to scene. The Tigger scene reflects the creative genius of the Imagineers as well as their technological expertise. As the hunny pots line up to listen to Tigger talk, he begins to bounce and the hunny pots begin bouncing up and down with him! The scenery also bounces in step giving the appearance that the hunny pots are bouncing even higher. The "Bluster Day" scene is also top–notch as the hunny pots are "blown" to the side by the wind. After an exhausting day, guests see Pooh sleeping and the room slowly transitions turns into starlit space – an amazing effect – while Pooh floats away. The hunny pots are close behind and guests find themselves surrounded by Pooh's dreams and the Heffalumps. Here, guests will find six hunny pots (the three from your "train" and three more from another) dancing around the scene. Hunny pots zig and zag, go forward, backward and then just spin in circles through Pooh's crazy and colorful dream. The movement of the hunny pot corresponds with the story from the wind pushing it around to the bouncing with Tigger. Given the random twists and turns of the hunny pots, there are show elements in every corner fully immersing guests in the attraction.

This attraction is the best Fantasyland ride Disney has developed to date. It is understandable that the wait often exceeds an hour even on days of lower attendance.

How it Compares – While the Many Adventures of Winnie the Pooh rides at Disneyland and Magic Kingdom are the same general theme, there is no comparison to the Tokyo Disneyland version. The secret? It's all in the hunny pot. While the hunny vehicles and interior queue for this attraction look very similar to those at the Magic Kingdom and the queuing area at Disneyland is thematically more interesting, the technology in this ride blows the other two away. Guests feel completely immersed in the story and given the hunny pots tendency to spin around and even head backward, every element of the scene is meant to bee seen. As a result, the rooms and the "road" are much larger and designed to be viewed from every angle.

Tips – This is among the most popular attractions at Tokyo Disneyland. Ride this attraction first thing in the morning or get a FASTPASS first thing in the morning. Otherwise, you can expect lines on busy days to reach two hours or more and that no FASTPASS will be available within a couple hours of the park opening.

Dining
Troubadour Tavern
Eatery Snapshot – Counter–service ice cream
Prices – $3.30 to $3.90
Capacity – 210
Priority Seating Availability – No
Description and Review – Step up to the window and order a soft serve cone, sundae or drink. Troubadour (defined as a "folk singer") Tavern shares a seating area with Captain Hook's Galley and is a great stop for a sweet snack.

Captain Hook's Galley
Eatery Snapshot – Counter–service pizza
Prices – $4.30 to $5.50 per slice
Capacity – 210
Priority Seating Availability – No

152

DESCRIPTION AND REVIEW – Captain Hook's Galley serves pizza with unusual toppings including seafood or bacon and pineapple. As with most things Tokyo Disneyland, the quality is high and the food is served hot….if these sound like your kind of toppings.

TIPS –Generally, seating is often difficult to come by due to the location. However, Captain Hook's Galley is located along the parade route. If you are lucky enough to commandeer a table with a view, this is an unbeatable place for location and comfort to watch the parade.

Queen of Hearts Banquet Hall

EATERY SNAPSHOT – Counter–service with a variety of western fare
PRICES – Entrees range from $10.30 to $15.65; kids' meals $9.90
CAPACITY – 460
PRIORITY SEATING AVAILABILITY – No
DESCRIPTION AND REVIEW – Finally! A whimsical restaurant fit for Disneyland – and Fantasyland is the perfect location. The theming is unbeatable as guests enter the Queen of Heart's labyrinth at the front door and are immersed in the magic and fantasy of Wonderland. From the checkerboard floor, to the deck of cards standing guard, every element is classic Disney theming. As you enter the restaurant, you will walk through the mouth of the door which Alice enters in the movie and head toward the open kitchen where selections ranging from rotisserie chicken and grilled swordfish, to heart–shaped meat patty with tomato–brown sauce await. The food here is tasty and the lines can be quite long. It is an excellent place to find well–prepared and healthier fare. Even if this restaurant is not somewhere you choose to eat, be sure to take a look inside.

TIPS – If possible, try to avoid prime eating times for this restaurant by eating a late lunch or late dinner.

Cleo's

EATERY SNAPSHOT – Counter–service drinks and snacks
PRICES – $2.50 to $3.20 drinks; $2.30 to $3.10 snacks
CAPACITY – 0
PRIORITY SEATING AVAILABILITY – No
DESCRIPTION AND REVIEW – Named after Pinocchio's goldfish, Cleo's offers an assortment of hot and cold drinks. Due to the limited offerings, lines tend to be short and the service quick. There are generally one or two sweet treats available for purchase including items like Italian Ice and cookies.

TIPS – This is a great place to grab a coffee or hot cocoa on cold nights.

Village Pastry

EATERY SNAPSHOT – Kiosk serving "Tipo Tortas"
PRICES – $3.90
CAPACITY – 0
PRIORITY SEATING AVAILABILITY – No
DESCRIPTION AND REVIEW – Village Pastry is a kiosk styled to look like Stromboli's wagon from Pinocchio. Tipo Torta, a long thin pastry shaped like a churro with filling, is served here. The fillings change seasonally and can include sweet potato or chocolate, among others.

Shopping
Fantasy Gifts

RETAIL SNAPSHOT – Souvenir stand
DESCRIPTION AND REVIEW – Located in a small cottage, Fantasy Gifts is a traditional souvenir stand offering the usual assortment including stuffed animals, Tokyo Disneyland candy, key chains, etc.

The AristoCats

RETAIL SNAPSHOT – Stuffed animals, t–shirts and souvenirs
DESCRIPTION AND REVIEW – The AristoCats is located in a charming alcove of Cinderella Castle. The grandeur of the façade is diminished once inside as the minimally themed shop offers the traditional assortment of stuffed animals, back scratchers, postcards and t–shirts.

The Glass Slipper

RETAIL SNAPSHOT – Glassware
DESCRIPTION AND REVIEW – Located within the walls of Cinderella Castle, the doorway to The Glass Slipper is under an intricately fashioned mosaic mural. As the name suggests, glass items for sale include slippers, castles, characters, engravable Mickey wine glasses and other unique glass–sculpted items. Guests may watch glassblowers at work as they heat, shape and mold many of the items for sale within the shop.

Baby Mine

RETAIL SNAPSHOT – Baby items
DESCRIPTION AND REVIEW – This cute shop named after the Dumbo song, Baby Mine, offers a broad selection of baby and toddler clothes, toys and accessories. The sign declares this shop a "Disney Baby Boutique" and given the choices and prices, this is an apt description. Where else can you find $30 terry cloth Minnie Mouse pants for an infant?

Pleasure Island Candies

RETAIL SNAPSHOT – Candy shop

DESCRIPTION AND REVIEW – Although guests do not turn into jackasses, there is a wide selection of treats at Pleasure Island Candies. From souvenir boxes, to a bag for a quick snack, selections include Disney and non–Disney themed items. While much smaller than the World Bazaar Confectionary, the lines tend to be significantly smaller in this Fantasyland shop with an adequate selection.

Stromboli's Wagon

RETAIL SNAPSHOT – Souvenir kiosk

DESCRIPTION AND REVIEW – Like Village Pastry, this Wagon looks like it is right out of the pages of Pinocchio. Stromboli's Wagon offers the normal selection of Tokyo Disneyland souvenirs.

Pooh Corner

RETAIL SNAPSHOT – Pooh Bear merchandise

DESCRIPTION AND REVIEW – Located at the exit to Pooh's Hunny Hunt, Pooh Corner is one of the best themed shops in Fantasyland. From the outside of this charming and delightful cottage to the exposed beams and wooden accents used inside and the beehive shaped lights, there are wall–to–wall Pooh Bear items to be found. The shop is filled with honey pots that are stuffed with merchandise. Selections include honey filled snacks and guests can pay for their purchases at honey pot themed cash registers.

TIPS – Due to its location at the exit of one of Tokyo Disneyland's most popular rides, Pooh's Hunny Hunt, navigating this store can be very difficult any time of day. The same items can be found at a variety of shops throughout the park, though it is worth a quick look inside.

Toontown

Overview

Nestled in the far corner of the park opposite Critter Country lies the home of Mickey, Minnie, Pluto, Goofy, Donald, Daisy, Chip 'N Dale and all "Toons". Inspired by Disney's 1988 film <u>Who Framed Roger Rabbit</u>, Toontown is the newest land at Tokyo Disneyland. Everything within its boundaries looks as if it came right out of a cartoon. The walls, columns, fountains, roads and hills are all puffed up, edges are rounded off, buildings lean at cartoon–like angles and, of course, guests are invited to explore the homes of some of Toontown's most famous residents. There are no square edges and no square buildings in Toontown and as guests enter this land, they are immersed into the middle of a cartoon. This land is set up like a giant cul–de–sac with one side featuring cityscape and most of the shops and restaurants, while the other half is primarily reserved for the homes of Toontown's inhabitants located under the Toontown hill–side sign (it resembles the Hollywood sign).Everywhere guests turn, there are comical Toon modifications. Signs offer plenty of humor, everything is zany and mixed–up, and the many buttons, knobs and levers will provide a surprise for playful guests. Sound effects are everywhere – from an explosion heard near Roger Rabbit's Car Toon Spin, to characters' voices on their mailboxes, to the sounds of Toontown residents talking or yelling at each other in various windows, mailboxes or telephones. It's one gag after another in Toontown.

Toontown:	
Attractions (8)	*Shops (2)*
Roger Rabbit's Car Toon Spin	Toontown Deliver Company
Minnie's House	Gag Factory/Toontown Five & Dime
Mickey's House and Meet Mickey	
Chip 'n Dale's Treehouse	*Restaurants (8)*
Gadget's Go Coaster	Dinghy Drinks
Donald's Boat	Toon Pop
Goofy's Bounce House	Out of Bounds Ice Cream
Toon Park	Huey, Dewey and Louie's
	Good Time Café
	Daisy's Snack Wagon
	Mickey's Trailer
	Goofy's Drink Stand
	Pop–A–Lot Popcorn

The center of Toontown sports a trolley station, a giant covered gazebo area and Toontown City Hall. The town's two fountains used to be connected by the Jolly Trolley, a bouncy trolley car that transported guests from one side to the other, but due to immense crowds and the limited usefulness of the trolley, guests must now walk the short distance. Toontown is singularly unique in architecture and is a delightful journey into Mickey and the gang's home. Like all things Disney, it is meant to be enjoyed by guests of all ages, though the scope and scale of the attractions is targeted directly at children where Fantasyland is directed at families. Even for those traveling without children, there is plenty to see in Toontown and it is absolutely worth a visit. The size and uniqueness of Toontown cause an obvious problem: congestion. Where Critter Country is small, it is home to one main attraction. In Toontown, everything is an attraction and guests flood the entire area. Couple this with Toontown's size and the immense popularity of Mickey Mouse and it is often crowded and jam–packed regardless of the size of crowds in the rest of the park. Toontown sports eight attractions, eight eateries and two stores.

How it Compares

Tokyo Disneyland's Toontown most closely reflects Toontown at Disneyland. Where Mickey's Toontown Fair at the Magic Kingdom offers fewer attractions and is geared primarily as a character greeting area, both Disneyland and Tokyo Disneyland's Toontown are set up like small towns. Both feature nearly identical facades, buildings, and attractions and are laid out in a mirror image of one another. One major difference in the layout is that at Disneyland, the entrance is located off to the "city" side of Toontown where Tokyo Disneyland, guests enter nearer the middle of Toontown City Hall and closer to the "residential" area. Both are excellent additions to their respective parks. Other differences include the vast amounts of trees, bushes and shrubs at Tokyo Disneyland's Toontown. Where Disneyland and the Magic Kingdom's versions feature a much more "Imagineered" environment, Tokyo Disneyland's town incorporates a lot of nature and has a much different feel as cartoon and "reality" live side by side.

> **NOT SO HIDDEN MICKEY ALERT**
> There is a red car parked in front of Mickey's House. The hood ornament sure looks familiar....

Tips

Toontown provides a touring enigma. It is crowded and lines can be very long, but the attractions do not rank as high as those in other areas of the park. If you are traveling with small children, a stop here is essential to let the little ones run around and get out their energy out. If not, save Toontown for late in the day when the little tykes have cleared out.

Attractions

Roger Rabbit's Car Toon Spin

TRAVELERS SERIES RATES IT – Yoshi (Good – make this a priority)
ENTERTAINMENT SNAPSHOT – Indoor dark ride through <u>Who Framed Roger Rabbit</u>
QUEUE – Set on the wrong side of the tracks in Toontown, the line for Roger Rabbit's Car Toon Spin takes guests through the alleys of Toontown at night. Guests will see characters and scenes from the Disney blockbuster and, as with all things Toon–related, the gag quotient is high. This is an extremely well–themed queuing area but is also quite misleading. It snakes further into the building than it appears from the entrance and what may look like a very short line can be quite long.

ATTRACTION LENGTH – 3 ½ minutes

DESCRIPTION AND REVIEW – Located on the "city" side of Toontown and inside The Cab Co. (with Benny the Cab about to fall off the second story), this attraction is based on the 1988 live–action and animated feature, <u>Who Framed Roger Rabbit</u>. Guests board Benny the Cab for a wacky and wild trip through Toontown to save Jessica Rabbit. The Cab includes an Alice's Tea Party-style wheel that allows guests to spin in circles while they move along their route. As a result, guests often travel backward and sideways and see each scene from a variety of perspectives. Roger Rabbit's Car Toon Spin thrusts guests in the middle of the cartoon action as they try to escape from the weasels and Judge Doom's dreaded "dip" – the only thing that can "kill" a cartoon. As in the movie, Roger is the hero and saves guests every time. This is a terrific Disney ride that everyone will enjoy and, like Pooh's Hunny Hunt, the technology offers a unique "spin" on a typical dark ride. The very limited dialogue is in Japanese but is barely noticeable as the dialogue is largely irrelevant to the story–line.

HOW IT COMPARES – This attraction is nearly identical in everyway to its Disneyland predecessor. The building, the queue, the loading area and the ride are the very similar.

Minnie's House
TRAVELERS SERIES RATES IT – Osanai (Young – experience if traveling with young children)
ENTERTAINMENT SNAPSHOT – Walk–through attraction of Minnie's house
QUEUE – N/A
ATTRACTION LENGTH – Self–directed

DESCRIPTION AND REVIEW – Minnie Mouse has opened up her home and invited everyone in Toontown to take a tour. Minnie's House is a quaint lavender and pink cottage style home with a beautiful garden and cartoonish shapes and structures. Guests enter through the front door and can take a walk through Minnie's entire ground floor from living room to kitchen. There are unique "mouse" decorations and plenty of pictures of her beau, Mickey. There are terrific photo ops throughout the home and guests can even relax for a few moments in Minnie's chair. This is a great place to explore a three–dimensional and interactive version of Minnie's House and there are a variety of knobs and levers to turn and pull throughout the attraction. Minnie's kitchen is the most interactive room in her home. Here, guests can open her refrigerator, start the dish washer, turn on the stove and bake a cake. Drop a coin in the wishing well in Minnie's back yard and you'll hear her talk.

How it Compares – Minnie's House is a near replica of her California residence in Disneyland. The shape and color of the home and the decorations within are the same. Offerings are similar to those at the Magic Kingdom, though Florida is home to Minnie's Country House which looks a bit different – both inside and out – from Tokyo Disneyland's version.

Mickey's House and Meet Mickey

Travelers Series Rates It – Abere–ji (Average – experience this attraction if time allows)

Entertainment Snapshot – Walk through attraction of Mickey's House and character greeting

Queue – The queue is the walk–through of Mickey's House and culminates in his barn where guests can meet Mickey and take a picture with him.

Attraction Length – Self–directed through the house; about one minute to meet Mickey and take a photo

Description and Review – Located directly beneath the Toontown sign, Mickey Mouse's house is the most popular stop on the residential side of Toontown. Like Minnie's home, Mickey's has all the creature comforts and even includes toys and a dog bed for Pluto. The home itself is fun to walk through, though Minnie's is more interactive. As guests leave Mickey's home, they are invited to walk through his backyard, past Pluto's doghouse to Mickey's Movie Barn to meet Mickey while he takes a break from filming his latest cartoon. There is a standard queuing area here where guests are entertained by Mickey cartoons wile they wait to get their picture taken with the famous homeowner.

Mickey Mouse is incredibly popular and the line to get through his home and take a picture with him can be daunting. Waits of 60–90 minutes or more on the busiest days is common.

> **HIDDEN MICKEY ALERT**
> The most obvious place for a Hidden Mickey is in the head cheese's house! There is a bookshelf in his living room with cheese bookends. Take a peak at the top of the left–hand side bookend and you'll see Mickey.

How it Compares – With the exception of the ridiculously long lines at Tokyo Disneyland, this attraction is a virtual carbon copy of Mickey's Disneyland home. As is the case with Minnie, Magic Kingdom is home to Mickey's Country House which looks quite different both inside and out.

Tips – Unless you absolutely, positively must have a one on one picture with Mickey Mouse, skip this attraction. Visit Minnie's House to get a sense of what Mickey's looks like on the inside and spend your time on the other Tokyo Disneyland attractions.

Chip 'n Dale Treehouse

TRAVELERS SERIES RATES IT – Osanai (Young – experience if traveling with young children)

ENTERTAINMENT SNAPSHOT – Walk–through attraction of Chip n' Dale's home

QUEUE – N/A

ATTRACTION LENGTH – Self–directed

DESCRIPTION AND REVIEW – Guests can explore Chip n' Dale's Treehouse by climbing up stairs at the bottom or side of the giant Redwood. While much smaller and less elaborate than Mickey or Minnie's house, this house is a cute area for kids to explore.

HIDDEN MICKEY ALERT
There is a cartoon car that has skidded to a halt in front of Chip 'n Dale Treehouse. Take a long hard look at the skid marks in the cement and you'll find dozens and dozens of little Hidden Mickeys.

HOW IT COMPARES – One difference between Tokyo Disneyland's Chip n' Dale's Treehouse and Disneyland's Chip 'n Dale Treehouse is that Disneyland's version is nestled into the corner of Toon Town near a cave whereas the Tokyo Disneyland versions occupies more open space. The only other noticeable difference is that there are more props in the Tokyo Disneyland version, particularly on the outside of the tree.

Gadget's Go Coaster

TRAVELERS SERIES RATES IT – Osanai (Young – experience if traveling with young children)

ENTERTAINMENT SNAPSHOT – Mild children's roller–coaster

QUEUE – Kids and adults will feel like a small Toon in line for Gadget's Go Coaster. The queue was created using gigantic household odds and ends and contains handrails made out of a comb and a toothbrush and another made out of a garden hose. The line snakes around Toon Lake – not much more than a small pond – and the whimsical house at the end of the line allows guests to board the coaster.

ATTRACTION LENGTH – 1 minute

DESCRIPTION AND REVIEW – Gadget's Go Coaster is a very mild child's roller coaster. Adults will find the seating fairly cramped, but this fun little coaster provides a wonderful exposure to coasters for children, though it is worth noting that adults are always smiling on this ride. Each train holds only 16 guests and a maximum of two trains can operate at the same time (one loads while the other races over the tracks). This limited capacity combined with the Toontown crowds can make a small line a very long wait for kids and adults alike.

HOW IT COMPARES – Essentially the same ride with different theming as The Barnstormer at Goofy's Wiseacre Farm at the Magic Kingdom, Tokyo Disneyland's Gadget's Go Coaster is identical to Disneyland's attraction of the same name. However, Tokyo Disneyland's version incorporates significant live foliage and is far more charming than its Disneyland counterpart.

TIPS – Gadget's Go Coaster is the same type of ride as Flounder's Flying Fish Coaster at Tokyo DisneySea. The major difference is the line is generally much shorter for Flounder's version.

Donald's Boat

TRAVELERS SERIES RATES IT – Osanai (Young – experience if traveling with young children)
ENTERTAINMENT SNAPSHOT – Walk–through attraction of Donald's boat
QUEUE – N/A
ATTRACTION LENGTH – Self–directed

DESCRIPTION AND REVIEW – Donald's Boat, the Miss Daisy, is moored in Toon Lake. Guests of all ages can climb aboard and explore Donald's boat. Kids can steer, ring the bell, blow the horn and look through a periscope made for a duck. While fanciful, there is relatively little to do and see in Donald's Boat compared to the other "homes". However, the view of Toontown form the top deck is worth a quick look.

HOW IT COMPARES – Donald's Boat at the Magic Kingdom is a water play area in addition to allowing guests to explore the boat. Like most of Toontown, Tokyo Disneyland version is virtually identical to Donald's Boat at Disneyland.

Goofy's Bounce House

TRAVELERS SERIES RATES IT – Osanai (Young – experience if traveling with young children)
ENTERTAINMENT SNAPSHOT – Children's bounce–house
QUEUE – The queue to jump around in Goofy's house winds outside through Goofy's garden. Here, guests will see a Goofy scarecrow protecting the sunflowers, corn and other crops grown by Goofy.
ATTRACTION LENGTH – 2 minutes

DESCRIPTION AND REVIEW – The craziest, zaniest and goofiest home in Toontown could only belong to one character. Goofy's house is extremely crooked, holes in the roof have been patched with an umbrella, and the entire structure is topped off with a giant Goofy hat. Inside the home is no different as Goofy has replaced his floor with a bouncy floor and inflatable furniture. Here, children can jump and bounce their energy out. Only guests under 132 cm (52 in) may bounce. Due to the limited number of children allowed to bounce at one time, lines will quickly hit the "not worth it" mark.

> **HIDDEN MICKEY ALERT**
> There are seats near the exit of Goofy's Bounce House where children sit to put on their shoes. Check out the stool with the tire inner tube for a seat and look closely at the pattern. Wavy lines make for an excellent Hidden Mickey.

HOW IT COMPARES – Goofy's Bounce House is the most original attraction in Tokyo Disneyland's Toontown. Disneyland closed the "bounce" portion of the house in 2006, replaced it with a playground, and renamed it Goofy's Playhouse. The Magic Kingdom never built a bounce house, but instead themed the roller coaster in Mickey's Toontown Fair to Goofy's house.

Toon Park

TRAVELERS SERIES RATES IT – Osanai (Young – experience if traveling with young children)
ENTERTAINMENT SNAPSHOT – Children's playground
QUEUE – N/A
ATTRACTION LENGTH – Self–directed

DESCRIPTION AND REVIEW – Toon Park is a padded play area where kids can run free in a fenced–in area while parents sit and try to recover from the day. The ground is padded and each of the animals and other items to climb on and over are soft, so bumps and scrapes are virtually non–existent. There is no need to explore this area unless you are traveling with very small children.

HOW IT COMPARES – Disneyland offers a unique play area at Goofy's Playhouse in Toontown and the Magic Kingdom has Pooh's Playful Spot in Fantasyland – both of which are far more charming, much better themed and a lot more fun than this benign Tokyo Disneyland play area.

Dining
Dinghy Drinks
EATERY SNAPSHOT – Kiosk offering drinks
PRICES – Drinks start at $2.50
CAPACITY – 0
PRIORITY SEATING AVAILABILITY – No
DESCRIPTION AND REVIEW – This dinghy is operated by Donald's nephews, Huey, Dewey and Louie. It offers an assortment of bottled water and soft drinks.

Toon Pop
EATERY SNAPSHOT – Kiosk serving popcorn
PRICES – $3.30
CAPACITY – 0
PRIORITY SEATING AVAILABILITY – No
DESCRIPTION AND REVIEW – This kiosk offers caramel popcorn.

Out of Bounds Ice Cream
EATERY SNAPSHOT – Kiosk offering frozen sweets
PRICES – $3.30 to $3.90
CAPACITY – 0
PRIORITY SEATING AVAILABILITY – No
DESCRIPTION AND REVIEW – This kiosk, made to look like a cartoon golf cart, offers guests a variety of frozen treats ranging from ice cream bars to frozen bananas.

Huey, Dewey and Louie's Good Time Café
EATERY SNAPSHOT – Counter–service theme park food
PRICES – $2.10 to $5.30
CAPACITY – 430
PRIORITY SEATING AVAILABILITY – No
DESCRIPTION AND REVIEW – This whimsical eatery is the only Toontown establishment offering a full meal and is adjacent to a large outdoor eating area. Huey, Dewey and Louie's Good Time Café serves up shrimp cutlet sandwiches, fried chicken sandwiches, tossed green salad, french fries, sausage on a stick and desserts. Among the most popular items for kids is Mickey Mouse-shaped pizza. The food here is not as good as other places and Toontown is probably not the best place to eat.

Daisy's Snack Wagon
EATERY SNAPSHOT – Kiosk serving snacks
PRICES – $2.75 to $3.90

CAPACITY – 0
PRIORITY SEATING AVAILABILITY – No
DESCRIPTION AND REVIEW – Daisy's roach coach – a cartoony car – offers a few quick items, including hot pretzels and cookies.

Mickey's Trailer
EATERY SNAPSHOT – Kiosk offering spring rolls
PRICES – $3.10
CAPACITY – 0
PRIORITY SEATING AVAILABILITY – No
DESCRIPTION AND REVIEW – Loosely themed after the trailer from one of Mickey's camping expedition cartoons, this small trailer offers spring rolls for the hungry guest. Egg and shrimp pizza are among the fillings.

Goofy's Drink Stand
EATERY SNAPSHOT – Kiosk serving cold drinks
PRICES – Drinks start at $2.50
CAPACITY – 0
PRIORITY SEATING AVAILABILITY – No
DESCRIPTION AND REVIEW – This stand is barely standing as it is held up by an oar, tennis racket and baseball bat right outside Goofy's Bounce House. Guests will find a variety of ice-cold drinks.

Pop–A–Lot popcorn
EATERY SNAPSHOT – Kiosk offering popcorn
PRICES – $3.30
CAPACITY – 0
PRIORITY SEATING AVAILABILITY – No
DESCRIPTION AND REVIEW – A small toony vehicle next to the gas station with popcorn popping through the roof, Pop–A–Lot Popcorn offers up popped kernels in a regular box or souvenir bucket.

Shopping
Toontown Delivery Company
RETAIL SNAPSHOT – Kiosk with traditional souvenirs
DESCRIPTION AND REVIEW – The air has been let out of the Toontown's Delivery Company tires and it is now a permanent "store front". Items include traditional souvenirs.

Gag Factory/Toontown Five & Dime
RETAIL SNAPSHOT – Two stores combined into one for a large variety of Disney merchandise

DESCRIPTION AND REVIEW – The Gag Factory and Toontown Five & Dime are two differently themed shops under one roof. The Gag Factory won't make you sick, but rather gives an industrial aura to this large store. Guests can see how Toon gags are made and see the Wacky Gag–O–Matic machine. Wares include clothes, stuffed animals, figurines, cups, mugs, pencils and just about anything else you would expect in a large Tokyo Disneyland store.

Tomorrowland
Overview
Tomorrowland is a combination of the future that might be and the future that never was. The white spires of Space Mountain tower above this land and are visible from nearly every corner. Whether guests enter through Center Street in World Bazaar, the main entrance off the plaza or from Fantasyland, it is clear that they have transitioned to visions of the future. Every type of creature and character resides in Tomorrowland from robots to aliens, Space Rangers and Monsters. A diverse utopian (and clean!) future is reality here.

Tomorrowland:	
Attractions (8)	*Shops (6)*
Star Tours	Cosmic Encounter
Space Mountain	Planet M
Captain EO	ImageWorks
StarJets	Stellar Sweets
Grand Circuit Raceway	Solar Ray's Light Supplies
Buzz Lightyear's Astro Blasters	Monsters, Inc. Company Store
Monsters, Inc. "Ride & Go Seek!"	
"One Man's Dream II – The Magic Lives On"	
Restaurants (7)	
Plaza Restaurant	Space Place FoodPort
Soft Landing	Lite Bite Satellite
Pan Galactic Pizza Port	The Popping Pod
Tomorrowland Terrace	

The buildings and architecture are from yesterday's tomorrow with whites, grays, silvers and blues being the general color theme. The walkways to Tomorrowland cross over a "futuristic" moat with mosaic-style rocks serving as the riverbed. Everything is shiny in Tomorrowland –

if it isn't stainless steel, it's white and pristine. Robotic technologies are everywhere in this land.

There are no fewer than five ways to enter Tomorrowland (World Bazaar's Center Street, three entrances off the Plaza including the "main" entrance, and Fantasyland). Entering through the main entrance provides an excellent representation of what the original Tomorrowland in Disneyland looked like in 1955. Two large buildings flank either side of the walkway with Space Mountain serving as the centerpiece at the end of the path. However, Tomorrowland is quite spacious. There are trees, shrubs and bushes throughout the area that inspire peace and comfort. Tomorrowland is home to more mega–attractions than any other land including Space Mountain, Star Tours, Captain EO and the new Monsters, Inc. Ride and Go Seek!. Tomorrowland's diverse offerings include eight attractions, seven eating establishments and six stores.

How it Compares

When Tomorrowland at Disneyland and the Magic Kingdom were upgraded in the 1990s, Tokyo Disneyland was left out. Tokyo Disneyland's Tomorrowland is somewhere between the Disneyland and Magic Kingdom's originals (premiering in 1955 and 1971, respectively) and the upgrades performed in the '90s. It is simultaneously retro–futuristic and whimsical. Given its size, Tomorrowland at Tokyo Disneyland more closely reflects the Magic Kingdom's version, but from there all comparisons are lost. What is missing is, at times, more noticeable than what is there. There are no monorails speeding overhead, no people movers circling the area – not even the leftover track of failed experiments like Disneyland's Rocket Rods. Instead, it's a sea of white sterility and still reflects the vision of the future circa 1960. Ambiance aside, Tokyo Disneyland's Tomorrowland offers excellent attractions and the brand new Monsters, Inc. Ride and Go Seek! attraction is exclusive to this park.

Tips

Tomorrowland really "pops" at night. Be sure to stroll through Tomorrowland and see the land lit up – it's stunning. Space Mountain remains the centerpiece with its lighting and colors. In fact, Tomorrowland – much like Tokyo city – looks much more futuristic at night.

Attractions

Star Tours

TRAVELERS SERIES RATES IT – Yuunaru (Outstanding! Disney at its best)
ENTERTAINMENT SNAPSHOT – Motion–simulator ride through outer space

QUEUE – Stars Wars fans and novices alike can appreciate the theming quality of this queue. The attraction is housed in a futuristic hangar and spaceport where Star Tours transport ships standby to launch for space destinations with guests aboard as passengers. Boarding announcements are made over the loudspeaker as guests walk past droids preparing ships for take–off. C3PO and R2D2 from Star Wars fame are visible working on the ships as are other lesser known Star Wars droids. As guests make their way through the spaceport to the boarding gates, they are shuffled in front of monitors for the pre–flight safety video as they prepare to take a flight to the Endor moon.

ATTRACTION LENGTH – 4 ½ minutes

DESCRIPTION AND REVIEW – Once the 40 guests take their seats and are buckled up, the pilot – a clumsy and insecure robot – announces that this is his first flight. It doesn't take long for his inexperience to show as the ship is immediately headed the wrong way trying to leave the spaceport and comes close to disaster time and time again. Once in space, light speed is initiated and the ship races toward the Endor moon. Of course, the ship passes the destination and the pilot gets caught in a meteor shower. Ultimately, the entire ship is weaving and winding its way through an asteroid only to break through the ice and fly out the other side. Just when the adventure seems to be winding down, the menacing Star Wars music cues and the Star Tours ship is caught in a tractor beam in the middle of a space fight against the evil Galactic Empire. Instead of taking the tourists to safety, the pilot, Rex, launches his ship in the middle of the battle and follows fighters over and through the Death Star. Dodging and weaving from enemy fire, the pilot navigates the ship until the shots that set off a chain reaction to destroy the Death Star can be seen. Once this evil space station is destroyed, the pilot engages light speed and brings the passengers back to the spaceport before nearly colliding with a propane truck as the attraction comes to a skidding halt. Dialogue is in Japanese, but in many ways this makes the comical fear expressed by the pilot even funnier and does not detract from the experience. Japanenglish takes front stage as many Star Wars words do not translate well as Rex says "light–ah–speed" and "tractor beam–ah" among others.

It is hard to tell where the undeniable genius of this ride comes from – George Lucas and his exceptionally talented team or the Disney Imagineers for hiring them. This attraction is Disney at its finest. The attraction is more than 20 years old (it originally opened at Disneyland in 1987) and still offers some of the best motion–simulation technology in theme parks today. This is an absolute must see!

How it Compares – Star Tours used to be the exact same attraction at Disneyland, Disney's Hollywood Studios (Walt Disney World Resort) and Tokyo Disneyland save for the Japanese dialogue. Disneyland's Star Tours closed in July 2010 and Disney's Hollywood Studios' attraction will close in the fall of 2010. Both are rescheduled to reopen in 2011 with the same concept and new ride. Prior to this upcoming conversion, the main comparisons lie in the queuing area and it is very similar to Disneyland. The biggest difference is the façade of the hangar which looks like a towering space–port in Tokyo instead of a small building in California. Tokyo's version was clearly built to accommodate very long lines as the space–port/hangar is much larger (and taller) than its Disneyland counterpart. The safety video presented once guests are seated is chopped in two at Tokyo – the first part shows the safety regulations and after the attraction ends, the second half explains how do unfasten the safety restraints; the entire video is presented at the beginning of the attraction in the U.S. Likewise, Rex does not have his "remove this tag before flight" tag hanging off of his body as he does in Disneyland. Odds are you have been on Star Tours in California or Florida before. For this reason, the Japanese dialogue spoken by Rex is actually a very funny experience because it's something different about the attraction. It is definitely worth experiencing!

Space Mountain (FASTPASS)

Travelers Series Rates It – Yuunaru (Outstanding! Disney at its best)

Entertainment Snapshot – Roller coaster ride through outer space

Queue – Space Mountain's queue transitions guests from Tomorrowland to a space station where they prepare to take a ride into outer space. The queue snakes through the inner corridors of the space station and the sounds indicate that you are on a space station and no longer on Earth.

Attraction Length – 3 minutes

Did You Know?
Space Mountain's top speeds do not exceed 35 miles per hour. The sensation of darkness and subsequent inability to see the track contributes to the feeling that the rockets travel much, much faster.

Description and Review – Guests board the rockets for take–off and are put in queue behind other rockets preparing for launch. As the train – three cars, each with two seats – approaches the launch pad, a series of effects give the illusion that the rocket ship is launching into outer space. Once there, the track is virtually impossible to see, but the stars, satellites and asteroids are all around. As the ride begins its rollercoaster action, heart racing music blasts from the seat. This music is a tremendous addition to the attraction and it is timed to each drop, rise, and turn of the rollercoaster. This ride is an absolute blast and demonstrates Disney's ability to combine creativity and imagination and turn a basic rollercoaster ride into an outer–space adventure. Do not miss this attraction!

HOW IT COMPARES – Tokyo Disneyland's Space Mountain – freshly upgraded – looks almost exactly like its Disneyland cousin. The track layout is nearly identical, the queue is similar, the trains are the same, the layout of the line is the same, the holding area and gates sport the same luminescent glow, though the main loading room's docked spaceship is being "charged" with energy that is far more "technologically advanced" and looks pretty cool. Space Mountain at Tokyo Disneyland still has the moving walkway heading up the second level that was removed from Disneyland years ago. It's a terrific retro–walk to the ride. Otherwise, the single track, interior loading area, the ramps, gates and exits are a clone of the California–based ride. Where Magic Kingdom's Space Mountain queue is quite different and cars seat people one in front of the other, the cars at Tokyo Disneyland seat two across, like those at Disneyland. Like Magic Kingdom, Tokyo Disneyland's Space Mountain does not have a soundtrack while the coaster is in motion.

Captain EO Tribute
(FASTPASS / ENGLISH SUBTITLES AVAILABLE)

TRAVELERS SERIES RATES IT – Yuunaru (Outstanding! Disney at its best)
ENTERTAINMENT SNAPSHOT – 4D show featuring Michael Jackson
QUEUE – The monitors in the holding area show scenes from the "making of" this Disney classic which originally appeared in Tokyo Disneyland from March 20, 1987 to September 1, 1996. A young (and thin) George Lucas can be seen producing he film as can director Francis Ford Coppola and many of the actors and dancers getting makeup and costumes. Instead of serving as a "pre–show" in traditional terms, the holding area highlights that this throwback is a tribute to a once–again popular attraction.
ATTRACTION LENGTH – 17 minutes

DESCRIPTION AND REVIEW – As guests are seated in the 369 seat theater, they are instructed to put on their 3D glasses as the Captain EO insignia turns to 3D outer space and the first asteroid circles into the middle of the theater. A ship comes into view as does its rag–tag crew. A set Siamese–twin aliens complete with '80s hair named Idey and Ody fly the ship and are accompanied by a large robot–man named Major Domo, a small robot named Minor Domo, a small flying butterfly/monkey named Fuzzball and a clumsy elephant alien named Hooter wearing a mesh tank top. Then, Captain EO (played by the King of Pop, Michael Jackson) appears and it quickly becomes clear that this group of misfits is constantly in trouble and

169

cannot complete any missions. After accidentally finding and crash landing at their destination, the crew disembarks in search of the Supreme Leader. The planet is void of any color or beauty and looks like an aluminum recycling plant. The clumsy crew gives away their location and the entire crew is caught and brought before the Supreme Leader; Angelica Huston dressed as a part woman, part Star Trek cyborg, and part creature from Aliens. She orders that Captain EO and his crew be imprisoned. Before her orders can be followed, Captain EO's crew begins playing "We are Here to Change the World" as Captain EO breaks into song and dance. Captain EO begins transforming the guards into outlandish 80s dancers who join him as they bring peace, goodness and beauty to this desolate planet. As color returns to the planet and all the guards have been transformed, Captain EO focuses all of his energy on the Supreme Leader, turning her into a beautiful queen. As Captain EO prepares to leave this lush and beautiful planet, he breaks into a few bars of "Another Part of Me" and then he and his crew depart. There are 4D effects like wind, smoke and lasers, but the best of them all is that the entire floor of the theatre moves in sync with the action. Guests can feel Captain EO's ship get shot and crash land, but the most fun is the when the theater rocks to the groove of Michael Jackson's music. Patrons do not take themselves too seriously in this retrospective, but everyone has a lot of fun singing along. Captain EO is scheduled to run from July 1, 2010 through June 30, 2011 and replaces MicroAdventure – the 4D attraction based on the Honey I Shrunk the Kids series that originally replaced Captain EO.

HOW IT COMPARES – Captain EO opened in Disneyland and Epcot in 1986 and is, in effect, the exact same show. The only differences lie in the queue. Disneyland's holding area is below the queue for Space Mountain. Epcot's queue is in the Imagination Pavilion in Future World. Tokyo Disneyland's queue is a standard holding consisting of a large room and an outside queuing area.

TIPS – Captain EO is a combination of two Japanese favorites – Disney and Michael Jackson. Crowds will be quite large, but given the substantial seating capacity and 20 minute cycle times, nearly 1,200 people can see this show every hour. Ride this attraction late in the day as the line dwindles. It is likely not worth utilizing a FASTPASS for this attraction.

StarJets
TRAVELERS SERIES RATES IT – Abere–ji (Average – experience this attraction if time allows)
ENTERTAINMENT SNAPSHOT – Outdoor circular ride aboard rocket ships

QUEUE – The line for StarJets is queued on the main level of Tomorrowland, though the rockets are located on the second story. Guests wait in a traditional covered chained queuing station and once it is their turn, they are directed into an elevator and sent to the second level for the ride. The line can move quite slow as a maximum of 24 people can experience each flight.
ATTRACTION LENGTH – 1 ½ minutes

DESCRIPTION AND REVIEW – StarJets is Dumbo on steroids. With the ride located high up on a second story deck, the "height" associated with the ride is significant and the views are wonderful. StarJets offers a full view of Tomorrowland, much of Fantasyland and Toontown. Like Dumbo, guests control their individual rockets, piloting them up and down as the attraction moves in a circle. If the line is reasonable, take a rocket for a spin. This attraction is fun for big and small kids alike and offers terrific views.

HOW IT COMPARES – A nearly identical StarJets ride used to be housed at Disneyland and Magic Kingdom. Both rides were rechristened Astro Orbiter with their respective launches of the "new" Tomorrowland. Magic Kingdom's Astro Orbiter is virtually identical to this Tokyo Disneyland attraction as it is located on a large flight deck platform. Disneyland's Astro Orbiter was moved from its second story roost to a street–level attraction at the entrance to Tomorrowland. Even with new theming, the ride is the same.

Grand Circuit Raceway
TRAVELERS SERIES RATES IT – Abere–ji (Average – experience this attraction if time allows)
ENTERTAINMENT SNAPSHOT – Self–driven cars
QUEUE – The queue for Grand Circuit Raceway will get guests revved up for the action. The line is a standard chain rope, but the smell of exhaust and the announcements over the loudspeaker begin to convince those in line that they are about to drive in a race. Loading speed is slow on Grand Circuit Raceway as the literal buckling and unbuckling is done at "guest speed" (and guests are generally a bit distracted).
ATTRACTION LENGTH – 5 minutes

DESCRIPTION AND REVIEW – This attraction is themed to a car race complete with grandstand, loudspeakers, cars with racing stripes and Cast Members wearing pit crew jumpsuits. Guests are seated in cars that anyone tall enough to push the gas and see over the steering wheel can drive. The cars' speed is regulated and they are on a guide rail for safety, but the course has numerous twists and turns as drivers cruise over and under a bridge and around the track.

HOW IT COMPARES – The queue and track layout of Grand Circuit Raceway is nearly identical to Tomorrowland Speedway in Magic Kingdom. There are very few props situated through the course and this attraction is all about driving. The theme, track layout and overall attraction is substantially different from Autopia at Disneyland. Overall, the basics of the attraction are the same in all three parks.

Buzz Lightyear's Astro Blasters (FASTPASS)

TRAVELERS SERIES RATES IT – Yuunaru (Outstanding! Disney at its best)
ENTERTAINMENT SNAPSHOT – Combination dark ride and shooting gallery featuring characters from Toy Story 2.
QUEUE – Guests begin walking through a Buzz Lightyear comic book-style queuing area where the drawings on the pages demonstrate how to collect power cells by aiming at targets to score points and destroy the evil Emperor Zurg. The green aliens from the Toy Story series are "good guys" who help Buzz Lightyear and the Space Rangers. As guests wind through the queue, they arrive at Star Command and an audio–animatronic Buzz Lightyear who thinks everyone is a Space Ranger explains the mission – collect power cells and defeat Zurg – and provides an overview of the Power Ranger attack strategy on Etch (the Etch–a–Sketch from Toy Story fame). The loading speed is fast on Buzz Lightyear's Astro Blasters as it is a continuously moving attraction where, like the Haunted Mansion, Space Rangers (guests) board via a moving walkway so that the ride does not stop.
ATTRACTION LENGTH – 4 minutes

> **HIDDEN MICKEY ALERT**
> In front of Buzz Lightyear's Astro Blasters are several statues of the green aliens from the Toy Story movies. Many of them are standing on pink rock formations and at the base of the formation, there are several green stones. Three of these alien rocks form a Hidden Mickey that is out of this world.

DESCRIPTION AND REVIEW – Once seated, Space Rangers grab their Astro Blasters (space guns) and get to work defeating Zurg. Fantastic and silly, the scenes in this attraction depict aliens, robots and Emperor Zurg and each has a giant target or multiple targets on them. Space Rangers aim and fire unlimited ammunition (a tiny red laser beam) at the targets and score points for each "hit". There are two blasters per vehicle and each has a display showing the guests their point total. There is also a joystick in the vehicle allowing Space Rangers to spin their vehicle 360 degrees to find and aim at targets on all sides. All the scenes are in vibrant fluorescent "dark ride" colors.

At Buzz Lightyear's Astro Blasters, Space Rangers often have a difficult time appreciating the scenes as they are busy blasting and scoring points. The creativity of the attraction is excellent and it is a must see.

HOW IT COMPARES – This attraction is very similar to Buzz Lightyear's Space Ranger Spin at Magic Kingdom and Buzz Lightyear Astro Blasters at Disneyland. The look, feel and experience are very similar in all three.

Monsters, Inc. Ride & Go Seek! (FASTPASS)

TRAVELERS SERIES RATES IT – Yuunaru (Outstanding! Disney at its best)
ENTERTAINMENT SNAPSHOT – Combination dark ride and interactive game featuring the Monsters, Inc. characters.
QUEUE – Guests enter the Monsters, Inc. building from the 2001 Disney/Pixar classic <u>Monsters, Inc.</u> and the fun picks up where the movie left off as evidenced by the removal of the "We Scare Because We Care" tagline and the addition of the new "It's Laughter We're After." There are large murals on the ceiling depicting a map of the world and the work done in the Monsters, Inc. factory. Jokester of the Month awards can be seen posted to the wall highlighting the funniest monsters. At the center of the room is a large Monsters, Inc. logo on the floor directly in front of Celia's reception desk. Guests may pose for pictures in front of the desk as they navigate the queue. Announcements may be heard over the PA system including many from Roz. Hearing her speak in Japanese is funny even if you cannot understand what is being said! Billed as a Monsters, Inc. "special event", many posters along the queue show the concept of "Flashlight Tag" and Mike Wazowski narrates a video further explaining how to play this game while experiencing the attraction. Guests begin to be introduced to Rocky – a small and cute furry orange monster. Guests exit the lobby through a door marked "Security" and the line breaks into two separate queues. It really does not matter whether guests go right or left, as the remaining portion of the line is very short and they both end at the loading area. Loading speed is moderate as guests board multiple cars simultaneously.
ATTRACTION LENGTH – 4 minutes

DESCRIPTION AND REVIEW – Sulley has brought Boo back to Monstropolis and wants to play Flashlight Tag with her. Boo, of course, runs off to hide. She is pursued by Randall, who is determined to get his revenge, and Sulley and Mike have to find her first to save her. Security (guests) is sent to find her. Guests board Monsters, Inc. security tram vehicles that look like small tractors and take a zany and interactive ride through the Monsters, Inc. factory and Monstropolis. Armed with a continuously shining flashlight (no button pushing required), guests points them at monsters located within the attraction. For each monster they "find" by shining their flashlight, the monster and scene comes to life. After chasing through the Monsters, Inc. factory floor, the alleys of Monstropolis and through scenes from the movie like Harryhausen's restaurant, Mike and Sulley rescue Boo and quash Randall's thoughts of revenge. As guests waits to exit the attraction, they stop in front of Roz who makes a snarky, albeit in Japanese, comment about the people in the security tram.

Monsters, Inc. Ride & Go Seek! is a very hi–tech combination of Buzz Lightyear's Astro Blasters and the Westernland Shootin' Gallery and this attraction is filled with humorous scenes. This attraction is wonderfully done from the impeccable theming, the state–of–the art ride system and the interactive features. Make sure you take the time to experience this attraction.

How IT COMPARES –Disney's California Adventure is home to Monsters, Inc. Mike & Sulley to the Rescue. The California version is based on scenes from the movie and follows the general plot of the movie (i.e. monsters are still scared of humans) where the Tokyo Disneyland version takes place after the movie. The California version is a typical dark ride and is not interactive, though both feature Roz talking to guests at the end of the attraction.

TIPS – Monsters, Inc. Ride & Go Seek! is extremely popular and its location – directly off Center Street and World Bazaar – makes it an early stop for many guests. This is a great attraction to run to first thing in the morning or collect a FASTPASS very early before they run out.

One Man's Dream II – The Magic Lives On
TRAVELERS SERIES RATES IT – Yuunaru (Outstanding! Disney at its best)
ENTERTAINMENT SNAPSHOT – Stage show featuring Mickey Mouse and the gang
QUEUE – Reserved seating tickets are required and are available via lottery each day. They are distributed at Tomorrowland Hall. There are two entrances to Tomorrowland Hall – enter the side marked One Man's Dream II. After waiting in a short line, proceed to an available lottery machine. Select English on the monitor, select the show time you want, scan the passports of everyone who wants a ticket (i.e. if there are six people in your party, scan all six tickets before proceeding to the next step). Select "okay". The lottery machines will tell you immediately whether or not you were

awarded tickets to your selected show. Win or lose, you can only attempt to get tickets one time per day. If you are issued tickets, collect them from the machine, exit the building and report to the show when indicated. The lottery is not held for the first show of the day. Guests interested in this performance should arrive at Showbase Theater at least 30 minutes before the show begins.

ATTRACTION LENGTH – 30 minutes

DESCRIPTION AND REVIEW – The Magic does live on in this live stage show. The first stage set is in black and white with Mickey as Steamboat Willie. As the music starts, the entire scene comes to life to kick off the show. Color is added and the music kicks into high gear. The sets and characters change frequently and include Mickey and his pals performing several numbers. The insects from A Bug's Life perform in a circus and then Peter Pan and Wendy take to the sky and fly to Neverland. Next, King Louie (<u>Jungle Book</u>) and Terk (<u>Tarzan</u>) perform together. The villains combine for a haunting number amidst several bubbling cauldrons followed by the princesses' performance. Mickey and the gang return to bring down the curtain. The dance numbers are energetic, the music is fun and the entire audience (with the help of a few Cast Members) claps along. Everything seems to work in this high energy tribute to Walt Disney's vision. Guests are treated to some of the most memorable moments from Disney Classics live on stage. The dialogue is in Japanese while the songs are in English, save for a couple renditions that are part English and part Japanese. One Man's Dream II – The Magic Lives on is a great Disney performance!

HOW IT COMPARES – This show is unique to Tokyo Disneyland.

> **NOT SO HIDDEN MICKEY ALERT**
> The stage's border pattern has a very familiar look.

TIPS – Work in a stop to Tomorrowland Hall at least an hour before the first show and try your luck at winning reserved seats. If you do not win tickets, plan for your entire party to arrive at least 30 minutes (45 during peak times) before the first show; this is the one show that does not require reserved seats. If possible, try to sit near the exit to allow your party to leave quickly after the show – this will save you time in exiting and allow you to get to the next ride before the throng of people behind you!

Dining
Plaza Restaurant

EATERY SNAPSHOT – Counter–service featuring Asian rice dishes

PRICES – Entrees range from $5.90 to $8.10; sets range from $10.30 to $12.50

CAPACITY – 730

PRIORITY SEATING AVAILABILITY – No

DESCRIPTION AND REVIEW – The Plaza Restaurant is located directly off Center Street from World Bazaar. It is an enormous counter–service eatery and offers a variety of dishes including pork rice over curry, fried chicken on a Chinese bun or beef and vegetables over rice. The adventurous can try chicken and scrambled eggs over rice! The inside looks like "the future" circa 1965. The interior color scheme is at complete odds with the rest of Tomorrowland with orange and yellow as the dominant colors; the restaurant looks anything but futuristic. The food is adequate and the seating area is quite spacious, especially considering that more than 700 seats are available.

TIPS – Skip this restaurant. There are better places to eat at Tokyo Disneyland for ambience and food.

Soft Landing

EATERY SNAPSHOT – Counter–service soft serve and drinks

PRICES – $3.33 for a soft serve cone

CAPACITY – 0

DESCRIPTION AND REVIEW – Perhaps one of the more futuristic looking areas of Tomorrowland. Futuristic soft serve flavors can change with the season and often include milk, green tea or milk and green tea swirl.

PRIORITY SEATING AVAILABILITY – No

TIPS – Soft Landing is most easily found as you exit Star Tours (just take a right once you've exited), otherwise to find it, you will have to go upstairs next to the Pan Galactic Pizza Port.

Pan Galactic Pizza Port

EATERY SNAPSHOT – Counter service Pizza

PRICES – $4.30 to $5.50 per slice; $8.75 to $9.30 for sets

CAPACITY – 590

PRIORITY SEATING AVAILABILITY – No

DESCRIPTION AND REVIEW – The Pan Galactic Pizza Port is owned by Tony Solaroni and is a very well themed and fun place to grab a slice or a snack. The enterprising alien, Tony, installed an enormous pizza machine that occupies the center of this restaurant. In addition to being food for the eyes, every few minutes a twist occurs. Tony gets a call from his wife, the machine explodes, or a television commercial for the Pizza Port plays. It's an entertaining way to enjoy some pretty good pizza. Options include chicken and vegetable pizza or sausage and mushroom pizza. Specialty slices are also available like red snow crab pizza. It also offers healthier options such as shrimp and tuna salad.

TIPS – Grab your food and head upstairs. There is more room to spread out as most people stay on the main floor and it offers a better view of Tony's show below.

Tomorrowland Terrace

EATERY SNAPSHOT – Counter–service Western–style theme park food
PRICES – $3.20 to $5.30 for sandwiches; $7.65 to $9.75 for sets
CAPACITY – 1,470
PRIORITY SEATING AVAILABILITY – No
DESCRIPTION AND REVIEW – Tomorrowland Terrace is enormous and has several large sections, all with a futuristic look. For the Westerner feeling deprived of traditional theme park fare, the cheeseburgers and french fries offered here will make amends. Other entrées include the shrimp cutlet sandwich, teriyaki chicken sandwich and a bacon–cheese double burger.

> **DID YOU KNOW?**
> Tomorrowland Terrace boasts the highest seating capacity of any Tokyo Disneyland eatery.

Space Place FoodPort

EATERY SNAPSHOT – Counter–service wrap sandwiches and snacks
PRICES – $3.10 to $5.50 for snacks; $2.50 to $3.20 drinks
CAPACITY – 100
PRIORITY SEATING AVAILABILITY – No
DESCRIPTION AND REVIEW – For guests who want to be in the middle of the action when they have a bite, Space Place FoodPort is a good choice. Situated under the StarJets, this counter–service restaurant features beef and Korean vegetable wrap sandwiches, star–shaped steamed buns available in shrimp or pork and "Mickey's Smile", a pastry shaped like the famous mouse and filled with either cheese or banana. A full selection of drinks including soda, teas, coffee and hot cocoa are available here.

Lite Bite Satellite

EATERY SNAPSHOT – Kiosk serving churros
PRICES – $2.75 churros, $2.20 drinks
CAPACITY – 0
PRIORITY SEATING AVAILABILITY – No
DESCRIPTION AND REVIEW – This futuristic churro stand offers… are you ready for this?...honey–lemon churros and bottled drinks.

The Popping Pod

EATERY SNAPSHOT – Counter –service popcorn
PRICES – $3.30

CAPACITY – N/A
PRIORITY SEATING AVAILABILITY – No
DESCRIPTION AND REVIEW – The future of popcorn is here. The changing menu at the Popping Pod shows that butter and caramel are not the only popcorn flavors of the future. Options include curry, caramel, and honey, among other flavors. Depending on the time of year, there may be only one option available. If nothing else, it's an inexpensive way to try something out of this world!

Shopping
Cosmic Encounter
RETAIL SNAPSHOT – Personalized Disney character tags
DESCRIPTION AND REVIEW – Cosmic Encounters is a very small shop selling customized items.

Planet M
RETAIL SNAPSHOT – Buzz Lightyear souvenir and toy shop
DESCRIPTION AND REVIEW – Planet M is appropriately located next to Buzz Lightyear's Astro Blasters. This shop is stuffed to the brim with Buzz and other galactic Toy Story characters from Zurg to the squeaky little green aliens. If souvenirs on your list call for anything related to Buzz Lightyear – shirts, hats, toys, blasters, remote controlled aliens, anything! – this is the place to be. The theme is perfect for Tomorrowland and this shop fits right in.

> **HIDDEN MICKEY ALERT**
> Inside Planet M is a display with Donald on a red spacecraft. To the lower left of the craft is a purple planet. Take a close look at the craters and see if you can spot the man…er…mouse in the moon.

ImageWorks
RETAIL SNAPSHOT – Personalized Photo Souvenirs
DESCRIPTION AND REVIEW – ImageWorks is for anyone who likes to wear their own picture or that of their true love – from the newlyweds to the extremely vain. There are several photo booths located throughout the store. After getting that "just right" pose, guests go to work customizing their memories and superimposing their faces into a choice of scenes with Disney characters. The final print can come in a variety of forms from an 8x10 picture to t–shirts, calendars, phone cards and lots more! These souvenirs are not cheap, but they are truly one–of–a–kind.

Stellar Sweets
RETAIL SNAPSHOT – Candy store

DESCRIPTION AND REVIEW – With a sign that is far more interesting than the sterile interior theme, the choice of candy available here is quite good. Stellar Sweets is designed for those with a sweet tooth or who want outer–space themed packaging for their sour balls.

Solar Ray's Light Supplies

RETAIL SNAPSHOT – Kiosk offering light–up souvenirs

DESCRIPTION AND REVIEW – Solar Ray's Light Supplies is the most technologically advanced store in Tomorrowland, though we're not sure the placement of the solar panels on the side, instead of the top, of the kiosk were quite on target. This small shop sports anything and everything Disney that lights up at night. From necklaces and bracelets to hats, swords and spinning light up characters, Solar Ray's sells it all. Other traditional souvenirs are also sold here.

Monsters, Inc. Company Store

RETAIL SNAPSHOT – Monsters, Inc. themed souvenir and toy shop

DESCRIPTION AND REVIEW – Monster vehicles are parked outside (these make great photo ops) indicating the popularity of this shop to the Monsters, Inc. employees. The inside of the shop, though not quite futuristic, is terrific. Boasting bright vibrant colors, Monsters, Inc. characters can be found everywhere and their logo or picture emblazoned on everything. If you need a souvenir themed to Monsters, Inc., there is no better option than Monsters, Inc. Company Store.

Upcoming Attractions

Walt Disney was adamant that his parks grow and change as people changed and new technologies became available. He famously proclaimed that Disneyland should never be completed and so it is with Tokyo Disneyland. Attractions are refurbished, upgraded, removed and replaced. New attractions are built that test the limits of engineering and imagination. New parades and shows can be found with the seasons and each year brings new attractions into the Disney fold. There are many upcoming attractions for Tokyo Disneyland.

Mickey's PhilharMagic – 2011

Mickey's PhilharMagic is scheduled to open in Fantasyland on January 24, 2011 and will replace the Mickey Mouse Review that closed in 2009. This 4D theater attraction follows Donald Duck as he attempts to right his wrongs after he uses Mickey's sorcerer's hat to create utter chaos at the symphony. Guests join Donald on a journey through Disney songs and movies to retrieve the hat and restore order to the concert. Guests don 3D glasses and experience a variety of gags. This attraction will be nearly identical to Mickey's PhilharMagic at Magic Kingdom. Accompanying this theater attraction will be a souvenir shop, Harmony Faire. The total budget for this attraction and shop is more than $61 million.

Cinderella's Fairy Tale Hall – 2011

Cinderella's Fairy Tale Hall is scheduled to open inside Cinderella Castle in 2011. This Fantasyland attraction will replace the Castle Mystery Tour that closed in 2006. This walk–through attraction will feature dioramas and paintings depicting the story of Cinderella and they promise to be replete with Disney magic. There will be a special effects laden recreation of the grand ballroom from this 1950 classic with Cinderella and Prince Charming appearing to dance. Many of the elements will be similar to the Sleeping Beauty Castle Walkthrough at Disneyland. This attraction is budgeted at more than $20 million.

SECTION 8: Tokyo DisneySea

Overview

Tokyo DisneySea opened in 2001 to much fanfare. Michael Eisner, then Chairman and CEO of the Walt Disney Company, was on hand to dedicate the park. Tokyo DisneySea is estimated to have cost more than $4 billion to construct – making it the most expensive theme park on the planet. The park has quickly become one of the most visited theme parks in the world and in 2009 ranked #5 with more than 12 million visitors. It ranked behind four Disney powerhouses: Magic Kingdom, Disneyland, Tokyo Disneyland and Disneyland Paris.

The Imagineers literally broke the mold on this park. Its nautical theming is not only unmatched by any other theme park, it is situated appropriately on Tokyo Bay. The park itself is decadent. The theming is rich and dense and is far superior to anything that has been done before.

> **TOKYO DISNEY FUN FACT**
> DisneySea was conceptualized as a park to be built along the ocean in Long Beach, California. At its center were to be huge glass domes that would allow guests to experience the wonders of the sea. Outside was to feature nautically themed attractions including an adventure ride through the center of an underwater volcano. Instead, Disney acquired land near Disneyland and built Disney's California Adventure at the Disneyland Resort while the initial ideas for DisneySea were used as the basis for Tokyo's new park.

ATTRACTIONS, RESTAURANTS AND SHOPS BY PORT

Mediterranean Harbor:

Attractions (6)
DisneySea Transit Steamer Line
Venetian Gondolas
Fortress Explorations
The Legend of Mythica
BraviSEAmo!
Meet & Smile

Restaurants (8)
Café Portofino
Zambini Brothers' Ristorante
Mamma Biscotti's Bakery
Ristorante di Canaletto
Gondolier Snacks
Magellan's
Magellan's Lounge
Refrescos

Shops (15)
Valentina's Sweets
Emporio
Galleria Disney
Fotografica
Il Postino Stationery
Nicolo's Workshop
Figaro's Clothiers
Merchant of Venice Confections
Venetian Carnival Market
Romeo's Watches & Jewelry
Juliet's Collections & Treasures
Miramare
Piccolo Mercato
Splendido
Rimembranze

American Waterfront:

Attractions (8)
Big City Vehicles
DisneySea Electric Railway
Turtle Talk
DisneySea Transit Steamer Line
Tower of Terror
Big Band Beat
Over the Waves
My Friend Duffy

Shops (5)
McDuck's Department Store
Steamboat Mickey's
Aunt Peg's Village Store
Newsie's Novelties
Tower of Tower Memorabilia

Restaurants (11)
S.S. Columbia Dining Room
The Teddy Roosevelt Lounge
Restaurant Sakura
Sailing Day Buffet
New York Deli
Cape Cod Cook–Off
Liberty Landing Diner
Barnacle Bill's
Papadakis Fresh Fruit
High Tide Treats
Delancey Catering

Port Discovery:
Attractions (3)
StormRider
Aquatopia
DisneySea Electric Railway
Shops (2)
Discovery Gifts

Restaurants (3)
Horizon Bay Restaurants
Seaside Snacks
Breezeway Bites

Skywatcher Souvenirs

Lost River Delta:
Attractions (6)
Indiana Jones Adventure:
　Temple of the Crystal Skull
DisneySea Transit Steamer Line
Mystic Rhythms
Restaurants (5)
Yucatan Base Camp Grill
Miguel's El Dorado Cantina
Expedition Eats
Tropic Al's
Lost River Cookhouse

Raging Spirits
"Saludos Amigos!" Greeting Dock
Musica Mexicana

Shops (4)
Lost River Outfitters
Expedition Photo Archives
Lookout Traders
Peddlers' Outpost

Arabian Coast:
Attractions (3)
Sinbad's Storybook Voyage
The Magic Lamp Theater
Caravan Carousel

Restaurants (3)
Casbah Food Court
Sultan's Oasis
Open Sesame

Shops (2)
Agrabah Marketplace

Abu's Bazaar

Mermaid Lagoon:
Attractions (8)
Flounder's Flying Fish Coaster
Scuttle's Scooters
Mermaid Lagoon Theater
Jumpin' Jellyfish
Blowfish Balloon Race
The Whirlpool
Ariel's Playground
Ariel's Greeting Grotto

Shops (6)
The Sleepy Whale Shoppe
Mermaid Treasures
Kiss de Girl Fashions
Mermaid Memories
Grotto Photos & Gifts
Sea Turtle Souvenirs
Restaurants (2)
Sebastian's Calypso Kitchen
Grotto Goodies

Mysterious Island:
Attractions (2)
Journey to the Center of the Earth
20,000 Leagues Under the Sea

Restaurants (3)
Vulcania Restaurant
Refreshment Station
Nautilus Galley

Shops (1)
Nautilus Gifts

Tokyo DisneySea occupies roughly 176 acres (121 of which are accessible to guests) – nearly 40% more acreage than Tokyo Disneyland – and includes 36 attractions, 35 shops, and 35 eateries. However, five of the "attractions" include multiple stops for two different transportation lines (DisneySea Electric Railway and DisneySea Transit Steamer Line) bringing the unique attraction count to 33. Given that there are fewer attractions (there are 46 at Tokyo Disneyland) to handle nearly the same number of guests, this park can get crowded and the lines quite long. The park is organized into seven highly themed ports of call. These ports include: Mediterranean Harbor, American Waterfront, Port Discovery, Lost River Delta, Arabian Coast, Mermaid Lagoon, and Mysterious Island.

Shows and Parades

The live entertainment and parade schedule is a moving target at Tokyo DisneySea. Like other Disney parks, some shows are permanent fixtures of the park while others change annually or with the season. Be sure to review the entertainment options before you depart on your trip so that you may plan any additional "must sees". Check the daily schedule for specific times and locations for these events.

Stroller and Wheelchair Rental

Strollers and wheelchairs (regular and motorized) are available to rent at Tokyo DisneySea. The rental kiosk is located in the building on the far left of the entrance court between the turnstiles and the entrance to Mediterranean Harbor. The daily rental fee is substantially lower than in the U.S.: strollers are $7.75, wheelchairs $3.30 and motorized wheelchairs $22.20. If you plan to visit both parks in the same day, keep your receipt and you will be issued the same item in the other park at no additional cost. One thing you will be sure to notice is how few people rent these items relative to the Disneyland or Walt Disney World Resorts.

Main Entrance

Tokyo DisneySea's Main Entrance is nearly identical in layout to Tokyo Disneyland. There is significant open space lined with rows of trees and shrubs between the transportation area and the Main Entrance where guests line up to be admitted through the turnstiles and into an open space courtyard before entering the first port, Mediterranean Harbor. The main courtyard in front of Tokyo DisneySea's main entrance is a sight unto itself. The nautical blue of the cement is set against the backdrop of the Old World Mediterranean–style DisneySea Hotel MiraCosta with the DisneySea AquaSphere at its center.

The AquaSphere is a fountain with a large globe at the center seemingly held up by water and is a symbol of DisneySea. This

> **HIDDEN MICKEY ALERT**
> From the entrance courtyard and AquaSphere, there is a wrought iron sign denoting the entrance to Galleria Disney. A border design runs around the outer edge of the sign – look closely at the corner and you will find a full–profile of Mickey Mouse.

courtyard helps set the tone for the park; adventure and elegance combined with remarkable architecture and works of art. Tokyo DisneySea is a renaissance park and everything within it and around it is unique. Even those attractions and areas that parallel other Disney parks have their own originality here. As you pass through the turnstiles, be sure to grab an English–language map and set sail for an amazing adventure.

> **TRAVEL TIP**
> Tokyo DisneySea stores that sell umbrellas and ponchos:
> *Mediterranean Harbor:* Emporio, Figaro's Clothiers, Il Postino Stationery (umbrellas only)
> *American Waterfront:* McDuck's Department Store, Steamboat Mickey's (umbrellas only), Aunt Peg's Village Store, Tower of Terror Memorabilia
> *Port Discovery:* Discovery Gifts
> *Lost River Delta:* Lost River Outfitters (umbrellas only), Peddlers' Outpost (umbrellas only)
> *Arabian Coast:* Agrabah Marketplace
> *Mermaid Lagoon:* Mermaid Treasures (umbrellas only), Kiss de Girl Fashions
> *Mysterious Island:* Nautilus Gifts (umbrellas only)

Mediterranean Harbor
Overview

Mediterranean Harbor is an Old World port town. Guests are immediately immersed into the setting from the charming "old" buildings to boats cruising the waterways, a docked 16th century Galleon and the towering centerpiece of Tokyo DisneySea just across the water – Mount Prometheus. Everywhere guests look, they will see the opportunity for adventure – whether it is boarding a ship, walking through the fishing village or exploring a Venice–like area complete with canals, to the incredible shows staged in the harbor including BraviSEAmo! The integration of the Tokyo DisneySea Hotel MiraCosta into the park adds to the ambiance substantially. The result is the appearance of "houses" along the port and it serves as to transport guests from the real world to this nautical wonderland.

Mediterranean Harbor:	
Attractions (6)	*Shops (15)*
DisneySea Transit Steamer Line	Valentina's Sweets
Venetian Gondolas	Emporio
Fortress Explorations	Galleria Disney
The Legend of Mythica	Fotografica
BraviSEAmo!	Il Postino Stationery
Meet & Smile	Nicolo's Workshop
	Figaro's Clothiers
Restaurants (8)	Merchant of Venice Confections
Café Portofino	Venetian Carnival Market
Zambini Brothers' Ristorante	Romeo's Watches & Jewelry
Mamma Biscotti's Bakery	Juliet's Collections & Treasures
Ristorante di Canaletto	Miramare
Gondolier Snacks	Piccolo Mercato
Magellan's	Splendido
Magellan's Lounge	Rimembranze
Refrescos	

The European roots are felt through the two main areas within Mediterranean Harbor: the port city that is immediately visible as guests enter the park, and the Venetian canals and waterways. Both are impeccably themed and there are moments when you will undoubtedly think you are in Italy (save for the Japanese–speaking gondoliers!).

Mediterranean Harbor is home to six attractions, eight restaurants and fifteen shops.

How it Compares

Mediterranean Harbor shares many similarities with the first "land" in any Disney park. There are places to pick up maps, a wide selection of restaurants and more shops than in any other area of the park. It is designed to help immerse guests into a whole new world. That's about where any similarities end. Mediterranean Harbor is truly one–of–a–kind and the use of water is unparalleled in any other Disney park. The amount of space is also substantial. Where World Bazaar in Tokyo Disneyland is clustered onto two streets or Main Street in the U.S. parks funnels guests in one direction, Mediterranean Harbor is spread out around the water similar to World Showcase at Epcot.

> **HIDDEN MICKEY ALERT**
> As you approach Mediterranean Harbor's main entrance from the AquaSphere courtyard, the top of the archway boasts a nautically themed piece of metal artwork (it almost looks like a compass). Within the center is a solid sphere with two small circular ears just above it.

Tips

If you are not careful, you can burn a lot of time in this area as other guests sprint to the attractions. Given the uniqueness of Mediterranean Harbor, many guests will stop and explore this area first and will not have the time to see some of the other attractions. Make sure you work time into your day to really explore the wonders of Mediterranean Harbor, but do so much later in the day to avoid long lines elsewhere.

Attractions

DisneySea Transit Steamer Line (to Lost River Delta)

TRAVELERS SERIES RATES IT – Abere–ji (Average – experience this attraction if time allows)

ENTERTAINMENT SNAPSHOT – Boat transportation

QUEUE – This covered queue is near the bridge to Mysterious Island and is themed in the Old World style of the rest of Mediterranean Harbor.

ATTRACTION LENGTH – 7 minutes

DESCRIPTION AND REVIEW – The Transit Steamer Line consists of a fleet of boats that thematically belong in the Lost River Delta – which is exactly where this ride transports guests. The short ride provides great views of the park from the water and serves as transportation to other ports. A different route may be found at the DisneySea Transit Steam Line's third port, American Waterfront. The Mediterranean Harbor route only goes to Lost River Delta.

HOW IT COMPARES – The DisneySea Transit Steamer Line is similar to the boats that transport guests around the World Showcase at Epcot. They are used for transportation and sightseeing.

TIPS – The DisneySea Transit Steamer Line does not operate when shows on the harbor are being set up or performed. Use these lines for transportation later in the day – it is quicker to walk to Lost River Delta for early day attractions.

Venetian Gondolas
TRAVELERS SERIES RATES IT – Abere–ji (Average – experience this attraction if time allows)
ENTERTAINMENT SNAPSHOT – Gondola boat ride
QUEUE – This covered queue is a traditional line themed to Venice.
ATTRACTION LENGTH – 12 minutes

DESCRIPTION AND REVIEW – Gondoliers wearing white shirts and black pants (funny, they do not look Italian) welcome guests aboard 16-person gondolas for a relaxing cruise through the canals of Mediterranean Harbor. A truly unique experience, this trip will transport you to the Old World. The peacefulness of the trip and the stunning views of the Mediterranean Coast make this a terrific experience. Gondoliers will often provide narration of the trip and even sing. Due to the relatively long ride and small capacity, lines can be very long for the Venetian Gondolas. While this attraction is unique, it may cause guests to miss out on more exciting adventures.

HOW IT COMPARES – There is not much of a comparison to be drawn for this attraction.

TIPS – The Venetian Gondolas do not operate when shows on the harbor are being set up or performed.

Fortress Explorations
TRAVELERS SERIES RATES IT – Yoshi (Good – make this a priority)
ENTERTAINMENT SNAPSHOT – Walk–through of a fortress and ship
QUEUE – There is no queue to enter Fortress Explorations.
ATTRACTION LENGTH – Self–directed

DESCRIPTION AND REVIEW – Docked on the opposite side of Mediterranean Harbor is the 16th century galleon, Renaissance. She is moored next to a fortress built during the Golden Age. Both the ship and fortress are open for exploration by adventurers of all ages. The detail of the ship is superb from the structure to the murals throughout. Everything above the Renaissance and in the fortress can be tugged, turned, pulled and played with. The fortress is much larger than it looks and is a labyrinth of interconnecting hallways and mystical rooms. The Solar System room contains a very large model of the solar system connected via pulleys and wheels. Guests can move individual planets to study their movements independent of one another. The War Room contains a large map with miniature galleons on it to be moved and positioned around the area for battle. Yet another room contains a pendulum that occupies most of the space and another hides a pool full of remote controlled galleons (you can drive them for $1.10). Fortress Explorations is almost a miniature port unto itself. There are fantastic machines and instruments to use for exploration around every corner. As guests step out onto the top of the Fortress, there are cannons to be fired into the Harbor and a Leonardo da Vinci style flying contraption that makes for terrific photo ops. The creativity of this area is a sight to be seen. Because of the number of places to explore within this attraction, there are rarely any lines and they can be enjoyed as quickly or as slowly as guests would like. Take the time to walk through this area and explore! Tokyo DisneySea has instituted a game within Fortress Explorations called The Leonardo Challenge. Guests must complete their mission by following clues on a map as they explore the attraction. Sadly, this game is only available in Japanese.

HOW IT COMPARES – Technically, Fortress Explorations is a kid's play area not unlike Tom Sawyer Island in concept. However, the theming is so unique that it cannot be compared to any other Disney attraction.

TIPS – Maps of Fortress Explorations are available from Cast Members in the area or on wall–mounted stands. These English and Japanese maps provide an overview of the Fortress and the rooms within.

The Legend of Mythica
TRAVELERS SERIES RATES IT – Yoshi (Good – make this a priority)
ENTERTAINMENT SNAPSHOT – Live stage show that takes place on Mediterranean Harbor
QUEUE – There is no queue to watch this show.
ATTRACTION LENGTH – 20 minutes

DESCRIPTION AND REVIEW – The Legend of Mythica is a terrific show that encompasses parade–style showmanship and floats on the Harbor. This show tells the story of mankind's interaction with mythical creatures and begins with a woman, speaking Japanese, telling the tale of the Legend of Mythica and how the gateway can be unlocked. As she finishes her story, flares shoot from the stage, music plays with a deep rhythmic beat, and purple–clad wave runners burst into the harbor riding circles around the center stage and gateway to Mythica. Meanwhile, five large floats make their way around the harbor taking up position facing the center "stage". Each has a connection with Mythica and they are shaped like a griffin, dragon, ram, frog and turtle and every float has a different colored giant enclosed egg–shaped container on the rear of the float. The antagonists on wave runners continue riding around the harbor in circles as the floats get into place while water shoots from all around the center stage. Once set, the egg–shaped containers open up and Disney characters emerge from each to unlock the gateway into Mythica's realm and interact with the creatures represented by their floats. Mickey emerges from the griffin; Goofy from the dragon; Chip n' Dale from the ram; Pluto from the frog and Donald from the turtle. In the climatic scene complete with water and small fireworks shooting from the stage, Minnie appears in the center float. Overall, this is a fast–paced show with plenty of action. Guests of all ages will enjoy this performance and it is not to be missed.

TIPS – Given the vast size of Mediterranean Harbor, there are plenty of great places to catch this show. The show is meant to be watched from any angle and guests will line the entire perimeter of the harbor including the Rimembranze bridge leading from Mediterranean Harbor to Port Discovery. There are great viewing areas on top of the turrets at Fortress Explorations as well as the area where guests can explore the boat and cargo next to the Fortress. On the opposite side of the Mysterious Island entrance from Fortress Explorations is a raised walkway along the base of the mountain. This area offers another good vantage point for the show and views are unobstructed from people lined up next to the water. During peak seasons, plan to arrive 30–40 minutes early to stake out a good viewing area. During off–peak times, arriving 10–15 minutes ahead of the show is sufficient to find a good viewing area. Disney rules prevent people from laying down blankets or ground coverings more than an hour before a show. This has little impact in The Legend of Mythica as most people stand for performances.

BraviSEAmo!

TRAVELERS SERIES RATES IT – Yuunaru (Outstanding! Disney at its best)
ENTERTAINMENT SNAPSHOT – Night time show on Mediterranean Harbor
QUEUE – N/A
ATTRACTION LENGTH – 15 minutes

DESCRIPTION AND REVIEW – BraviSEAmo! Is a spectacular nighttime show on the waters of Mediterranean Harbor. As the lights dim and the fog rolls in, Mickey appears holding a triton and riding on a water chariot pulled by giant seahorses. The triton shoots fireworks and the show begins. The stars are Bellisea (the "Spirit of Water") and Prometeo (the "Spirit of Fire"). Either "character" on its own could be a stunning show, but together they make BraviSEAmo! a must see. Water dominates a very tall float representing Bellisea. It spills over the top and out of the sides of the float to provide a "body" to the spirit. The water dances and sprays high into the sky over Mediterranean Harbor and is accented by colorful lights and music. Then fire begins emanating from the water and from the center of the fire, red steel beams begin to appear and slowly take shape into a dragon; this is Prometeo, the Spirit of Fire. Fire continues to rage from the water and from the dragon and its warmth can be felt all around the harbor. Thus the tale of love between Bellisea and Prometeo is told. The two spirits try to find a way to be together, but Bellisea's water puts out the fire and hurts Prometeo. The music blares during the emotional scenes as the two spirits discover how to be together in harmony. The combination of these two spirits interacting is nothing less than spectacular. Through interpretive movements, music and lights, the story is told without words, yet there is never a question about what is happening.

The show is scheduled to be closed at various times during the year. If possible, schedule your trip so that you can experience BraviSEAmo!

HOW IT COMPARES – There are no other shows in the Disney arsenal like BraviSEAmo! The most likely comparison can be made to Fantasmic! at Disneyland and Disney's Hollywood Studios. Unlike Fantasmic!, BraviSEAmo! does not feature cartoons or Disney characters as heroes. It is a world class production on a unique "stage". The water urging guests to use their imagination as water and fire combine with lighting and music to create a memorable experience. Fantasmic! will replace BraviSEAmo! in 2011 as a part of Tokyo DisneySea's 10th anniversary celebration.

TIPS – This show can be enjoyed from nearly any place around Mediterranean Harbor. The two spirits are massive and can be seen from quite a distance. The cargo next to the Renaissance ship in Fortress Explorations provides both a great vantage point and a place to sit. The top of the Fortress, the Rimembranze bridge and the raised pathway at the base of Mount Prometheus are all great spots. Anywhere there is space along the water will work for this show. Plan to stake out a spot 30–40 minutes early during periods of high attendance and 15–20 minutes during moderate attendance.

Meet & Smile
TRAVELERS SERIES RATES IT – Osanai (Young – experience if traveling with young children)
ENTERTAINMENT SNAPSHOT – Live stage show
QUEUE – Guests wait in front of the stage to see the show
ATTRACTION LENGTH – 25 minutes

DESCRIPTION AND REVIEW – Mickey, Minnie, Donald, Daisy, Pluto, Goofy and Chip 'n Dale are among the dancing and singing characters of this upbeat and lively stage show. The Disney crew dances and sings to a variety of numbers while having some fun with each other. Meet & Smile performances are typically held on Lido Isle, a small stage in Mediterranean Harbor just off the walkway near the beginning of the Rimembranze bridge. This show's production is not nearly as grand as other shows held on the harbor. Seating is available on Lido Isle and the show can be seen from the portions of the main walkway closest to the stage. This show is geared toward children and, though energetic, is probably not worth the time commitment.

Dining
Café Portofino
EATERY SNAPSHOT – Table service Mediterranean fare
PRICES – $11 to $16 for entrees and $19.75 for a set; $9.90 for kids' meals
CAPACITY – 540
PRIORITY SEATING AVAILABILITY – No
DESCRIPTION AND REVIEW – Guests who step into this Italian–themed eatery will think they are dining in Italy. From the floor to the rustic barrels, counters and banisters to the tile and faux finish on the walls and exposed beams, everything here is in order. Rotisserie chicken is turning on an open spit. Other items include veal and pork

> **DID YOU KNOW?**
> The legal drinking age in Japan is 20. Alcohol is not served at Tokyo Disneyland, but is available at many restaurants throughout Tokyo DisneySea.

meatloaf, seafood and rice casserole, and spaghetti with eggplant and ham sauce. The food and the atmosphere at Café Portofino are very good.

Zambini Brothers Ristorante
EATERY SNAPSHOT – Counter–service pizza, pasta and risotto
PRICES – Entrees range from $6.60 to $8.10 and sets are $16.10
CAPACITY – 750
PRIORITY SEATING AVAILABILITY – No

DESCRIPTION AND REVIEW – The remnants of the old winery that used to occupy this area have been incorporated into Zambini Brothers Ristorante. The non–descript courtyard in front of the restaurant is decorated with an olive tree and shrubs while the back sports stone pillars and a rustic pergola. The interior has brick floors and wine barrel-shaped cashier stands. There are three lines so be sure you get in the right one for pizza, pasta or risotto dishes. Pizza toppings include smoked salmon and potato as well as salami and Italian sausage. Seafood and rice casserole, spaghetti Bolognese and rigatoni in cream sauce with pancetta are also available as are soups and salads. The food is good and the setting is great. There is available seating inside, outside and upstairs.

Mamma Biscotti's Bakery

EATERY SNAPSHOT – Counter–service bread and pastries
PRICES – $2 to $5.40 for pastries; $2 to $3.20 for drinks
CAPACITY – 160
PRIORITY SEATING AVAILABILITY – No
DESCRIPTION AND REVIEW – This early 20th century Italian bakery looks like a traditional Italian outdoor café. Inside the tiled checkerboard floor surrounds a very small counter offering Italian pastries, fresh–baked bread, and coffee. The tables out front all have umbrellas and offer a quaint setting to enjoy a quick breakfast or snack of breads and pastries or an afternoon dessert. A variety of coffee drinks – both hot and iced – are available.
TIPS – The tables closest to the walkway offer terrific seating for The Legend of Mythica. Although very difficult to come by, if you nab one near show time – stay put!

Ristorante di Canaletto

EATERY SNAPSHOT – Table service Italian food
PRICES – Entrees range from $15 to $20
CAPACITY – 220
PRIORITY SEATING AVAILABILITY – Yes
DESCRIPTION AND REVIEW – Located among the Venetian canals, the Ristorante di Canaletto offers great food and amazing views. Wood–fired pizza and pastas are the main dishes and the view from upstairs is near perfection. Guests can sit near open arches and look out over the canals and footbridges of this Venetian corner. There are several varieties of salads and soups (minestrone is offered, of course). Pizza options include margherita, seafood or the day's special. Other entrees include grilled sirloin, spaghettini with vegetable–duck ragu, spaghettini with seafood–tomato sauce, and vegetarian spaghettini with caponata sauce among others.
TIPS – Request a seat on the balcony near the water.

Gondolier Snacks
EATERY SNAPSHOT – Counter–service gelato, coffee and snacks
PRICES – $3.30 to $4.20 for gelato; $2.00 to $3.20 for drinks
CAPACITY – 120
PRIORITY SEATING AVAILABILITY – No
DESCRIPTION AND REVIEW – Gondolier snacks is located across from the Lido Isle stage. This is a great place to grab a gelato or fresh–brewed coffee for your journey. Gelato is available in an assortment of flavors and drinks include soda, tea, espresso, cappuccino, iced coffee, milk and hot or iced cocoa. Pistachio gelato is highly recommended!

Magellan's
EATERY SNAPSHOT – Table service Mediterranean food
PRICES – Entrees range from $23.30 to $38.90 and sets from $31 to $49; kid's meals range from $16.10 to $21.65
CAPACITY – 200
PRIORITY SEATING AVAILABILITY – Yes
DESCRIPTION AND REVIEW – Aptly named, this restaurant is inside Fortress Explorations near the 16th century galleon, Renaissance (a ship similar to the one Magellan used as the first person to circle the globe). This restaurant makes excellent use of the circular rooms throughout its interior. The style here is elegant and the rich burgundy colors enhance the ambience. At the center of the main dining room is an enormous two–story globe supported by four seahorses. Above it is a stained glass dome celebrating astronomy and the images found amongst the stars. The archways and columns are framed in hand–carved dark woods and rustic candle stands provide for an intimate and even romantic setting. Oil paintings and tapestries on the wall continue the theme. Sautéed king salmon, grilled chicken, veal cordon bleu and beef bourguignon are among the entrees available. The food and service here are excellent.

Magellan's Lounge
EATERY SNAPSHOT – Light appetizers and cocktails
PRICES – Appetizers range from $8.30 to $13.30
CAPACITY – 70
PRIORITY SEATING AVAILABILITY – No
DESCRIPTION AND REVIEW – Located on the mezzanine just above Magellan's dining area is Magellan's Lounge. Shrimp and avocado, shaved scallops and kiwi, cream of pumpkin soup and asparagus salad with prosciutto are among the appetizers available. Guests here will include those looking for light appetizers or who are waiting for their table at Magellan's.

TIPS – Magellan's Lounge is a great alternative for those who don't want to spend the time or money to eat at Magellan's, but would like an intimate setting and upscale atmosphere.

Refrescos

EATERY SNAPSHOT – Counter service churros and snacks
PRICES – $2.75 to $4.65 for snacks; $2 to $3.20 for drinks
CAPACITY – 60
PRIORITY SEATING AVAILABILITY – No
DESCRIPTION AND REVIEW – Explorers must eat and so it is that Refrescos is located within the courtyard of the Fortress. This small snack counter offers some interesting fare. Maple churros and black pepper pork rib are the snacks of choice. A variety of hot and cold drinks are also available.

Shopping
Valentina's Sweets

RETAIL SNAPSHOT – Candy shop
DESCRIPTION AND REVIEW – Located under a non–descript stone archway and through a pair of wooden and glass door lies the bright and airy décor and delicious treats of Valentina's Sweets. A mural of the sky covers the ceiling and a painted rose vine winds along the ceiling. Artful mosaics serve as both the centerpiece and border of the Tuscan–styled tile. The store is filled with chocolates, candies, and packaged cookies, many of which are packaged in souvenir tins.

Emporio

RETAIL SNAPSHOT – Large store stuffed with Disney merchandise
DESCRIPTION AND REVIEW – Emporio in Italian is Emporium. Tokyo DisneySea's Emporio is essentially Tokyo Disneyland's Grand Emporium placed in an Italian setting. This shop, the largest in Tokyo DisneySea, is brimming with stuffed animals, toys, household goods, t–shirts, and hats. If

> **HIDDEN MICKEY ALERT**
> Make sure to look at the Hidden Mickeys on the sconces in the four sides of each ceiling mural.

it's a Disney souvenir, you are likely to find it here. The store's interior boasts cartoonish and whimsical columns. The décor is enhanced by the sky painted on the ceiling. Emporio is quite spacious with generous amounts of walking room throughout the store.

Galleria Disney

RETAIL SNAPSHOT – Large shop selling all things Disney

DESCRIPTION AND REVIEW – Through the Old World archways of Mediterranean Harbor sits a shop that is "Under the Sea". Disney characters abound in this fantasy sea–themed store. The walls are painted a bright ocean turquoise and the lighting assists in the illusion that guests are under water. The ceiling is covered with mosaic tile coral and fanciful seaweed, and the floor is made to look like sand. Murals, oil paintings and other artistic representations of Disney characters are placed throughout the store. The shop itself is unique, though the wares within are no different that other stores. Although a little out of sync with its European surroundings, this store is masterfully done.

> **HIDDEN MICKEY ALERT**
> Check out the display windows for two Hidden Mickeys incorporated into the red and green artwork.

Fotografica

RETAIL SNAPSHOT – Camera and photo print shop
DESCRIPTION AND REVIEW – Don't let the posters depicting old black and white photos fool you - Fotografica offers state-of-the-art merchandise including camera accessories, photo development and digital printouts. Antique photo equipment lines the shelves and small framed black and white prints cover the walls. Like Camera Center in World Bazaar, this outlet is also sponsored by Fuji Film and offers everything you may need or have forgotten related to your camera including film, batteries and an assortment of accessories and disposable cameras. Camera Corner allows guests to develop and print film (is anyone using film?) as well as print digital camera pictures complete with Disney "frame" – a border printed directly on your picture. These digital kiosks are easy to use and make a great one–of–a–kind souvenir.

Il Postino Stationery

RETAIL SNAPSHOT – Stationery and Postcard shop plus Silhouette Portraits
DESCRIPTION AND REVIEW – Il Postino Stationery is very similar to World Bazaar's House of Greetings. Offerings include stationery, small gifts and postcards. The floor is rustic European and the exposed beams and faux finish highlight the mailboxes–turned–display shelves in this old post office. Writing desks are available for guests who want to pen a letter or postcard to friends and family back home. Within the shop is a portrait studio where, like its Tokyo Disneyland counterpart, Cast Members use special scissors to cut out instantly recognizable profiles of guests and their group. Your silhouette may even appear alongside that of Mickey or Minnie.

Nicolo's Workshop
RETAIL SNAPSHOT – Handmade glassware shop
DESCRIPTION AND REVIEW – Nicolo's Workshop is a store and working studio where craftsmen are busy making, etching or polishing souvenir glassware. Guests are invited to watch these people at their work and it is often quite interesting when they are heating and shaping the glass to make items to sell. The cobbled floor, faux- painted walls – sometimes chipped to reveal the stone supports – weathered and exposed beams, rustic chandeliers and cashier stands add to the intimacy of Nicolo's.

Figaro's Clothiers
RETAIL SNAPSHOT – Clothing store
DESCRIPTION AND REVIEW – In a terrific play on words to the operatic Figaro, this shop is themed to the opera and characters are displayed wearing costumes of famous opera roles. The floral tile "rugs", chandeliers and overall décor have an almost art deco vibe. Merchandise includes t–shirts, sweatshirts, hats and accessories.

Merchant of Venice Confections
RETAIL SNAPSHOT – Cookie, candy and kitchenware shop
DESCRIPTION AND REVIEW – In case the canals outside were not a strong enough clue, Mickey and Minnie riding in a gondola – with a Goofy gondolier – in the front window will remind you of your Mediterranean location. This Venetian–themed shop displays its wares under small canopies and atop a stone and brick floor. The shop is spacious and wonderfully themed. Offerings include packaged cookies and candies – often in collectible tins – as well as kitchenware.

Venetian Carnival Market
RETAIL SNAPSHOT – Clothing store
DESCRIPTION AND REVIEW – This upscale clothing shop is decorated to the Italian festival, Carnevale. Along the walls, guests will find streamers, masks and flags depicting this festive event. Wares within the store include brand–name apparel with a Tokyo DisneySea flare – these items were produced exclusively for Tokyo DisneySea and can only be found in the park.

Romeo's Watches & Jewelry
RETAIL SNAPSHOT – Watch and jewelry shop
DESCRIPTION AND REVIEW – Destined to never be together, Romeo's Watches & Jewelry is immortalized next to Juliet's Collections & Treasures. Romeo's is truly elegant. The floor is beautiful parquet–style

wood, the counters and displays are a deep cherry and the ceiling is ornately decorated with wood. A large selection of clocks, watches and jewelry are offered here. Despite the shop's appearance, there are many items that are fairly inexpensive (and plenty that are very expensive). This store is worth a visit, even if just to see the luxurious décor.

Juliet's Collections & Treasures
RETAIL SNAPSHOT – Bath goods and cosmetics
DESCRIPTION AND REVIEW – Where Romeo's Watches & Jewelry is masculine, Juliet's Collections & Treasures is decidedly feminine. Themed to a Shakespearean garden, Juliet's décor is decorated with cream colors accented with the greens of vines and topiaries. The floral tile mosaics on the floor are works of art as is the stunning garden mural on the ceiling. Wares include ladies' bath goods, cosmetics, and hair accessories. Juliet's is connected to Romeo's through an interior doorway and is also a must see.

Miramare
RETAIL SNAPSHOT – Kiosk selling souvenirs
DESCRIPTION AND REVIEW – This harbor–side kiosk offers the usual selection of souvenirs and light–up toys.

Piccolo Mercato
RETAIL SNAPSHOT – Kiosk selling souvenirs
DESCRIPTION AND REVIEW – This café–side kiosk sells show merchandise, hair ties and a variety of other souvenirs and toys.

Splendido
RETAIL SNAPSHOT – Kiosk selling hats
DESCRIPTION AND REVIEW – Hats are always a Disney park staple. Splendido offers an assortment of different hats to purchase or for great photo ops!

Rimembranze
RETAIL SNAPSHOT – Kiosk selling souvenirs
DESCRIPTION AND REVIEW – This tiny kiosk parked halfway across Rimembranze bridge offers a small selection of traditional park souvenirs.

American Waterfront
Overview
   Built along the side of Tokyo Bay to give the illusion of being in a port city, American Waterfront depicts the Northeastern United States in the early 1900s. From New York to New England, this port celebrates the

impact of the sea on America. This port is essentially split into two areas. The Cape Cod side of American Waterfront is a New England-styled town sporting authentic looking buildings and the brick sidewalks found in this part of the U.S. Turn of the century police cars are seen transporting guests up and down the streets of while a row of buildings overlooks a small harbor where resident's sailboats are docked and row boats are beached. This sleepy town is perfect for a leisurely walk – and that is a good thing because there is not much else to occupy your time here.

New York circa 1912 is the theme for the other portion of American Waterfront. Anchored by the Liberty Fish Market, this area features many charming buildings and an old and "terror–fying" hotel. Theater shows are the mainstay in New York as is one of Tokyo DisneySea's best attractions – Tower of Terror.

American Waterfront:	
Attractions (8)	*Restaurants (11)*
Big City Vehicles	S.S. Columbia Dining Room
DisneySea Electric Railway	The Teddy Roosevelt Lounge
Turtle Talk	Restaurant Sakura
DisneySea Transit Steamer Line	Sailing Day Buffet
Tower of Terror	New York Deli
Big Band Beat	Cape Cod Cook–Off
Over the Waves	Liberty Landing Diner
My Friend Duffy	Barnacle Bill's
	Papadakis Fresh Fruit
Shops (5)	High Tide Treats
McDuck's Department Store	Delancey Catering
Steamboat Mickey's	
Aunt Peg's Village Store	
Newsie's Novelties	
Tower of Tower Memorabilia	

The S.S. Columbia, preparing for her maiden voyage, is docked in New York Harbor and is nearly an attraction itself. It is an enormous replica of a 20th century steam–powered luxury liner. Its three smoke stacks tower above everything else in American Waterfront and the inside reflects Titanic–style luxury. The wood moldings, statues, tile and intricately decorated ceilings combine to complete the elegance of the S.S. Columbia. The ship is worthy of exploration and the top decks provide excellent views of the park and Tokyo Bay. On clear days, guests can even see Mount Fuji.

S.S. Columbia is also home to two restaurants and its wharf hosts a live stage show.

The American Waterfront is spectacularly themed and boasts seven attractions, eleven restaurants and five shops. It must be noted that of the seven attractions, only one is an adventure ride – three are forms of transportations and three are shows. Although great to walk around and experience, American Waterfront lacks a strong selection of attractions. American Waterfront is accessible by foot from Mediterranean Harbor or Port Discovery and can be accessed via DisneySea Electric Railway from Port Discovery.

How it Compares
American Waterfront is a Disney Imagineering original.

Attractions
Big City Vehicles
TRAVELERS SERIES RATES IT – Abere–ji (Average – experience this attraction if time allows)
ENTERTAINMENT SNAPSHOT – Early 1900s replica vehicle transportation
QUEUE – Guests line up outside behind street signs in one of three different locations – two are located on the New York side at the foot of the Rimembranze bridge and the other is in the Cape Cod section.
ATTRACTION LENGTH – 6–12 minutes depending on the route

DESCRIPTION AND REVIEW – There are two places within American Waterfront where guests can board early 20th century vehicles for a one–way trip between Cape Cod and New York and another that takes guests on a round–trip sightseeing tour of New York. Vehicles include a police wagon, delivery truck, and town car. The ride in the vehicles can be pretty long (up to 12 minutes) and is a relaxing alternative to get from area to another.

HOW IT COMPARES – Tokyo DisneySea's Big City Vehicles are very similar in concept and design to the Omnibus at Tokyo Disneyland or the Main Street Vehicles of Disneyland and the Magic Kingdom. The most striking differences include the unique design of the vehicles at Tokyo DisneySea and the route. Like its U.S. cousins, Tokyo DisneySea's Big City Vehicles are used for transportation. But where the California and Florida versions take guests from one part of Main Street U.S.A. to another navigating throngs of people, Tokyo DisneySea's attraction moves a much larger distance and through wide–open and sparsely populated streets. This makes for a much more interesting ride and Big City Vehicles are a legitimate mode of transportation. Overall, these vehicles' routes make this the best of the "old cars" in the Disney fleet.

DisneySea Electric Railway

TRAVELERS SERIES RATES IT – Abere–ji (Average – experience this attraction if time allows)

ENTERTAINMENT SNAPSHOT – Elevated trolley transport

QUEUE – Guests queue on the top floor of the depot. This open air line is covered with fans for warmer days.

ATTRACTION LENGTH – 2 ½ minutes

DESCRIPTION AND REVIEW – Guests in the American Waterfront may choose to travel to Port Discovery via this elevated electric trolley. This attraction is a combination monorail and trolley car and offers great views along its route. Boarding occurs near New York Harbor under the bridge next to Broadway Theater. The stylized red brick entrance is reminiscent of early 20th century train depots (except it is a lot cleaner!). The interior of the trolley cars have two benches; each faces the opposite side of the trolley. One side provides a view of the sea as guests move from New York through the Cape Cod areas of American Waterfront before arriving in Port Discovery. The other side offers views of Mount Prometheus and the Mediterranean Harbor. The DisneySea Electric Railway is worth a trip if the line is not too long.

HOW IT COMPARES – The DisneySea Electric Railway is a traditional "transportation" attraction, but the views make it unique and unlike other Disney offerings.

TIPS – Because guests tend to tour American Waterfront before Port Discovery, the lines are often shorter at the Port Discovery station for a one–way trip to American Waterfront.

DisneySea Transit Steamer Line

TRAVELERS SERIES RATES IT – Abere–ji (Average – experience this attraction if time allows)

ENTERTAINMENT SNAPSHOT – Round–trip boat ride

QUEUE – Under the rusted roof of the Grand Banks Cannery lies a traditional covered queue with an alarming amount of space for guests to line up.

ATTRACTION LENGTH – 13 minutes

DESCRIPTION AND REVIEW – The Transit Steamer Line consists of a fleet of boats themed more to the Lost River Delta than American Waterfront. The Steamers leaving from the American Waterfront dock take guests on a round–trip tour of the Tokyo DisneySea's seven ports. The tour is in Japanese and focuses on pointing out the attractions and ports seen along the route. Different routes are available from the other two DisneySea Transit Steamer Line docks located in Mediterranean Harbor and Lost River Delta.

HOW IT COMPARES – The DisneySea Transit Steamer Line is similar to the boats that transport guests around the World Showcase at Epcot. They are used for transportation and sightseeing.

TIPS – The American Waterfront DisneySea Transit Steamer Line does not begin operation until one hour after the park opens. Likewise, it does not operate directly before or during shows on Mediterranean Harbor.

Turtle Talk

TRAVELERS SERIES RATES IT – Yuunaru (Outstanding! Disney at its best)
ENTERTAINMENT SNAPSHOT – Guests interact with undersea creatures including Crush, the turtle from <u>Finding Nemo</u>
QUEUE – As guests board the S.S. Columbia, they are immediately transported back to turn-of-the-century America. Posters, pictures and newspaper articles – all in English – are framed throughout this indoor queue. They show the S.S. Columbia being launched and information from her maiden voyage. They also show the wonders of the latest discovery - the one guests have been invited aboard to witness - the hydrophone. Billed as "The Invention of the Century", scientists have discovered a way to speak with undersea creatures. The posters and schematics further show that in the bow of the ship, there is a hydrophone set up and part of the steel frame of the ship has been replaced with glass so that humans and sea animals can see each other while they speak. As guests move into the pre–show area, one of the Japanese speaking crew members discusses the invention of the hydrophone. They go on to humorously describe the "Hydrophone Translation Apparatus" and how it works to translate animal voices into a language humans can understand and vice–versa. Lastly, the crew member teaches all the guests how to speak whale the same way Dory does in Finding Nemo – long and overly enunciated words.
ATTRACTION LENGTH – 12 minutes

DESCRIPTION AND REVIEW – As guests are admitted to the theater, they will see rows of benches throughout and may choose any seat they like. There is not a bad seat in the theater, though children have a much better view from the front and guests who may wish to participate in the show should consider sitting closer to the front. On the far left wall is the Hydrophone Translation Apparatus and directly in front is a glass wall with views into the ocean where guests can see a microphone swaying in the water. Fish begin swimming by and the crew member, with help from the audience, calls Crush the turtle. As Crush the "surfer dude" talking turtle appears, he begins speaking to the audience. Crush makes comments about people in the audience – what they are wearing how they are sitting, etc. The audience can ask him questions and Crush answers them often playing up the differences of how humans see things and how sea turtles see things. Crush's face is filled with expression as he looks around the room and talks to the audience. The show is filled with gags like when Crush puts on a bikini top and doesn't realize what it is until someone from the audience tells him; he becomes surprised and then embarrassed as he gets rid of it. Dory arrives to interact with the audience and works with them on speaking as a giant whale shows up and accidentally pins Dory to the glass. The smooshed Dory humorously asks the audience for help and using the "whale talk" they learned in the pre–show, the audience communicates with the whale who then swims away.

Turtle Talk is an audience-driven show and demonstrates the creative ingenuity of the Disney Imagineers. Though the show, at a cost of $13.2 million was not expensive by Disney attraction standards, its concept and execution are outstanding. The show is difficult to follow in Japanese, but the English language posters do a fine job in laying out the basics of the show and it is clear throughout the show what is happening.

HOW IT COMPARES – Turtle Talk is very similar to Turtle Talk with Crush at Disney's California Adventure and Epcot. The biggest difference is the location of Tokyo DisneySea's version inside a ship and the concept of the Hydrophone Translation Apparatus. Additionally, the pre–show and theming are much more in–depth at Tokyo DisneySea and the appearance of Dory is unique. Due to cultural differences, Crush himself is less expressive in his looks and less sarcastic – he doesn't do the "dead–pan" nearly as often as he does in the U.S.

Tower of Terror (FASTPASS)

TRAVELERS SERIES RATES IT – Yuunaru (Outstanding! Disney at its best)
ENTERTAINMENT SNAPSHOT – Thrilling elevator ride through an abandoned hotel
QUEUE – The queue and pre–show begins the moment guests walk onto the property of the Hotel Hightower – now dubbed the Tower of Terror. Although the hotel has just been restored by the New York Preservation

Society, there is an eerie feel in the courtyard that all is not right with this hotel. Public tours of the hotel are available and as guests wind their way through the queue, the music and the screams heard overhead set the dramatic tone for this hair–raising attraction. Newspaper clippings are located throughout the queue and begin to give some hint as to what happened on New Year's Eve 1899. Then, guests enter the lobby and can see the dusty remnants of this luxurious hotel and begin to learn more about the cursed statue that the hotel's wealthy founder – explorer and collector Harrison Hightower III – recovered on an expedition to Africa. The most worrisome feature in the lobby is the roped off elevator that crashed on that fateful December evening and was not fixed during the restoration, but left for show during tours. It is said that Harrison Hightower III was taking the Shiriki Utundu statue that he brought back from Africa to his penthouse apartment when the accident occurred. When the elevator was recovered, all that was found was the Shiriki Utundu statue – Mr. Hightower had vanished and no trace of his body was ever found. From the lobby, guests are directed to Hightower's private office where the full story – told in Japanese – of the cursed statue is learned. Lightning strikes and the Shiriki Utundu makes it clear that no one is welcome here. Shaken from this dramatic revelation and ghostly encounter, guests are directed through a warehouse. Here, Hightower's extensive collections, such as ancient Chinese and Egyptian artifacts consisting of statues, vases, masks, furniture and more, are stored. As guests navigate this collection and wind through the queue, they are directed to storerooms with access to an elevator.

ATTRACTION LENGTH – 2 minutes

> **HIDDEN MINNIE ALERT**
> That's right, a Hidden Minnie profile can be found within the private office of Harrison Hightower III. There is a tall stained glass window depicting the famous explorer that changes to black and white with Hightower holding the Shiriki Utundu statue. Just above Hightower's head and over the far left–hand spires of the hotel is a white cloud (black once the picture changes) that shows the profile of Minnie Mouse looking to the right.

DESCRIPTION AND REVIEW – Guests board a service elevator with direct access to the penthouse apartment – a place not visited since Mr. Hightower disappeared in the elevator shaft years earlier on December 31, 1899. Twenty two guests are seated in three rows and once they all buckle up, the elevator begins to take them up to the penthouse. The elevator suddenly stops on the way up, where the cursed statue Shiriki Utundu appears and guests learn how powerful this artifact truly is. The statue casts a spell upon the entire group and windows open to reveal that the elevator is high enough to be near the penthouse (guests can see much of the park from here). The view is short–lived as the elevator shakes and falls straight down the shaft and rises as fast as it fell back to the penthouse and then straight down again. Ultimately, everyone survives the adventure and has now learned the horrifying secret of the Tower of Terror.

The theming continues through the exit as guests are directed to the final stop on their tour, The Rajah's Pool. The room that once housed this decadent facility has been transformed into a gift shop, but there are still remnants of the pool. Murals near the ceiling depict various scenes while the tile perimeter of the pool is still visible on the floor with the pool filled in with hardwood planks.

The ride is exhilarating and unmatched in its theming and storytelling. This ride is an absolutely must–see and cannot be missed. Everything about this attraction is Disney at its best and the Japanese dialogue does nothing to take away from this attraction.

HOW IT COMPARES – Tokyo DisneySea's Tower of Terror is modeled after the Twilight Zone Tower of Terror at Disney's Hollywood Studios in Florida and Disney's California Adventure in California. The elevator ride itself is more similar to the California version; both are watered down versions of the spectacular effects in the original Walt Disney World Resort attraction. At Disney's Hollywood Studios, the elevator car ascends and then detaches from the shaft and navigates through the building with scenes of the Twilight Zone before entering another shaft and beginning the freefall. The California and Tokyo version's elevators never leave the original shaft and primarily travel up and down. The theming and back story of Tokyo DisneySea's Tower of Terror is also significantly different. Whereas, the U.S. versions are based in Hollywood and surround the mysterious disappearance of several hotel guests, Tokyo's hotel is based in New York and surrounds the disappearance of the hotel's founder. Also, the Tokyo DisneySea Tower of Terror does not include the "Twilight Zone" narration and has replaced it with a trip into Harrison Hightower III's study.

> **DID YOU KNOW?**
> The "freefall" in the Tower of Terror is actually must faster than a "freefall" and the elevator is accelerated down the shaft. Disney Imagineers did not believe a freefall was fast enough for the excitement of this attraction!

TIPS – Tower of Terror is one of the most popular attractions at Tokyo DisneySea and often commands the longest waits. Run here to grab a

FASTPASS first thing in the morning as lines will quickly reach 90–120 minutes, even on days of moderate attendance.

Big Band Beat

TRAVELERS SERIES RATES IT – Yoshi (Good – make this a priority)

ENTERTAINMENT SNAPSHOT – Live stage show

QUEUE – Reserved seating tickets are required and are available via lottery each day. They are distributed at Biglietteria across from the Lido Isle stage in Mediterranean Harbor. After waiting in a short line, proceed to an available lottery machine. Select English on the monitor, select the show time you want, scan the passports of everyone who wants a ticket (i.e. if there are six people in your party, scan all six tickets before proceeding to the next step). Select "okay". The lottery machines will tell you immediately whether or not you were awarded tickets to your selected show. Win or lose, you can only attempt to get tickets one time per day. If you are issued tickets, collect them from the machine and report to the Broadway Music Theatre at the time indicated. The lottery is not held for the first show of the day. Guests interested in this performance should arrive at the Broadway Music Theatre at least 30 minutes before the show begins.

ATTRACTION LENGTH – 30 minutes

DESCRIPTION AND REVIEW – Guests enter the Broadway Theatre into an elegant marble–floored lobby. The chandeliers and murals all tastefully accent this spacious room as guests move through it to the theatre. Big Band Beat provides big band sound to a large Broadway production as performers tap and dance their way through this jazz revue. Disney characters are the center of the show and tap, dance and sing with the best of them. Mickey takes to the drums in an unforgettable performance. Overall, the show is high–energy and a lot of fun.

TIPS – The doors are closed five minutes before the show's start time or, in the case of the first show, when the theatre reaches its 1,500 person capacity.

Over the Waves

TRAVELERS SERIES RATES IT – Abere–ji (Average – experience this attraction if time allows)

ENTERTAINMENT SNAPSHOT – Live stage show

QUEUE – Guests wait outside next to the S.S. Columbia.

ATTRACTION LENGTH – 30 minutes

DESCRIPTION AND REVIEW – Set against the S.S. Columbia on Dockside Stage, Over the Waves is a fun Disney character filled musical. The story surrounds two children who stow away on a cruise and the antics the Disney characters go through to ensure everything is okay. The show is kicked off by a couple of crew members announcing a Dream Cruise. Two young stowaways watch the rich and famous board the ship – the Japanese version of Marilyn Monroe is our favorite – and decide to dress like crew members to get aboard. Once there, they encourage many of the passengers to loosen up and have fun through music. The ship's crew members and passengers are quickly joined by Mickey, Minnie, Donald, Daisy, Chip n' Dale, Goofy and Pluto and all of them sing and dance. Songs are in English and Japanese and include a variety ranging from the musical theme from Rocky, to a rendition of Flashdance's Maniac to Madonna's Vogue and Express Yourself. The show also includes beats created from props like the Broadway show Stomp. The longest running gag has the crew members bring out a set that looks like the ship's hallway with doors to several state rooms. The stowaways have been discovered and are chased in and out of doors in a Scooby Doo–style chase. Goofy catches the stowaways with a giant net and the crew members try to decide what to do with them. In a moment of forgiveness, the passengers and Disney characters insist they are set free and the show transitions into the finale where they all sing about the Sea of Dreams as confetti drops, signaling the end of the show.

Over the Waves is big on music and fun, but the show is too long and not worth the 45–60+ minute time commitment during peak periods when you must arrive early to ensure a seat.

My Friend Duffy

TRAVELERS SERIES RATES IT – Abere–ji (Average – experience this attraction if time allows)

ENTERTAINMENT SNAPSHOT –Live stage show that may be enjoyed with a meal

QUEUE – Guests order food from Cape Cod Cook–Off before proceeding to the dining and show area.

ATTRACTION LENGTH – Continuous shows are 10 minutes with 5-minute breaks in between.

DESCRIPTION AND REVIEW – Situated in the Duffy section of the Cape Cod Cook–Off restaurant, is the My Friend Duffy show. This is a continuous show that tells the tale of Duffy the bear; how he came to live with Mickey and his adventures. Mickey and the gang are on stage throughout the performance. This is a terrific way to combine a campy show with a meal. The show is silly, but fun. A great alternative to Over the Waves, My

Friend Duffy saves time by combining a meal and a show. Not to mention, it will provide you with some insight as to the affection the Japanese feel for this bear.

TIPS – With the unbridled popularity for Duffy, finding a seat can be a challenge, especially during "meal times". Consider seeing My Friend Duffy with a late lunch or an early dinner. The last show is typically around 6:00 pm.

Dining
S.S. Columbia Dining Room
EATERY SNAPSHOT – Table service steak and seafood
PRICES – Entrees range from $25 to $40.50; kid's meals range from $16.10 to $21.65
CAPACITY – 200 indoors
PRIORITY SEATING AVAILABILITY – Yes
DESCRIPTION AND REVIEW – Located on the S.S. Columbia's third level (Deck B) is the elegant S.S. Columbia Dining Room. This is not a typical cruise ship dining room, but rather the room is open and airy. The walls are white and are accented with ironwork ranging from traditional designs to 10 foot high trees. Crafted moldings adorn both the walls and ceilings and. A large mural celebrating the steam liner's destinations are on the wall with Panama Canal as the highlighted trip. Luxurious drapes accent each window and the center of the dining room is domed with a large chandelier. The mood is accented by a live piano player.

> **HIDDEN MICKEY ALERT**
> Pay close attention to those crackers in your soup, they sport the famous mouse ears!

Fare includes grilled chicken, steak, and seafood with a wide variety of sides. The food and service are very good, though it is quite expensive.

The Teddy Roosevelt Lounge
EATERY SNAPSHOT – Table service lounge featuring light meals and appetizers
PRICES – $7.75 to $13.30 for appetizers; $13.30 to $32.75 for entrees
CAPACITY – 180 indoors and outdoors
PRIORITY SEATING AVAILABILITY – No
DESCRIPTION AND REVIEW – Aboard the S.S. Columbia's second level (Level C), guests will find The Teddy Roosevelt Lounge. Celebrating the 26th President of the United States, who was an avid outdoorsman, this lounge reflects a hunting lodge that Teddy would have enjoyed. Steeped in dark woods – from the bar to the floor to the ceiling to the hand–carved

statues to the fireplace and bookshelves, the Lounge is elegant and rich. Heads of animals, black and white photos, oil paintings of Teddy and intricate carvings line the walls while hand–carved statues of bears sit atop the bar. Past the bar and tables is a "den" complete with dark leather sofas and chairs surrounding a small table in front of a fireplace flanked by built–in bookshelves. Overhead is a small dome with a mural and large chandelier. Dining options include light meals and appetizers such as roast beef sandwiches on graham, deep–fried prawn sandwiches on Danish and selected sirloin steak with yuzu–pepper. If the option is available, sit in the "den" to enjoy a meal or cocktail.

DINING TIP – Whether you are interested in having a cocktail, eating a meal or just touring the S.S. Columbia, be sure to check out The Teddy Roosevelt Lounge as it is exceptionally well themed.

> **HIDDEN MICKEY ALERT**
> One of the more unique Hidden Mickeys may be found in the bar of The Teddy Roosevelt Lounge. The cognac bottles have been arranged in such a way that a shadow depicting a nearly perfect Hidden Mickey appears between the top and bottom shelf.

Restaurant Sakura

EATERY SNAPSHOT – Table service Japanese food
PRICES –Sets range from $19.40 to $24.40; kids' meals are $16.10
CAPACITY – 320 indoors and outdoors
PRIORITY SEATING AVAILABILITY – Yes
DESCRIPTION AND REVIEW – Located harbor–side and within the old Liberty Fish Market brick building, Restaurant Sakura offers Japanese fare. The interior of the restaurant still sports some of the items that were used in the old fish market. From the small white and black tiled floor to the rustic but clean "feel", Restaurant Sakura could just as well be located on a pier in San Francisco – the

> **DID YOU KNOW?**
> Sushi is generally rice topped with a single item, like raw fish. Chirashi–zushi is a bowl of sushi rice with multiple toppings.

theming is spot on. Options include seasonal udon, assorted tempura, teriyaki chicken with vegetables, and assorted deep–fried skewers of meat, seafood and vegetables.

TIPS – As one of the few Japanese options at the Tokyo Disney Resort, Restaurant Sakura is quite popular. If you do not take advantage of Priority Seating, plan either a late lunch or early dinner to avoid the rush.

Sailing Day Buffet
EATERY SNAPSHOT – Western style buffet
PRICES – $31 for adults; $18.90 for children 7 to 12; $11 for children 4 to 6
CAPACITY – 440 indoors and outdoors
PRIORITY SEATING AVAILABILITY – Yes
DESCRIPTION AND REVIEW – The United States Steamship Co. is celebrating the maiden voyage of the S.S. Columbia by offering a festive atmosphere in its warehouse. Racks and pallets are loaded with items for the ship and the floor has been cleared out and set with tables for guests to enjoy their fare. Traditional Western–style buffet options are available here and there is often live musical entertainers that walk through the restaurant.

New York Deli
EATERY SNAPSHOT – Counter service sandwiches, sides and desserts
PRICES – Sandwiches range from $7.55 to $9.90
CAPACITY – 520 indoors and outdoors
PRIORITY SEATING AVAILABILITY – No
DESCRIPTION AND REVIEW – New York Delicatessen is a counter–service restaurant located down a brick–lined alley near the Broadway Music Theatre. This small and seemingly innocuous entrance does not reflect the 500 seat restaurant behind the façade. Eats include traditional sandwiches like sliced turkey on ciabatta and grilled Reuben to smoked salmon on a soft bagel. The food is good and New York Deli is a nice alternative to "fast food" or the slow pace of a table service restaurant.
TIPS – Seating can be a bit tricky to locate – not finding an available seat, but locating the actual seats. Many are located behind the deli to the right of the front entrance and around a small corner. There are 520 seats nearby so you're sure to find an open seat if you keep looking.

Cape Cod Cook–Off
EATERY SNAPSHOT – Counter service hamburgers, soups and salads
PRICES – $3.45 to $4.10 for entrees; $7.90 to $11 for sets
CAPACITY – 910 indoors and outdoors
PRIORITY SEATING AVAILABILITY – No
DESCRIPTION AND REVIEW – Cape Cod Cook–Off is located in the tallest building of the Cape Cod section of American Waterfront and, though unnoticed from the outside, it occupies the interior space of the houses on both sides and the warehouses behind. The first impression of Cape Cod Cook–Off is of the massive open space within the eatery. The walls are painted white with four large murals in the recessed ceiling. Once guests get their food, they have several options of where to dine. Most are themed to the Cape Cod style, except for the warehouse in back. Themed like an old

warehouse with cargo suspended from the rafters and ship steering wheels holding the lights, it is in here that Duffy and the Disney gang put on live entertainment continuously throughout the day. My Friend Duffy lasts 10 minutes with a 5-minute intermission between performances. It plays continuously with the final show starting around 6 pm. The food at Cape Cod Cook–Off is standard theme park food. If traveling with children, it's a great way to entertain them (and perhaps skip one of the other shows). If not, there are much better places to eat within Tokyo DisneySea, unless you are craving a theme park hamburger.

Liberty Landing Diner

EATERY SNAPSHOT – Counter service Japanese
PRICES – $2.65 to $4.20
CAPACITY – 0
PRIORITY SEATING AVAILABILITY – No
DESCRIPTION AND REVIEW – Located water–side next to the Liberty Fish Market (Restaurant Sakura), this renovated boat repair shop offers a small selection of Japanese food items. Specialties include grilled sushi rolls with roast pork and mustard and mini chirashi–zushi (rice bowls with multiple toppings). The food is good and Liberty Landing Diner offers a great "quick" option for guests on the go.

Barnacle Bill's

EATERY SNAPSHOT – Kiosk offering snacks, beer and wine
PRICES – $2.45 to $4 for snacks; $2.55 to $6.70 for drinks
CAPACITY – 0
PRIORITY SEATING AVAILABILITY – No
DESCRIPTION AND REVIEW – Barnacle Bill's is a small snack shack on the dock and offers a few snacks like sausages or assorted nuts and pretzel bits, as well as beer, sparkling wine and hot wine. The oil drums and crates nearby have been converted into areas to stand and take in the view of the American Waterfront while enjoying a snack.

Papdakis Fresh Fruit

EATERY SNAPSHOT – Fruit stand
PRICES – $2.10 to $2.30
CAPACITY – 0
PRIORITY SEATING AVAILABILITY – No
DESCRIPTION AND REVIEW – Papdakis Fresh Fruit is located near the entrance to the S.S. Columbia and offers, well, fresh fruit. Unlike typical fruit stands, items here may be ordered whole or cut to order and often include selections like oranges, apples, kiwis and grapefruit.

TIPS – Papdakis is open seasonally.

High Tide Treats
EATERY SNAPSHOT – Kiosk serving brownies
PRICES – $2.75
CAPACITY – 0
PRIORITY SEATING AVAILABILITY – No
DESCRIPTION AND REVIEW – Located in a remote section of the American Waterfront under the DisneySea Electric Railway tracks near Port Discovery, High Tide Treats offers brownies.
TIPS – High Tide Treats is open seasonally.

Delancey Catering
EATERY SNAPSHOT – Hot dog stand
PRICES – $4.20
CAPACITY – 0
PRIORITY SEATING AVAILABILITY – No
DESCRIPTION AND REVIEW – This bright yellow truck turned hot dog stand offers a New York and Japanese favorite – hot dogs!
TIPS – Delancey Catering is open seasonally.

Shopping
McDuck's Department Store
RETAIL SNAPSHOT – Large store stuffed with Disney merchandise
DESCRIPTION AND REVIEW – Money is the symbol of Scrooge McDuck, the proprietor of this department store and uncle of Donald Duck. McDuck's combines both New York 5th Avenue elegance with American Waterfront's dock–side roots with weathered hardwood floors and brick wall interior. Offerings include the traditional souvenirs as well as boxed cookies and candies, t–shirts, stuffed animals, cups, mugs, key chains, etc. McDuck's Department Store offers the same wares as Emporio but is often much less crowded.

Steamboat Mickey's
RETAIL SNAPSHOT –Souvenir shop
DESCRIPTION AND REVIEW – Named after the first Disney cartoon to feature synchronized sound, <u>Steamboat Willie</u>, Steamboat Mickey's offers a selection of traditional souvenir options. For guests who want a stuffed Mickey that reflects one of his many looks through the years, this shop has a great selection.

Aunt Peg's Village Store
RETAIL SNAPSHOT – Duffy accessories and confections
DESCRIPTION AND REVIEW – Aunt Peg's Village Store is a large red house in the middle of the Cape Cod section of American Waterfront. The beautiful brick entrance invites guests into this country shop where an amazing selection of Duffy accessories are available. From outfits, shoes or the bear himself, Aunt Peg's has it all. Additional wares on the country–weathered and worn shelves and cases include packaged cookies and candies.
TIPS – The line to enter Aunt Peg's Village Store can often run 100 people or more deep as guests check out the latest in Duffy fashions.

Newsie's Novelties
RETAIL SNAPSHOT – Kiosk selling souvenirs
DESCRIPTION AND REVIEW – This New York newsstand has been converted to sell traditional Disney souvenirs and mementos.

Tower of Terror Memorabilia
RETAIL SNAPSHOT – Personalized photos of your party on the Tower of Terror and traditional gift shop
DESCRIPTION AND REVIEW – The luxurious Rajah's Pool & Spa, which used to delight and relax guests of the Hotel Hightower has been converted to sell personalized photos and other themed memorabilia from your "tour" of the Tower of Terror. Remnants of Rajah's Pool are still present including the murals that adorn the walls and the tile band around the pool.

Port Discovery
Overview

The perimeter of Port Discovery sits less than 100 yards off Tokyo Bay. There is a water gate with a good sized leak giving the illusion that the port gates are closed off directly from Tokyo Bay until the port operators open them to allow ships in or out. Port Discovery is a "marina of the future" where scientists and researchers are celebrating the completion of their latest inventions. The festivities are open to guests from around the world who have been invited to sample these adventures firsthand. Port Discovery is a relatively small, futuristically themed port. It shows the future as an ultra–modern area filled with fantastical transportation concepts. The colors inject this same feeling into the area as deep reds, gold and patina greens dominate the palette. Discovery Port is accessible from American Waterfront by foot or DisneySea Electric Railway and by footpath from Mysterious Island and Lost River Delta. It is home to three attractions, three restaurants and two shops.

Port Discovery:
Attractions (3)   Shops (2)
StormRider   Discovery Gifts
Aquatopia   Skywatcher Souvenirs
DisneySea Electric Railway

Restaurants (3)
Horizon Bay Restaurants
Seaside Snacks
Breezeway Bites

How it Compares

Although the overriding them of Port Discovery retains its originality, this area is inspired by Jules Verne, much like Tomorrowland at Disneyland and Magic Kingdom (as well as Hong Kong Disneyland and Disneyland Paris' version called Discoveryland). The theming of Port Discovery could explain why the Tokyo Disney resort elected to keep the retro look of Tomorrowland at Tokyo Disneyland it – keeps both Port Discovery and Tomorrowland relatively unique in the Disney family.

Attractions
StormRider (FASTPASS)

TRAVELERS SERIES RATES IT – Yuunaru (Outstanding! Disney at its best)
ENTERTAINMENT SNAPSHOT – Motion–simulator flight into a storm
QUEUE – The indoor queuing area for StormRider sets the mood and provides the background for the attraction, albeit in Japanese. StormRider is set in the middle of the Center for Weather Control's tower. It is the invention of a "Storm Diffusion Device" – called a Fuse – that is the reason for the festivities in Port Discovery. This device is meant to be transported and detonated into the middle of violent storms to diffuse their energy before the storms make landfall and causes damage. The pre–show, complete with English subtitles scrolling on a screen, features crew members discussing this new technology. They perform a demonstration of the Fuse to show its effects on a simulated hurricane. The crew members then inform everyone that a massive typhoon is approaching Port Discovery. Guests have been invited to fly in a transport behind the Fuse and head for the middle of the storm and observe the detonation and breaking apart of the storm.
ATTRACTION LENGTH – 14 minutes

DESCRIPTION AND REVIEW – Once aboard the motion-simulator transport, 122 guests immediately take off via plane for the typhoon. Take off is very smooth and the visibility is great through the giant screen in front. Small portals along the side of the transport provide guests with views of the water and landscape as the transport flies toward to storm. The transport follows closely behind another aircraft when suddenly it falls victim to the storm and everyone watches as the other transport goes down. The Fuse is launched, but as a result of the turbulence and chaos, it misfires and comes crashing through the ceiling of the transport. As a result, the transport carrying guests from Port Discovery begins to break apart with hoses hissing, sparks flying and panels falling from the ceiling. The StormRider transport is flying out of control amidst the turbulence as crew members work remotely to get the Fuse dislodged from plane and into the storm before it explodes. In the final moments, the Fuse is finally extracted and the transport gains enough control to get out of the storm, just as the Fuse detonates. The transport is hit with aftershocks and nearly goes down into the ocean. Once control is regained, the transport heads back to see sunny skies and a few remnants of the storm that has been blown apart. Port Discovery has been saved!

The dialogue in this attraction is Japanese, but the suspense translates in all languages. The ride is thrilling, bumpy and noisy – and a fantastic Disney attraction.

HOW IT COMPARES – The easiest comparisons for StormRider are to Star Tours at Disneyland and Disney's Hollywood Studios at the Walt Disney World Resort. However, the technology used in StormRider is light–years beyond that of Star Tours and includes "4D" effects. StormRider is wild, yet smoother than Star Tours. Given the upcoming enhancements to Star Tours in the U.S. parks, it is a safe bet that they will incorporate some of the StormRider effects.

Aquatopia

TRAVELERS SERIES RATES IT – Abere–ji (Average – experience this attraction if time allows)
ENTERTAINMENT SNAPSHOT – Boating adventure
QUEUE – The queue is a standard covered queue and the entire attraction is visible from line or from the rails on the side of the attraction.
ATTRACTION LENGTH – 2 ½ minutes

DESCRIPTION AND REVIEW – Aquatopia grabs the attention of all those who walk by. The Center for Weather Control is allowing guests to test new types of navigation systems. As one, two, or three guests board these water craft, they set out on an aquatic adventure navigating fountains, rocks, light poles and whirlpools. The water craft guide themselves and seem to have a mind of their own and they twist, turn, back up and spin around as they narrowly miss the objects in their path.

> **HIDDEN MICKEY ALERT**
> There are several rock formations within the waters of Aquatopia and each has holes and crevices to make them look weathered. Find the large formation toward the end of the ride. At the base of this formation, there are three distinct holes that form a Hidden Mickey.

Aquatopia's bark is better than its bite. This attraction looks wonderfully creative, and is, but the "fun" quotient was lost in translation from concept to the final product. Given the long lines that are typical due to the slow loading speed and limited capacity, this attraction is not worth a long wait. Spend a few minutes watching from the guardrail and you can pretty well imagine what it's like to ride.

HOW IT COMPARES – There isn't really anything in the Disney arsenal quite like Aquatopia. It shares technology with Tokyo Disneyland's Pooh's Hunny Hunt and has the same "random" motions as it moves forward, backward, and spins in a circle. This attraction seems more akin to Disneyland's ill–fated Rocket Rods in that the attraction focuses on new transportation technology, looks fantastic and had an exciting concept for Imagineers to develop. In the end, it's a relatively dull ride set in an imaginative concept and world–class theming.

TIPS – There are times when lines for Aquatopia are very short. Should you pass by the attraction during these times, take the water craft for a spin!

DisneySea Electric Railway

TRAVELERS SERIES RATES IT – Abere–ji (Average – experience this attraction if time allows)
ENTERTAINMENT SNAPSHOT – Elevated trolley transport
QUEUE – Guests queue on the top floor of this futuristic station. This covered queuing area provides shade. Two vibrant murals painted on the walls depicting the adventure and fantasy of the sea in this futuristic port, are worth taking the time to admire.
ATTRACTION LENGTH – 2 ½ minutes

DESCRIPTION AND REVIEW – DisneySea Electric Railway provides one–way transportation to the New York section of American Waterfront. This elevated trolley car offers great views along its route. Boarding occurs just opposite Aquatopia. Because of the their vibrant red and blue colors and elevated tracks, these 20th century trolleys look oddly appropriate in this futuristic port. The interior of the trolley cars have two benches, each which face out the opposite side of the trolley. One side provides a view of American Waterfront and Tokyo Bay while the other side offers views of Mount Prometheus and the Mediterranean Harbor. The DisneySea Electric Railway is worth a trip if the line is not too long.

HOW IT COMPARES – The DisneySea Electric Railway is a unique attraction and is unlike other Disney offerings. Though it is a fairly standard "transport", the views and theming are exclusive to Tokyo DisneySea.

TIPS – Because guests tend to tour American Waterfront before Port Discovery, the lines are often shorter at the Port Discovery station for the one–way trip to American Waterfront.

HIDDEN MICKEY ALERT

While waiting in line, take the time to admire the two large murals for a variety of Hidden Mickeys. There are no fewer than five hidden between these two murals. 1) Take a close look at the steam coming out of the futuristic train's smokestack. 2) On the opposite wall, the spots on the sea turtle swimming underwater form a Hidden Mickey. 3) Between the red flying machine and Pegasus, there are ominous clouds. The dark cloud near the tail of the flying machine looks a lot like a Hidden Mickey. 4) Check out the riveting picture of the red Golden Gate bridge…the rivets form a Hidden Mickey. 5) A blimp contraption is flying through the sky, just above and to the right of the blue–haired goddess. Inside the windows is a profile of Mickey Mouse looking out over the water.

Dining

Horizon Bay Restaurant

EATERY SNAPSHOT – Buffeteria serving seafood, soups and salads

PRICES – $9.90 to $14.55 for entrees; $9.90 for kids' meals

CAPACITY – 600 indoors and outdoors

PRIORITY SEATING AVAILABILITY – No

DESCRIPTION AND REVIEW – Set in a futuristic yacht club, Horizon Bay Restaurant has a contemporary futuristic look. Honey colored hardwood floors and chairs are complimented by stainless steel columns and vents running through the restaurant. The building's architecture is inspired and the outdoor seating is on the water. Fare here is served buffeteria style and consists of grilled salmon with fresh tomato sauce, sautéed chicken with onion sauce, cordon bleu–style pork cutlet, braised beef, deep–fried prawns with tartar sauce as well as salads and soups.

Seaside Snacks

EATERY SNAPSHOT – Kiosk serving shrimp buns
PRICES – $4.45
CAPACITY – 30 outdoors
PRIORITY SEATING AVAILABILITY – No
DESCRIPTION AND REVIEW – Seaside Snacks is located just past the American Waterfront Lighthouse at the transition into Port Discovery. This snack shack offers ukiwah buns. These pink and white life saver-shaped rings are steamed buns filled with shrimp.
TIPS – The lines can be incredibly long for these snacks. If you encounter such a line, find something else to eat…they are not worth the wait.

Breezeway Bites

EATERY SNAPSHOT – Kiosk offering pastries
PRICES – $2 to $3.75
CAPACITY – 20 outdoors
PRIORITY SEATING AVAILABILITY – No
DESCRIPTION AND REVIEW – This futuristic snack shack is located behind the Horizon Bay Restaurant and nestled against the base of Mount Prometheus. This out of the way kiosk offers a small variety of pastries.

Shopping
Discovery Gifts

RETAIL SNAPSHOT – Souvenir shop featuring Port Discovery items
DESCRIPTION AND REVIEW – Discovery Gifts cannot be missed with the giant wind machine sitting atop its roof. Inside this small shop are gifts and souvenirs, many of them themed to StormRider and Aquatopia. There are also some very unique gifts related to the weather theme of Discovery Port from paper and model airplanes to mini–experiments that can be done at home. Some of the items here are not available elsewhere at Tokyo DisneySea.

Skywatcher Souvenirs

RETAIL SNAPSHOT – Kiosk offering souvenirs
DESCRIPTION AND REVIEW – Skywatcher Souvenirs is a futuristic kiosk offering traditional souvenirs as well as several items themed exclusively to Port Discovery. One of the most "who the heck would ever need this" items is a holder for your FASTPASS tickets. Considering guests may only have one FASTPASS at a time (two if they time it well), it would seem that a pocket or wallet would do just fine.

218

Lost River Delta
Overview

Lost River Delta is a port for the adventurous. The center of this area is an ancient Central American pyramid situated along "El Rio Perdido", the Lost River, and it can be seen from nearly anywhere within Lost River Delta's boundaries. This port is set in the 1930s and is surrounded by the lush landscape of the Central American jungle. The bridge that crosses the Lost River is "hastily" constructed of wooden logs and ropes. Water planes can be seen beached in the nearby river – a clue that explorers are in the jungle and searching for treasure. All around are ancient artifacts and archeological dig sites. This port gives the feeling of isolation and the few buildings that exist look like remote outposts. Everything here is mysterious and the theming is spectacular – it looks like the jungle where Indiana Jones escapes at the beginning of Raiders of the Lost Ark. Take the opportunity to see the Lost River Delta at night when the camps and bridge are lit up; the scene is beautiful.

Lost River Delta:
Attractions (6)
Indiana Jones Adventure:
   Temple of the Crystal Skull

DisneySea Transit Steamer Line
Mystic Rhythms

Musica Mexicana
"Saludos Amigos!" Greeting Dock
Raging Spirits

Restaurants (5)
Yucatan Base Camp Grill
Miguel's El Dorado Cantina
Expedition Eats
Tropic Al's
Lost River Cookhouse

Shops (4)
Lost River Outfitters
Expedition Photo Archives
Lookout Traders
Peddlers' Outpost

The Lost River Delta encompasses areas on both sides of the Lost River and can be accessed on foot from Port Discovery, Mermaid Lagoon or Arabian Coast. This port can also be reached via DisneySea Transit Steam Liner from Mediterranean Harbor. The Lost River Delta sports six attractions, five restaurants, and four shops.

How it Compares

The closest thing to Lost River Delta is the lush Central American jungle areas of Disneyland's and Magic Kingdom's Adventureland (as opposed to the African portions of Adventureland). The portion of

Disneyland where Indiana Jones and the Temple of the Forbidden Eye and the Jungle Cruise are housed is a good reference point as is the Jungle Cruise attraction within the Magic Kingdom. Overall, Lost River Delta has a much more mysterious feel than the Adventurelands. In essence, it feels like Indiana Jones Land.

Attractions
Indiana Jones Adventure:
Temple of the Crystal Skull (FASTPASS / SINGLE RIDER)
TRAVELERS SERIES RATES IT – Yuunaru (Outstanding! Disney at its best)
ENTERTAINMENT SNAPSHOT – Motion simulator powered dark ride
QUEUE – Indiana Jones Adventure: Temple of the Crystal Skull begins with the queue. Guests enter the interior labyrinth of the Central American pyramid and are immersed in adventure. Drawings, paintings and carvings on the walls depict the story of the Fountain of Youth – the very prize explorers are chasing in this attraction. Archeologists have clearly been here and have set up lighting and walkways as they explored the inter sanctum of this temple. The theming could not be more realistic and the queue does an outstanding job setting the stage for this Indiana Jones Adventure. As guests approach the attraction, a short film – made to look like it was created in the 1930s – alerts guests to the details of their search for the Fountain of Youth and the safety features of the vehicles that will transport them.

> **HIDDEN MICKEY ALERT**
> There is a standard Disney sign near the entrance of the Indiana Jones Adventure warning guests about the attraction. The sign is directly in front of a leaning column. At the base of the column, just behind the sign is an ancient Hidden Mickey.

ATTRACTION LENGTH – 3 minutes

DESCRIPTION AND REVIEW – Guests enter large jeep–like vehicles and fasten their seat belts. The transports take them deep within the Temple of the Crystal Skull and these vehicles follow a path forward, like a dark ride, though each one provides a different experience. These motion simulators give the vehicles the ability to bounce over rough terrain, shake as they descend stairs, and tilt into turns giving the feeling that they are traveling faster than they are. These old vehicles seem to stall even before taking off into the temple. The interior of the pyramid is covered with booby–traps, filled with bugs, rats and....wait for it....snakes – the creatures Indiana Jones fears most. Once into the center of the temple, guests can see the wonders of the Crystal Skull and the mysterious power that protects it. Guests journey over a collapsing bridge, into hoards of bugs, past a giant snake, through a giant smoke ring and into the Disney magic. Perhaps one of the greatest effects of any Disney attraction in the world is the climactic ending. The transport speeds around a corner to find Indiana Jones hanging from a rope. He sees the transport full of guests and immediately yells at them to go turn around and go back. Seconds later a giant boulder (remember the opening scene from Raiders of the Lost Ark?) begins rolling toward Indy and the transport. The vehicle attempts to drive backward, but stalls. The boulder is nearly on top of the vehicle and in a flash of light the transport lunges toward the ball and under it to safety. This ride is an amazing adventure and ranks as an absolute must see!

HOW IT COMPARES – Tokyo DisneySea's Indiana Jones Adventure: Temple of the Crystal Skull is nearly identical in theming and execution to Disneyland's Indiana Jones Adventure. The look and feel are the same, though there are some differences that make this attraction unique. The story line in Disneyland is set in the jungles of India's Lost Delta and adventurers are chasing wealth, youth or knowledge…depending on which door they enter. Tokyo's version focuses on Central America and an expedition searching for the Fountain of Youth. Additionally, the queue is the same overall idea, but the props and set up are different just as some of the props are different on the attraction itself. Notably, mystical spirit power can be seen emanating from the floor of the pyramid during the collapsing bridge scene at Tokyo DisneySea where this scene features fire in Disneyland's Indiana Jones Adventure.

DisneySea Transit Steamer Line (to Mediterranean Harbor)

TRAVELERS SERIES RATES IT – Abere–ji (Average – experience this attraction if time allows)
ENTERTAINMENT SNAPSHOT – One–way Boat transportation to Mediterranean Harbor
QUEUE – This covered queue is located across the Lost River opposite the Indiana Jones Adventure.
ATTRACTION LENGTH – 6 minutes

DESCRIPTION AND REVIEW – The Transit Steamer Line consists of a fleet of boats that belong here in the Lost River Delta. The short ride provides great views of the park from the water and serves as one–way transportation to Mediterranean Harbor. A different route is available from a third port in American Waterfront. The Lost River Delta route goes only to Mediterranean Harbor.

HOW IT COMPARES – The DisneySea Transit Steamer Line is similar to the boats that transport guests around the World Showcase at Epcot. They are used for transportation and sightseeing.

TIPS – The DisneySea Transit Steamer Line does not operate when shows on Mediterranean Harbor are being set up or performed.

Music Rhythms

TRAVELERS SERIES RATES IT – Yoshi (Good – make this a priority)

ENTERTAINMENT SNAPSHOT – Live stage show

QUEUE – The queue is a standard outdoor waiting area, though Lost River Delta is so well themed that even the wait provides an opportunity to enjoy the surroundings.

ATTRACTION LENGTH – 25 minutes

DESCRIPTION AND REVIEW – Mystic Rhythms is a live stage show located in an abandoned hangar in Lost River Delta. Parts of Hangar Stage have been destroyed and overgrown with rock formations, trees and a waterfall. The animals and the spirits tell a story about this mysterious port. Smoke and water effects spice up the rhythms and dance of this high–energy show.

TIPS – Plan to arrive with your entire group at least 30 minutes prior to the scheduled start time (45+ minutes on days of high attendance). The doors close 5 minutes prior to the start time or when the 1,140 seat theatre reaches capacity.

Raging Spirits (FASTPASS / SINGLE RIDER)

TRAVELERS SERIES RATES IT – Abere–ji (Average – experience this attraction if time allows)

ENTERTAINMENT SNAPSHOT – Roller coaster

QUEUE – Guests queue in the ruins on the side of the ancient temple. Smoke and fire are visible from the front of this ancient burial site including a waterfall – with a few flames – running down the center steps. From here, guests can see most of the attraction and hear the screams of the current riders.

ATTRACTION LENGTH – 1 ½ minutes

DESCRIPTION AND REVIEW – Set in the ruins of an ancient ceremonial site, guests board mine cars for a turbulent roller coaster ride. The intruders who excavated this sacred site have made the spirits angry and the spirits make their displeasure known as guests ascend the first hill. Smoke, bursting flames and a 360 degree loop demonstrate just how violent these spirits can be. Raging Spirits is themed wonderfully, though the ride itself is just okay. Disney Imagineers have long prided themselves with their design and ride operation and one of their rare attempts to create a legitimate roller coaster resulted in a second–rate ride. The style of the coaster is that of a mouse – it's relatively compact and the track overlays on top of itself. Additionally, and most disappointingly, the ride is quite violent and is reminiscent of older coasters and not typical of the smoothness associated with coasters built over the past 15 years. The turbulence causes guests' heads to hit side to side and can give you a bit of a headache. This design flaw is the primary reason this attraction rates only so–so. If you dare to tackle this mysterious attraction, be sure to press your head back against the headrest – hard – to avoid the side to side impact. If you do not experience this attraction, be sure to walk by Raging Spirits at night when the lighting effects combined with the smoke and fire make for a terrific site.

HOW IT COMPARES – There is no attraction like Raging Spirits in any of the U.S. parks. An attraction very similar in nature was originally Imagineered for Disneyland and would have run through the Indiana Jones Adventure. However it is nearly identical to Indiana Jones and the Temple of Peril at Disneyland Paris from the layout to the jarring trip through the sacred burial site.

> **HIDDEN MICKEY ALERT**
> As you disembark your mine car, look at the ladder leaning against the wall next to the tracks. On the wall at its base and just to the right on are three rocks that form a Hidden Mickey.

TIPS – This attraction is very popular with teenagers and, as a result, can be flooded with kids early on. If this is a "must see" for your party, be sure to get here early to experience it or get a FASTPASS – they will run out.

Musica Mexicana

TRAVELERS SERIES RATES IT – Abere–ji (Average – experience this attraction if time allows)
ENTERTAINMENT SNAPSHOT – Live music that may be enjoyed with a meal
QUEUE – Guests order food from Miguel's El Dorado Canteen before proceeding to the dining and show area.
ATTRACTION LENGTH – 30 minutes

DESCRIPTION AND REVIEW – Musica Mexicana serves up Latin music performed by Mexican musicians to those dining in Miguel's El Dorado Cantina. Performances are in 30 minute sets and occur every 1–2 hours. If you are already dining in Miguel's El Dorado Cantina and a set is about to begin, have a seat and listen. Otherwise, do not bother working one of the performances into your day.

TIPS – If you plan on eating at Miguel's El Dorado Canteen, plan your meal around a performance and enjoy the music while you dine.

"Saludos Amigos" Greeting Dock

TRAVELERS SERIES RATES IT – Osanai (Young – experience if traveling with young children)
ENTERTAINMENT SNAPSHOT – Character greeting and store
QUEUE – Traditional rope line
ATTRACTION LENGTH – 30 seconds

DESCRIPTION AND REVIEW – "Saludos Amigos" Greeting Dock does not deserve to have the moniker "attraction" associated with it. Essentially, this Latin themed covered area is part shop, selling sombreros, blankets, maracas and other Latin souvenirs and part character greeting. The highlight of this attraction is the ability to pose with Disney characters wearing Latin American styles and colors.

TIPS – "Saludos Amigos" Greeting Dock opens one hour after the park and closes before the rest of the park. Be sure to check the entertainment schedule if you plan on visiting.

Dining
Yucatan Base Camp Grill

EATERY SNAPSHOT – Counter service BBQ
PRICES – Entrees range from $8 to $8.90; sets range from $12.40 to $13.30; kids' meals are $8.90
CAPACITY – 690 indoors and outdoors
PRIORITY SEATING AVAILABILITY – No
DESCRIPTION AND REVIEW – The Yucatan Base Camp Grill is a remote outpost in the middle of this Central American Jungle. Located next to an archeological dig site, this eatery has been constructed for members of the exploration team. This seemingly temporary structure is themed as a giant tent constructed against two of the pyramid's ancient walls of the dig site. Supplies can be seen stored in corners of the tent as well as overhead. The fare is includes cabbage rolled in cream sauce, smoked pork or smoked chicken all served with Mexican rice and vegetables. There are a selection of side dishes and the food here is quite good. After getting your food, grab a seat outside – the lush scenery and archeological dig make for an excellent backdrop for this meal.

> **HIDDEN MICKEY ALERT**
> There is a restroom near Yucatan Base Camp Grill. The backsplash of the drinking fountains located in front of the restrooms shows many ancient symbols. Look closely in the far left–hand corner of the backsplash to spot a Hidden Mickey.

Miguel's El Dorado Cantina
EATERY SNAPSHOT – Counter service Mexican food
PRICES – $8.65 to $10.90 for entrees; $10.55 for sets; $8.90 for kids' meals
CAPACITY – 600 indoors and outdoors
PRIORITY SEATING AVAILABILITY – No
DESCRIPTION AND REVIEW – Located alongside El Rio Perdido is a run–down warehouse that has been converted into a two–story Mexican restaurant. Guests enter the restaurant on the top level and place their orders at old oil drum cashier stations. The outside seating area is right along the river and offers a view of the Disney Transit Steamer Line and the mystical pyramid across the water. There is also an elevator to the bottom floor as stairs and trays of food often do not mix. The Mexican food served here is good and includes soft tacos and fajitas.
TIPS – Live music from Musica Mexicana can be heard in one of the dining areas. Check the schedule for show times.

Expedition Eats
EATERY SNAPSHOT – Kiosk serving Sausage Rolls
PRICES – $4.65
CAPACITY – 0
PRIORITY SEATING AVAILABILITY – No
DESCRIPTION AND REVIEW – Parked directly in front of the Temple of the Crystal Skull, this archeological roach coach looks like a truck out of an Indiana Jones movie. The limited fare here includes Yucatan Sausage Rolls – think hot dog inside a steamed bun roll. These make a great meal on the go and are quite tasty. Expedition Eats is also very popular and the line can be extremely long.

Tropic Al's
EATERY SNAPSHOT – Kiosk serving snacks and drinks
PRICES – $3.10 to $3.35 for snacks; $2.55 to $3.20 for drinks
CAPACITY – 0
PRIORITY SEATING AVAILABILITY – No
DESCRIPTION AND REVIEW – Tropic Al's (get it? Tropical is Tropic Al) is a run–down wagon on the path to Mermaid Lagoon. This kiosk serves cheesecake chimichangas and frozen treats to eat, and soda and hot and cold cocoa (including hot almond cocoa) to drink.
TIPS – Tropic Al's is open seasonally.

Lost River Cookhouse
EATERY SNAPSHOT – Counter service with chicken legs and dessert
PRICES – $4.45 to $5.30

CAPACITY – 30 outdoors
PRIORITY SEATING AVAILABILITY – No
DESCRIPTION AND REVIEW – Built at the base of the ancient ceremonial site, this snack shack was constructed to feed members of the excavation team and guests alike. Counter service fare includes spicy smoked chicken legs, passion fruit mousse or a mango drink with grape jelly and tapioca. Given the limited selection and long lines, guests would do better to grab items from the other eateries in Lost River Delta.

Shopping
Lost River Outfitters
RETAIL SNAPSHOT – Lost River Delta themed and non–themed merchandise
DESCRIPTION AND REVIEW – Located along El Rio Perdido next to Miguel's El Dorado Cantina, Lost River Outfitters offers a wide selection of items not found elsewhere in the park. Guests can find authentic   Indiana Jones hats and jackets and other souvenirs of the famous archeologist. Additional wares include hand–crafted Central American souvenirs and non–themed hats and clothes. Disney character merchandise designed to the ancient Central American theme of Lost River Delta can also be found in this riverside shop. Lost River Outfitters sells personalized leather goods here and the line to purchase these can rival that of many attractions.

Expedition Photo Archives
RETAIL SNAPSHOT – Personalized photos of your expedition team aboard Indiana Jones Adventure: Temple of the Crystal Skull
DESCRIPTION AND REVIEW – Remember that climactic flash of light during the bolder scene in Indiana Jones Adventure? That was your picture being taken. Guests exiting the ancient pyramid will walk through part of the archeological dig site where they can view a picture of themselves at the most thrilling moment of the Indiana Jones Adventure: Temple of the Crystal Skull.

Lookout Traders
RETAIL SNAPSHOT – Kiosk offering light–up items and souvenirs
DESCRIPTION AND REVIEW – This small shack-turned-kiosk offers a limited variety of light–up novelties and basic souvenirs.

Peddler's Outpost
RETAIL SNAPSHOT – Kiosk selling Indiana Jones-themed merchandise and traditional souvenirs

DESCRIPTION AND REVIEW – This small kiosk set in an outdoor corner of the Temple of the Crystal Skull offers traditional souvenirs as well as a selection of Indiana Jones-themed apparel and souvenirs.

Arabian Coast

Overview

Arabian Coast is set downriver from the Lost River Delta. This port is accessible by footpath from Lost River Delta or Mermaid Lagoon. Heavily influenced from the likes of Aladdin, the architecture here is stunning. Expansive and ornate buildings line the waterfront – each with distinctive spires and domes. Tile archways lead guests in and out of each structure. This port makes guests feel as if they have stepped into Aladdin's city of Agrabah; the crest of this area even features the famous blue Genie. Arabian Coast is a large port with lots of detail buried into the nooks, crannies and corners of the buildings. There are a variety of benches throughout the area that allow guests to relax and study the architecture, murals and mosaics, or to people watch. Beautiful tile fountains are placed in the center of courtyards while other smaller fountains were built against the walls. Arabian Coast transports guests into a whole new world of adventure. Boats docked and beached in the harbor provide hints that expeditions have arrived and that excitement awaits those explorers who venture deep into this Arabian fantasyland. The theming here is top notch and every detail is accounted for. Within the border of Arabian Coast, guests will find three attractions, three eateries and two shops.

Arabian Coast:	
Attractions (3)	*Restaurants (3)*
Sinbad's Storybook Voyage	Casbah Food Court
The Magic Lamp Theater	Sultan's Oasis
Caravan Carousel	Open Sesame
Shops (2)	
Agrabah Marketplace	
Abu's Bazaar	

Be sure to view Arabian Coast from across the water at night. The lighting effects are spectacular and the view of this port, including it's reflection in the water, is breathtaking.

How it Compares

Arabian Coast is a unique "land" in the Disney arsenal considering its size and scope. Certainly, some of the design can be paralleled to the

Morocco Pavilion at Epcot. The closest comparison, however, is the entrance to Adventureland from Main Street at Disneyland Paris which is also heavily themed to Aladdin. Again, the grandeur and style of Arabian Coast is unmatched and it is a masterfully constructed port of call.

Attractions
Sinbad's Storybook Voyage
TRAVELERS SERIES RATES IT – Yoshi (Good – make this a priority)
ENTERTAINMENT SNAPSHOT – Indoor boat ride
QUEUE – As guests enter the palace that houses the attraction, the story and legend of Sinbad the Sailor begins to unfold before them. The story is told in English and Japanese through scrolls, maps and murals depicting the scenes from Sinbad's adventures. Guests are treated to sneak peeks of the attraction as they wind through the corridors to the dock to prepare to set sail.
ATTRACTION LENGTH – 10 minutes

DESCRIPTION AND REVIEW – Guests board small boats and enter the magical world of Sinbad. Just as Tokyo DisneySea as a whole and Arabian Coast in particular are spectacularly themed, so is this attraction. Guests journey through a number of strange and far–off lands and each is rich in color, detail and fantasy. As the boat cruises slowly through the attraction, guests become immersed in busy marketplaces, travel past hoards of treasure, encounter mermaids, battle monkey people and come face to face with a genie. Each of these scenes carries its own look and feel and is filled with audio–animatronic characters that bring the story to life. These characters are remarkably life–like; not for their look, but because of their movements. This fanciful journey is a joy. While the limited dialogue is in Japanese, the story line is clearly spelled out in the scenes and guests will have no problem understanding the basics of the plot.

HOW IT COMPARES – Sinbad's Storybook Voyage is a very unique Disney attraction and is a blend of It's a Small World and Pirates of the Caribbean – Pirates of a Small World would be an appropriate title. Parallels may be drawn to It's a Small World due to the look of the boats, the bright colors of the scenes and the diminutive characters that guests see along the ride. However, Sinbad's Seven Voyages is much more like a dark ride and the attraction's length at 10 minutes provides ample time to tell a full story much more akin to Pirates of the Caribbean.

TIPS – Given the high capacity of the boats and the location of this attraction, there are rarely long lines to contend with. Sinbad's Storybook

Voyage should be ridden later in the day after the marquee attractions have been experienced.

The Magic Lamp Theater
(FASTPASS / ENGLISH SUBTITLES AVAILABLE)

TRAVELERS SERIES RATES IT – Yoshi (Good – make this a priority)

ENTERTAINMENT SNAPSHOT – Combination live action and 3D animated stage show starring Genie

QUEUE – Guests line up outside the Magic Lamp Theater. You will see banners portraying a snake charmer who can do magic. These advertisements proclaim the show to be Fantastic! Baffling! Incredible! Once into the courtyard, guests are ushered into the main tent for the show. Around the walls are several cartoonish murals of desert landscape. In the middle is a very large snake basket surrounded by several large vases. As guests file come inside, a big, but humorous turban–wearing cobra pops up occasionally to look at the crowd collecting. There are a very limited number of benches located next to the center "stage" and a few more around the perimeter of the tent. Guests may stand anywhere in this "theater in the round" as the view is the same from any angle. Once all the guests are inside, the lights dim and the cobra's head emerges from the basket. He begins to tell the audience a story and as he does, the murals around the perimeter of the wall come to life and show the story as told by the Cobra. The story is of Assim, a magician's assistant who discovers a magic lamp. The magician, Master Shaban, took the lamp from Assim and discovered a Genie inside when he rubbed it. Master Shaban's first wish was to become the world's greatest magician. Master Shaban quickly became jealous of Genie and locked the magic lamp in a chest. Today's show is to be Master Shaban's first without Genie. As the pre–show ends, guests are told to line up by the curtains and are lead into a theater. There is not a structured queue here, and the other patrons will stand very close together and push forward for a seat. Don't worry about getting a seat; if you were admitted to the pre–show, there are enough seats to accommodate everyone and there is not a bad seat in the house. Guests who request English subtitles from the Cast Members will receive a flyer with an overview of the show written in English.

ATTRACTION LENGTH – 9 ½ minutes

DESCRIPTION AND REVIEW – As guests are seated into the theater, the characters move from the cartoon walls of the pre–show to being live on stage. Master Shaban begins interacting with the audience and joking with people as they enter. He is confident in his newfound abilities and wants to show the world. Meanwhile, Assim – with his exaggerated bow and oversized silly glasses – wants to help the Genie and begins involving the audience in his quest to find the key to the chest. With the Genie freed, front and center, and animated in 3D, the usual pranks and gags associated with 3D and 4D begin to take shape. Jokes are abundant, though in Japanese, and include physical comedy which plays well with the non–Japanese speaking crowd. One of the highlights is the 3D Genie singing a Japanese rendition of <u>Friend Like Me</u>!

HOW IT COMPARES – This is a unique Disney attraction.

TIPS – Lines here tend to dwindle late in the day. Find the time to experience the Magic Lamp Theater, but only after other high profile attractions have been experienced.

Caravan Carousel
TRAVELERS SERIES RATES IT – Osanai (Young – experience if traveling with young children)
ENTERTAINMENT SNAPSHOT – Merry–go–round
QUEUE – The queue is a covered traditional queue.
ATTRACTION LENGTH – 2 ½ minutes

DESCRIPTION AND REVIEW – Caravan Carousel is a Disney–fied carousel themed with creatures from the Arabian Coast, including Sinbad's Story Book Voyage and Genie from Aladdin (who is present in multiple colors). This two–story carousel is housed under a giant blue dome and is exceptionally large – it has 126 "creatures" that guests may ride. Disney Cast Members wave to riders while the carousel is in motion and will wave to you over, and over, and over, and over – throughout the entire 2 ½ minute attraction! The attraction itself is more interesting to look at than to ride. In the end, this is a traditional merry–go–round.

HOW IT COMPARES – Caravan Carousel is unique because of the characters that guests can ride, its two–story platform and the beautiful architecture that houses the attraction. Outside of these cosmetic items, the attraction is the same as the Fantasyland carousel rides it emulates and the ride itself is no different.

TIPS – Given the relatively high capacity and short running time, there is rarely a line to experience Caravan Carousel. It may be worth a spin if you don't have to wait.

Dining
Casbah Food Court
EATERY SNAPSHOT – Counter service middle–eastern dishes
PRICES – $8.10 to $11 for entrees
CAPACITY – 850 indoors
PRIORITY SEATING AVAILABILITY – No
DESCRIPTION AND REVIEW – Rock the Casbah! Rock the Casbah! No, Casbah Food Court is not named after the Clash's 80s song depicting a small bar in San Diego, California. Casbah is an Arabic term meaning citadel – an appropriate description of the Arabian Coast. Themed to a covered Arabian marketplace complete with wood slat roof, this counter service food court offers a selection of Middle Eastern food from chicken and beef curries with rice and naan (a flat, leavened bread made in a tandoor or clay oven) to seafood chow mein. The outside of the restaurant features beautiful tile work and arches as well as a wall fountain featuring Jasmine from Aladdin. The dining area is quite large and appears very upscale from the dramatic columns around the dome, to the carved chairs, tiled tables and décor lining the walls.

Sultan's Oasis
EATERY SNAPSHOT – Counter service pita sandwiches
PRICES – $3.30 to $4.65 for snacks; $2 to $4.20 for drinks
CAPACITY – 140 outdoors
PRIORITY SEATING AVAILABILITY – No
DESCRIPTION AND REVIEW – Located on the Arabian Coast waterfront, Sultan's Oasis has dramatically designed columns and is situated under an ornate ceiling. The tile work on the walls is stunning. The seating is outdoors, though covered seating is available as are plenty of umbrella-covered tables. Fare here includes spiced meat buns, curried bacon and vegetable soup, fruit jelly topped with coconut soft serve as well as orange juice, coffee and strawberry tea.

Open Sesame
EATERY SNAPSHOT – Kiosk serving sesame churros and drinks
PRICES – $2.75 for churros; $2.55 to $3.20 for drinks
CAPACITY – 0
PRIORITY SEATING AVAILABILITY – No
DESCRIPTION AND REVIEW – Open Sesame is a small snack shack located near Sinbad's Storybook Voyage. Fare includes sesame churros, soda, coffee and apple cinnamon tea.
TIPS – Open Sesame is open seasonally.

Shopping
Agrabah Marketplace

RETAIL SNAPSHOT – Disney character merchandise

DESCRIPTION AND REVIEW – Agrabah Marketplace is sandwiched between the elegant royalty of Princess Jasmine's living quarters and those of the poor orphan Aladdin. Wares include a wide variety of Aladdin and Sinbad-themed stuffed animals and merchandise as well as additional Disney character offerings and magic tricks. The outside of this shop is, as expected, an Arabian marketplace while the inside is whimsical and includes Aladdin-themed displays throughout.

Abu's Bazaar

RETAIL SNAPSHOT – Carnival games of skill

DESCRIPTION AND REVIEW – Abu, Aladdin's friend and monkey, is always trying to take money from marketplace guests. So why should it be any different here? Inside this corner building are two games of skill – The Cobra's Trap and Journey to the Palace. For $5.50, guests can test their skill and try to win a prize.

> **HIDDEN MICKEY ALERT**
> Just around the corner from Abu's Bazaar facing the water is a wheelbarrow and old chest. Look closely at the carvings on the old chest and you will see a Hidden Mickey.

Surprisingly, Tokyo DisneySea did not try to position these as "attractions" (see "Saludos Amigos" Greeting Dock).

Mermaid Lagoon
Overview

Mermaid Lagoon's fanciful colors and design set it apart from any other port within Tokyo DisneySea. Themed to the 1989 Disney Classic The Little Mermaid – and built before the blockbuster Finding Nemo was released – this area brings a Disney sea–based classic to Tokyo DisneySea.

> **HIDDEN MICKEY ALERT**
> There is a blue bridge leading from Mysterious Island to Mermaid Lagoon. From this direction, on the right hand side of the bridge – directly across from the smoking section – are knee–high blue lines next to fanciful carvings in the taller blue of the bridge. In center of this lined section is a Hidden Mickey.

King Triton's castle stands out with its sea shapes, towering coral, giant shells and pink and purple hues and is a whimsical centerpiece to Mermaid Lagoon. The décor is brightly colored and the design is magical. Accessible by footpath from Lost River Delta, Arabian Coast or Mysterious Island, there are two sections to Mermaid Lagoon: The "above the sea" part of Mermaid Lagoon and Triton's Kingdom, an "under the sea" indoor area.

<u>Mermaid Lagoon:</u>

Attractions (8)
Flounder's Flying Fish Coaster
Scuttle's Scooters
Mermaid Lagoon Theater
Jumpin' Jellyfish
Blowfish Balloon Race
The Whirlpool
Ariel's Playground
Ariel's Greeting Grotto

Shops (6)
The Sleepy Whale Shoppe
Mermaid Treasures
Kiss de Girl Fashions
Mermaid Memories
Grotto Photos & Gifts
Sea Turtle Souvenirs

Restaurants (2)
Sebastian's   Calypso
Kitchen
Grotto Goodies

The indoor area uses the same whimsical themes, but the colors are even richer and seem to glow in full light. Guests feel immersed in the ocean with "water" overhead and they are surrounded by seaweed, coral, reefs, rocks and a variety of colorful fish and sea creatures. Although the design is incredible and enjoyable for guests of all ages, the attractions are geared toward children. Either way, Mermaid Lagoon is a must see especially at night when the fiber optic effects on King Triton's castle accent this masterpiece. Mermaid Lagoon boasts eight attractions, two restaurants and six shops.

HIDDEN MICKEY ALERT
Outside the exit from the underwater Triton's Kingdom are several beds of kelp. On the kelp are mosaic leaves – tan in color and made of dozens of very small pieces of tile. At the tip of the leaf is a very tiny Hidden Mickey.

How it Compares
Mermaid Lagoon is a mixture of Fantasyland and A Bug's Land from Disney's California Adventure. The artistry is truly amazing, but the attractions are really geared for the little ones. Many of the attractions are the same as those found in A Bug's Land, which are themed to <u>The Little Mermaid</u>.

Attractions
Flounder's Flying Fish Coaster
TRAVELERS SERIES RATES IT – Osanai (Young – experience if traveling with young children)
ENTERTAINMENT SNAPSHOT – Children's roller coaster

QUEUE – Outdoor queue with views of the entire attraction.
ATTRACTION LENGTH – 1 minute

DESCRIPTION AND REVIEW – Located in the "above the sea" Lagoon area, Flounder's Flying Fish Coaster is a kid's coaster ride between the coral and rock formations of Mermaid Lagoon. This attraction, as expected, is a smooth if uneventful coaster ride. The lines are generally short and if there is little or no wait, it may be worth a spin. Otherwise, like much of Mermaid Lagoon, looking at it will suffice.

HIDDEN MICKEY ALERT
There are no less than ten Hidden Mickeys incorporated into the large mosaic tile work just outside the entrance to Triton's Kingdom. One is located on the far left and is about head level. The three rocks forming the Hidden Mickey actually protrude from the wall, making it easier to find. Just as the mosaic wall transitions from pink to dark blue to sea green, two more Hidden Mickeys can be spotted in the dark blue section and, again, these round rocks stick out from the flat tiles. Additional Hidden Mickeys may be found in the mosaic tile column. Keep looking and see how many you can spot. Additionally, there are blue tiles that feature different sea creatures on each tile. Study these closely and you will find Donald and Goofy have their own tiles just above a traditional Hidden Mickey made from bubbles on one of the tile pieces.

HOW IT COMPARES – Flounder's Flying Fish Coaster looks (and is) just like Tokyo Disneyland's Gadget's Go Coaster from its surroundings to the body of water under the attraction. If anything, this ride is even less eventful than its Toontown cousin. The biggest difference is that the line is generally shorter.

Scuttle's Scooters
TRAVELERS SERIES RATES IT – Osanai (Young – experience if traveling with young children)
ENTERTAINMENT SNAPSHOT – Circular spinning ride
QUEUE – The queue is very well themed – as is all of Mermaid Lagoon – but otherwise it is an ordinary line where the entire attraction can be seen.
ATTRACTION LENGTH – 1 ½ minutes

DESCRIPTION AND REVIEW – Guests board brightly colored sand crabs for a circular journey up and down a small incline. About half–way through, the sand crabs rotate 180 degrees and allow guests to travel the same course backward. Unless you are traveling with children, take a quick peek and move on.

HOW IT COMPARES – There are not any attractions with direct parallels in the Disney library. Scuttle's Scooters are more like a traditional circular carnival ride.

Mermaid Lagoon Theater
(FASTPASS / ENGLISH SUBTITLES AVAILABLE)

TRAVELERS SERIES RATES IT – Yuunaru (Outstanding! Disney at its best)

ENTERTAINMENT SNAPSHOT – Live Stage Show

QUEUE – Guests line up in a traditional roped queuing area inside Triton's Kingdom. They enter the holding area through a hole in the hull of a sunken ship and sit or stand until directed into the theater. There is not much to see here, though guests will still have the sensation of being under water with pearls substituting as lights. Instrumental versions of songs from The Little Mermaid are heard while waiting. Guests may request English subtitles and will be given a device to bring with them into the theater. This small hand–held device is synched with the performance and provides English subtitles during the performance except when songs are performed in English.

ATTRACTION LENGTH – 14 minutes

DESCRIPTION AND REVIEW – Guests are directed, one group at a time, into the theater while the rest wait to be seated even as their doors open. Mermaid Lagoon Theater is a fantastic theatrical experience set in the shimmering blues and silvers under the sea. A sort of Cirque du Soleil meets The Little Mermaid, this live stage show features brightly colored puppetry, performers flying through the air, heart–pounding music and outstanding special effects. Like King Triton's Kingdom, the interior of the theater is deigned to be under the sea next to Ariel's treasure cove from the movie. It is clear from the surroundings that the theater is on the ocean floor. This "theater in the

> **HIDDEN MICKEY ALERT**
> Near the exit doors as you leave the Mermaid Lagoon Theater, you can spot a Hidden Mickey in the rock formation on the wall.

round" features a giant treasure chest on circular stage in the center, though most of the action takes place in the "water" above the stage and above the audience. The puppeteers are fully visible and dressed in black, but do a spectacular job keeping the oversized puppets front and center. Ariel swims (via wires) throughout the performance. Most of the songs are in English and the story is very easy to follow, especially with English subtitles. Cast Members are readily available to remind the audience when to applaud and lead the way by clapping when appropriate.

The story loosely follows the movie as Ariel longs to be part of the above water world. She interacts with Sebastian and Flounder between songs. There is a hint of chauvinism here with Sebastian making comments like "I hope this girl has not been boring you with her tiresome talk". Ursula is a character to be reckoned with as she appears in the form of a large face and finger nails. Her tentacles float down from above to provide the outlines of her body – an amazing accomplishment with limited mass. Her face looks like an enormous Christopher Radko ornament and is extremely expressive with giant shiny pale gold eyebrows that move in harmony with her voice. Although her voice is in Japanese, it is a dead ringer for Ursula and her character steals the show. She tries to convince Ariel to trade her voice for a chance to go above the sea. Ariel swims and sings while considering the offer. In a major departure from the motion picture (and in accordance with Japanese culture) Ariel decides not to enter a deal with the sea witch, but instead decides that while life above the water may be good, her place is here under the sea. Despite this significant change, this is a must-see show for guests of all ages.

HOW IT COMPARES – Disney's Hollywood Studios in Florida showcases Voyage of the Little Mermaid which features some of the same concepts – notably the puppeteers dressed in black performing a show themed to The Little Mermaid. The storylines are roughly similar considering they are based on the same movie. The execution, however, is wildly different. In many ways, this performance is much closer in nature to Finding Nemo – The Musical at Walt Disney World's Disney's Animal Kingdom. The colors, puppeteer involvement and the sheer size of the theater mirror Nemo. The theater in the round set up of Tokyo DisneySea's Mermaid Lagoon Theater, combined with the overhead performances, provides significant differences from either Walt Disney World show.

TIPS – As this area is themed primarily for children, enjoy Mermaid Lagoon Theater late in the day. Many of the children will have had their fill of Mermaid Lagoon and moved on to different areas. There is no need to utilize a FASTPASS on this attraction if you time your visit correctly.

Jumpin' Jellyfish

TRAVELERS SERIES RATES IT – Osanai (Young – experience if traveling with young children)
ENTERTAINMENT SNAPSHOT – Indoor children's parachute ride
QUEUE – The line is a traditional queue inside King Triton's underwater Kingdom and the entire attraction is visible from the queue.
ATTRACTION LENGTH – 1 minute

DESCRIPTION AND REVIEW – Guests sit on giant seashells attached to colorful glowing jellyfish and "swim" with them. The Jumpin' Jellyfish go up and down in a stationary vertical motion in a half–hearted attempt to mimic the motion of jellyfish. This attraction is geared for kids; if you are traveling without them, don't waste our time on this attraction.

HOW IT COMPARES – Jumpin' Jellyfish is identical to the Jumpin' Jellyfish attraction at Disney's California Adventure. The only difference is that the Tokyo DisneySea version is inside.

Blowfish Balloon Race
TRAVELERS SERIES RATES IT – Osanai (Young – experience if traveling with young children)
ENTERTAINMENT SNAPSHOT – Circular children's ride
QUEUE – Inside queue is a traditional rope line.
ATTRACTION LENGTH – 1 ½ minutes

DESCRIPTION AND REVIEW – Guests board brightly colored seashells tethered to equally colorful blowfish by seaweed. As the attraction begins, the fish rise into the air and gently swing guests in a circular motion similar to Dumbo. Each seashell can hold up to four guests – two facing backward and two facing forward. This attraction, like all of Mermaid Lagoon, is wonderfully themed. Unless your children are begging you to ride, don't bother with this attraction.

> **HIDDEN MICKEY ALERT**
> As guests enter the indoor wonders of Triton's Kingdom, there is a decorative sign placed against a pink wall. The wall contains fossilized imprints from old sea shells and creatures. Just to the left of the seahorse on the bottom left of the sign are three imprints that form a Hidden Mickey.

HOW IT COMPARES – Blowfish Balloon race is a redecorated version of Flik's Flyers at Disney's California Adventure. The largest differences are that the Tokyo DisneySea attraction is indoors and themed to life under the sea.

The Whirlpool
TRAVELERS SERIES RATES IT – Osanai (Young – experience if traveling with young children)
ENTERTAINMENT SNAPSHOT – Children's spinning carnival ride
QUEUE – Impeccably themed, this queue is a standard rope line and offers views of the entire attraction.
ATTRACTION LENGTH – 1 ½ minutes

DESCRIPTION AND REVIEW – Guests are seated in "kelp cups" with a wheel situated in the center of each cup. These cups sit upon one of two platforms and as the platforms begin to spin in a circle, the kelp cups spin along. The cups move in a figure eight pattern and switch from one side of the platform to the other. This ride has an extremely small capacity and is not worth any wait.

> **HIDDEN MICKEY ALERT**
> Within Triton's Kingdom on a purple wall located just outside Ariel's Playground is an imprint of a Hidden Mickey.

HOW IT COMPARES – The most obvious comparison for The Whirlpool seems to be Alice's Tea Party at Tokyo Disneyland and its brethren in the U.S. However, the attraction is a re–themed replica of Francis' Ladybug Boogie at Disney's California Adventure where guests cannot control how quickly the cups spin.

Ariel's Playground

TRAVELERS SERIES RATES IT – Yoshi (Good – make this a priority)
ENTERTAINMENT SNAPSHOT – Children's playground
QUEUE – There is rarely a line to enter Ariel's Playground except on days of very high attendance

> **HIDDEN MICKEY ALERT**
> Look closely at the maps at either entrance to Ariel's Playground. On the far right–hand side just below the sea dragon and eels and just to the right of the Starfish Playpen and turtle riding the water spout from the whale is a tiny rock formation drawn onto the map. That shape sure looks familiar! A second Hidden Mickey can be found carved into the rocks along the stair handrail leading into Ariel's Playground.

ATTRACTION LENGTH – Self directed

DESCRIPTION AND REVIEW – Ariel's Playground is a fantastically themed children's play area. Themed to The Little Mermaid, it is an expansive area where guests of all ages and sizes can climb, touch, crawl and explore nine different areas. There is a colorful map that displays each of the areas that guests can explore; a souvenir copy of the map may be obtained from a Cast Member. Guests can check out Fisherman's Nets to climb rope bridges; Kelp Forest and it's maze of kelp; Galleon Graveyard; Ariel's Grotto to see the statue of Prince Eric in Ariel's treasure filled cavern; Cave of Shadows where guests can explore a cave lined with glowing jellyfish; Ursula's Dungeon; Sea Dragon; Starfish Playpen; and Mermaid Sea Spray where guests can get wet. Even without children, take a few moments to walk through this incredibly themed playground – it is worth five minutes to explore the different areas either before or after experiencing Mermaid Lagoon Theater.

HOW IT COMPARES – Ariel's Playground is very unique. Of the Disney play areas, it is most similar to Disney's Hollywood Studios' Honey I Shrunk the Kids Movie Adventure Set or The Boneyard in Disney's Animal Kingdom in size and scope. Ariel's Playground is full of places to explore like these two areas, though is geared for smaller children.

Ariel's Greeting Grotto

TRAVELERS SERIES RATES IT – Osanai (Young – experience if traveling with young children)
ENTERTAINMENT SNAPSHOT – Character greeting station for Ariel
QUEUE – The queue is a traditional, if impeccably themed, line
ATTRACTION LENGTH – 1 minute

DESCRIPTION AND REVIEW – Guests in love with Ariel will have the opportunity to meet her and have a photo taken. Lines for this photo op can be extremely long.

> **HIDDEN MICKEY ALERT**
> After snapping your photo with Ariel, look at the blue and purple column along the exit path and you will spot a Hidden Mickey carved into it about four feet off the ground.

HOW IT COMPARES – Ariel's Greeting Grotto is a traditional character greeting photo op in the vein of those throughout Disney parks.

TIPS – Ariel is generally available from 9:00 am to 6:00 pm. On busy days, the line is closed off earlier than 6:00 pm.

Dining
Sebastian's Calypso Kitchen

EATERY SNAPSHOT – Counter service pizza
PRICES – Entrees range from $5.90 to $7; sets are $11
CAPACITY – 580 indoors
PRIORITY SEATING AVAILABILITY – No
DESCRIPTION AND REVIEW – Sebastian the crab is the proprietor of this restaurant. The theming and décor are in line with the rest of the Triton's

> **HIDDEN MICKEY ALERT**
> Find the two crabs – one with a blue shell and one with a red shell – next to each other along the bottom of the Little Mermaid wall mural at Sebastian's Calypso Kitchen. The markings on the red crab's shell form a Hidden Mickey.

Kingdom, though the walls in the dining area depict animated characters from <u>The Little Mermaid</u> including Sebastian and Ariel. Offerings include seafood pizza, sausage pizza, calzones and a creamy scallop croquette sandwich.

Grotto Goodies
EATERY SNAPSHOT – Kiosk offering cookies
PRICES – $3.55
CAPACITY – 0
PRIORITY SEATING AVAILABILITY – No
DESCRIPTION AND REVIEW – This tiny kiosk is themed in the seaweed and seashells that make up the outdoor portion of Mermaid Lagoon. The mainstay here are little madeleines – spongy seashell shaped cookies.

Shopping
The Sleepy Whale Shoppe
RETAIL SNAPSHOT – Disney character merchandise
DESCRIPTION AND REVIEW – One of the most creatively themed shops in Tokyo DisneySea, The Sleepy Whale Shoppe is accessible through the open mouth of this snoozing purple mammal. The Whale's rib cage makes up the interior of the Shoppe and items this creature has swallowed are used to display the standard Disney merchandise and souvenirs offered here.

Mermaid Treasures
RETAIL SNAPSHOT – Clothing accessories
DESCRIPTION AND REVIEW – Mermaid Treasures is an excellent recreation of the dressing room in which Ariel and her sisters prepare for their concert in The Little Mermaid. This shop is located in a brightly lit cavern. Wares are themed to The Little Mermaid and include jewelry, perfumes and cell phone straps and accessories.

Kiss de Girl Fashions
RETAIL SNAPSHOT – Clothing store
DESCRIPTION AND REVIEW – This shop sells a variety of adult and children's clothing and accessories. The theming here is much more reserved than the rest of Mermaid Lagoon. The result is an attempt to provide a more upscale boutique within Triton's Kingdom. Unfortunately, the attempt falls a little flat.

Mermaid Memories
RETAIL SNAPSHOT – Kiosk selling Little Mermaid souvenirs

DESCRIPTION AND REVIEW – This tiny kiosk is located in the "above the water" Lagoon area and offers small toys and souvenirs featuring characters from The Little Mermaid.

Grotto Photos & Gifts

RETAIL SNAPSHOT – Photos of your groups encounter with Arial and souvenirs

DESCRIPTION AND REVIEW – Located in the outside Lagoon area, Grotto Photos & Gifts sells personalized photos from your character greeting with Ariel. Additionally, Ariel-themed merchandise is sold here, though the same items may be found at The Sleepy Whale Shoppe.

Sea Turtle Souvenirs

RETAIL SNAPSHOT – Kiosk selling hats

DESCRIPTION AND REVIEW – This small hat shack is designed to look like a turtle is swimming overhead. Wares primarily consist of different styles of hats. This kiosk provides the perfect transition from Mermaid Lagoon to Mysterious Island, as it fits the themes of both ports.

Mysterious Island

Overview

Guests cannot help but be immensely curious about Mysterious Island. At the center of this port sits the marquee landmark of Tokyo DisneySea – Mount Prometheus. This industrial and Jules Verne-inspired area calls to adventurers. The patina colored steel bridges, handrails, light posts, and archways leading in and around Mount Prometheus have a decidedly Parisian flare. Their unique design and placement around the lagoon where none other than Captain Nemo's Submarine is docked provides a retro–futuristic vibe to Mysterious Island. The caverns are a mixture of intrigue and foreboding. The earth moving contraption emerging from the side of Mount Prometheus as well as other objects suspended above the harbor indicates that this port is dedicated to exploration. The entire area is built into the side of this "active" volcano. The cracks along the mountain spew steam and warn guests of the fire burning within. Geysers force water high into the air as Prometheus releases pressure before spewing fire. Mysterious Island is accessible by footpath from both sides of Mediterranean Harbor and from Mermaid Lagoon. This is the smallest port within Tokyo DisneySea and is home to two attractions, three restaurants and one shop.

Mysterious Island:
Attractions (2)
Journey to the Center of the Earth
20,000 Leagues Under the Sea

Restaurants (3)
Vulcania Restaurant
Refreshment Station
Nautilus Galley

Shops (1)
Nautilus Gifts

How it Compares
Nothing like Mysterious Island exists outside of Tokyo DisneySea. It is a one–of–a–kind area built into the park's most prominent landmark, Mount Prometheus.

Attractions
Journey to the Center of the Earth (FASTPASS)
TRAVELERS SERIES RATES IT – Yuunaru (Outstanding! Disney at its best)
ENTERTAINMENT SNAPSHOT – High speed dark ride adventure
QUEUE – The queue is an integral part of Journey to the Center of the Earth and sets the stage for the attraction as guests wind their way deep within the interior of Mount Prometheus. Upon entering the mountain through towering patina archways, guests walk past several labs and can view artifacts from previous expeditions. From here, guests board a high–speed elevator and descend into the lower levels of the volcano. The elevators shake and rattle as engines and bells can be heard indicating that work continues as explorers dig into the core of the earth. As guests exit the elevator, they find themselves in a second queuing area and finally lay their eyes on the machines and equipment needed for the journey. Chief among these are giant drilling machines similar to the one visible from outside Mount Prometheus.
ATTRACTION LENGTH – 3 minutes

DESCRIPTION AND REVIEW – Guests board retro–futuristic excavating machines and sit two to a row, three rows deep. These rugged vehicles are encased in metal and the front has a shovel–nose to push dirt and rocks out of the way. Once the Journey is underway, guests wind down and through the earth's core at speeds of up to 47 mph (75 km/hr). The speed changes constantly throughout the attraction and the transitions from slow to fast and fast to slow are incredibly smooth. This expedition takes guests through crystal–filled caverns where many strange creatures resembling big bugs from Jules Verne's <u>Journey to the Center of the Earth</u> can be seen. The exploration seems benign until a giant monster – half tyrannosaurus rex and half giant bug – shows up. He's clearly hungry to eat the passengers! The vehicles blast off up a steep incline to escape the monster and go through steam from the Mount Prometheus before racing down the outside of the mountain, around the perimeter of Mysterious Island and into the dark caverns. The only downside is that there are not enough fantasy elements and the time racing through the caverns is too short. Even so, this attraction is outstanding, a lot of fun, extremely popular and an absolute must see.

HOW IT COMPARES – There is no other Disney attraction quite like Journey to the Center of the Earth. It is a Tokyo DisneySea original. The technology for the vehicles is similar to Epcot's Test Track and Disneyland's former Rocket Rods though the attraction itself is closer to that of the Indiana Jones attractions. The theming and actual attraction are unmatched.

20,000 Leagues Under the Sea (FASTPASS / ENGLISH SUBTITLES AVAILABLE / SINGLE RIDER)

TRAVELERS SERIES RATES IT – Yuunaru (Outstanding! Disney at its best)
ENTERTAINMENT SNAPSHOT – Board a Jules Verne-style submarine to explore underwater ruins
QUEUE – The queue for 20,000 Leagues Under the Sea is a circular ramp that winds down over the lagoon and through parts of the mountain into the loading area. One exploration vehicle is visible from the walkways of Mysterious Island, and one can be seen suspended above the lagoon as guests walk down the ramp. Once in the area below, guests can view equipment from earlier explorations. Upon request, Cast Members will provide an English–language pamphlet that helps explain the story.
ATTRACTION LENGTH – 5 minutes

DESCRIPTION AND REVIEW –Designed by Captain Nemo, these mini–subs called Neptune are capable of taking guests to extreme oceanic depths. Neptune seemingly offers close quarters, though the seating is comfortable with two sitting together looking through the forward window, two looking through the left and two through the right. Overall, these submarines hold up to six people. The design detail within these subs in fantastic and each seat is fashioned with a joystick in front of the accompanying window. Each "station" is given an opportunity to control the direction the spotlight points with the joystick. The seating area is surprisingly comfortable for such a

HIDDEN MICKEY ALERT
About 30 feet before guests approach the final left–hand turn leading to the boarding area of 20,000 Leagues Under the Sea is a waist-level Hidden Mickey. It blends very well with the rocks and you have to keep your eyes peeled or you will walk right on by.

small space and any concerns over size are immediately forgotten as the subs plunge into the depths of the ocean. The attraction begins as guests descend to the dark depths of the ocean. They explore ruins of ships and then the sub is attacked by a giant squid. Just as it looks like the squid will crush the submarine, Neptune's defense system kicks in and emits an electrical charge that runs through the squid like lightening and everything goes dark. Contact has been lost with the control center. As the subs continue, a faint illuminating light can be seen and then another and another. Voyagers can begin to observe alien–like mer–people with big black eyes peeking at them from behind rocks and ruins. The subs continue their journey through ancient ruins as more of these creatures can now be seen and they are holding powerful glowing crystals. The mer–people recognize the need for the Neptune to get back in contact with the control center. Shadows of these creatures can be seen pushing the Neptune to safety where it can once again communicate with the control center.

> **SPOILER ALERT**
> You may want to read this after you experience 20,000 Leagues Under the Sea. While experiencing this attraction, guests feel as if they are under water. The sub rocks gently and creatures and props "float" gracefully through the water. However, as the sub ascends and the attraction ends, the subs are bone dry! The only water in this attraction is located under the subs in the queuing area and in the space between two sheets of glass in each of the windows. This gap allows for the flow of bubbles and guests feel as if they are ascending and descending from the illusion of viewing everything through water. It is a terrific effect and most guests do not realize they were never under water.

There are a couple of suspenseful moments that may be frightening for children (and adults), but nothing scary happens. Overall, this attraction is excellent and the execution is top–notch.

HOW IT COMPARES – 20,000 Leagues Under the Sea is a unique attraction, though it borrows many elements from Disneyland's old Submarine Voyage (prior to being converted to Finding Nemo Submarine Voyage) and starts out in the shallow reefs only to see unusual sea creatures and a run–in with a giant squid. Still, the attraction is unlike any other.

TIPS – Because this attraction is located next to *the* marquee attraction Journey to the Center of the Earth, it tends to be a honing beacon for guests early in the day. The lines tend to grow much shorter late in the day.

Dining
Vulcania Restaurant
EATERY SNAPSHOT – Buffeteria serving Chinese fare
PRICES – $7.60 to $10.50 for entrees; $17.50 for sets; $9.90 for kids' meals
CAPACITY – 480 indoors
PRIORITY SEATING AVAILABILITY – No
DESCRIPTION AND REVIEW – Vulcania Restaurant has been carved into the side of Mount Prometheus and is a spectacular site. The interior of the restaurant is surrounded by rock and overhead lighting has been installed by the excavation crew. Machines are generating geothermal power to provide energy to the rest of Mysterious Island. Entrees include shrimp in chili sauce, sweet and sour pork, fried chicken with soy–vinegar sauce, spicy tofu and fried rice. The Chinese cuisine offered at Vulcania Restaurant is quite good. The theming here is impeccable and it is an enjoyable place to eat.
TIPS – Lines for the attractions die down later in the day and Vulcania is a good choice for dinner before or after you experience the attractions of Mysterious Island.

Refreshment Station
EATERY SNAPSHOT – Kiosk serving Gyoza Sausage Buns
PRICES – $4.65
CAPACITY – 16 outside
PRIORITY SEATING AVAILABILITY – No
DESCRIPTION AND REVIEW – Refreshment Station is located in the canyon connecting Mermaid Lagoon to Mysterious Island. This industrial-themed snack shack offers gyoza sausage buns. They are unbelievably popular, but not worth more than a few minutes' wait.
TIPS – The lines can be incredibly long for these snacks. If you encounter such a line, check out Nautilus Galley or Expedition Eats (Lost River Delta) for a snack.

Nautilus Galley
EATERY SNAPSHOT – Counter service offering snacks and drinks
PRICES – $3.35 to $5.55 for snacks; $2.55 to $6.40
CAPACITY – 130 outdoors
PRIORITY SEATING AVAILABILITY – No
DESCRIPTION AND REVIEW – Nautilus Galley is located on the lower dock level near Captain Nemo's submarine, Nautilus. Like everything else in Mysterious Island, Nautilus Galley has an industrial look and feel. Fare includes smoked turkey legs, pork gyoza and dried shrimp and seaweed

soup while drinks include soda, tea, draft beers and cocktails. It's a great place to grab a quick snack and they offer a variety of Gyoza dumplings.

TIPS – Nautilus Galley's pork gyoza is one of our absolute favorite snacks at the Tokyo Disney Resort. The gyoza is not crescent–shaped, but instead a long rectangle. They are served fresh and piping hot and are a great value. Due to its location, there is rarely a line at Nautilus Galley and it offers a great hot snack and a terrific view.

Shopping
Nautilus Gifts
RETAIL SNAPSHOT – Mysterious Island themed merchandise
DESCRIPTION AND REVIEW – Located inside a retro–futuristic steel and glass dome, Nautilus Gifts cannot be missed. The interior is even more spectacular than the exterior and boasts science fiction décor. Merchandise includes items themed to the 20,000 Leagues Under the Sea and Journey to the Center of the Earth attractions as well as general character wares.

Upcoming Attractions
Walt Disney was adamant that his parks grow and change as people changed and new technologies became available. He famously proclaimed that Disneyland should never be completed and so it is with Tokyo DisneySea. Attractions are refurbished, upgraded, removed and replaced. New attractions are built that test the limits of engineering and imagination. New parades and shows can be found with the seasons and each year brings new attractions into the Disney fold. There are many upcoming attractions for Tokyo DisneySea.

Jasmine's Flying Carpets – 2011
Jasmine's Flying Carpets is scheduled to open next to Sinbad's Storybook Voyage in Arabian Coast during the summer of 2011. This attraction, based on the Disney film Aladdin, will allow guests to climb aboard and control magic carpets as they soar up and down and tilt back and forth through the sky. Accompanying this attraction will be an elevated viewing deck. Based on The Magic Carpets of Aladdin at Magic Kingdom, this attraction is for guests of all ages and is similar to Dumbo. This attraction is budgeted at approximately $22 million.

Fantasmic! – 2011
Fantasmic! is scheduled to premier in the Mediterranean Harbor in 2011 as a part of Tokyo DisneySea's 10th anniversary celebration and will replace BraviSEAmo! Fantasmic! is a spectacular show combining animation shown against water screens with floats and live performers. The story

follows Mickey Mouse into his nightmares where he must battle many of the Disney villains. This high–energy and effects laden show will be based on versions at Disneyland and Disney's Hollywood Studios, though it will likely be modified for 360 degree viewing on Mediterranean Harbor. The show is budgeted at more than $33 million.

Toy Story Mania – 2012

Toy Story Mania is scheduled to open near the New York section of American Waterfront in 2012. Early press releases indicate a waterfront amusement park-styled area will be added within this port. This attraction, based on the three Disney / Pixar blockbusters, is an interactive 3D adventure. Based on the same attraction at Walt Disney World Resort's Disney's Hollywood Studios and Disneyland Resort's Disney's California Adventure, guests board vehicles, don 3D glasses and are immersed in an interactive game. Guests utilize the same controller to throw darts at balloons, toss rings at aliens, and throw balls to break plates in virtual games of skill. Toy Story Mania and the new area are budgeted at $116 million.

SECTION 9: Tokyo Highlights

Overview

Tokyo is an incredible city that comes to life at night. The crowds, the food and the neon lights are all a part of this incredible culture. You have already traveled a substantial distance and should take advantage of your location. Spend some time – a day, two or three – exploring the city and experiencing the people. Even a half–day of riding the subway and walking in the city will be worthwhile. This is a great thing to do your first day in Japan as you begin to adjust to the time change (it may not be time to hit Space Mountain!). It is also a good way to spend any weekend or holidays when the crowds at the park are sure to be at their peak. There are many guidebooks on things to do in Tokyo. Some offer walking tours and great ways to experience the Tokyo beyond Disney. Be advised that even the most popular guide books are often difficult to navigate and short on details (we speak from experience!). If your mindset is one of adventure and exploration, you are sure to have a great time....and you will probably get a little turned around as you explore the city. Fret not, there is always a Metro station nearby and you can always head to the subway to regain your bearings and get to your next stop. Do some research, go to the library and review the sites that are most important to

> **TRAVEL TIP**
>
> Bring a small plastic trash bag with you as you tour Tokyo. There is a very limited availability of public trash cans. If you are traveling with kids or anyone who eats snacks, it's no fun walking around Tokyo for 20 minutes holding an apple core!

248

you. We listed just a couple of our favorites below and think these are at the top of the list if you have limited time. Wikipedia (www.wikipedia.com) is a great place to review these and other destinations.

Riding on the Metro

No matter where your explorations take you, be sure to take the Metro. It is a great place to people watch and learn about Japan. Don't forget to look at all the advertisements! You can see a lot by walking around the larger subway/train stations, looking in the shops and watching people coming and going.

Tsukiji Fish Market

This wholesale market opens in the wee hours of the morning (3am) as 400 different types of seafood arrive from all over the world via boat, truck, train and plane. There are roughly 900 dealers who operate stalls and the entire operation employees more than 60,000 people. Arrive around 5 am to witness the auction and then tour some of the small stands/shops afterwards. Experiencing the Tsukiji Fish Market early in your trip is best as you will likely be up in the middle of the night due to the time change! Be sure to confirm the market is open and its hours of operation and verify that tourists are allowed on the date you plan to visit.

Meiji Shrine

This shrine is a must see. The walk to the shrine will take you into a forest setting secluded from the hustle and bustle of the city. There are wide open spaces to enjoy or for kids to run around. The monuments are large and impressive and the shrine will infuse some history into your trip. There is a small snack shack near the entrance that serves drinks, ice cream and other eats.

Sensoji Temple

There is a lot to do and see near the Sensoji Temple. In addition to a beautiful temple and shrine, there is a Japanese Pagoda and the Kaminarimon Gate, with its bright red structure and enormous 200 pound lantern. Sandwiched in between the gates is the Tokiwado Kaminari Okoshi, an open–air market stuffed with vendors selling gifts, candy, treats and a myriad of other Japanese snacks. There are several stands where you can watch the food being made and witness a cook in a very small enclosed room with glass allowing onlookers to see. As always, be prepared to eat what you buy while you stand near the store or put it in a bag to enjoy later; you will not see people walking and eating.

Sumo Wrestling

This 1,500 year old sport is Japan's most popular. The professional Tokyo–based matches occur only three times each year – January, May and September. They begin on a Sunday and run for 15 consecutive days. If your timing is such that you are lucky enough to be in Tokyo during a tournament, make attending one of these bouts a top priority. You may need to rely on the concierge at your hotel to help you obtain tickets well in advance of your trip. Also, take the time to study up on Sumo history as you will be able to make more sense out of the chaos this way.

Appendix A – Japanese Words to Know

Communicating in English is not difficult at the Tokyo Disney Resort. Here are a few terms that you will have the opportunity to practice throughout your trip:

Hello   *Konnichiwa*
Goodbye   *Sayonara*
Please   *Kudasi*
Thank you   *Domo arrigatoo*
You're welcome   *Doo-itashimmashite*
Yes   *Hai*
No   *Iie*
Good morning   *Ohayo gozaimasu*
Good afternoon   *Konnichiwa*
Good evening   *Konbanwa*
Today   *Kyoo*
Tomorrow   *Ashita*
Restaurant   *Resutoran*
Menu   *Menyu*
Breakfast   *Chosoku*
Lunch   *Hirugohan*
Dinner   *Yushoku*
Water   *Mizu*
Excuse me or Pardon me   *Sumimasen*
Where is the toilet?   *Toire wa, doku desu ka?*
How much does it cost?   *Ikura desu ka?*
1   *Ichi*
2   *Ni*
3   *San*
4   *Shi*
5   *Go*
6   *Roku*
7   *Shichi*
8   *Hachi*
9   *Kyuu*
10   *Juu*
Sunday   *Nichiyoobi*
Monday   *Getsuyoobi*
Tuesday   *Kayoobi*
Wednesday   *Suiyoobi*
Thursday   *Mokuyoobi*

APPENDIX A: JAPANESE WORDS TO KNOW

Friday *Kinyoobi*
Saturday *Doyoobi*
Airport *Kuukoo*
Train station *Eki*
Subway *Chika-tetsu*
Ticket *Kippu*

Appendix B – List of Web Sites

Appendix B consists of an alphabetical list of all the sites in Travelers Series Guide to the Tokyo Disney Resort.

Airport Limousine Bus Service: www.limousinebus.co.jp/en/index.html
Expedia: www.expedia.com
Go Mobile: www.gomobile.co.jp
Hilton Tokyo Bay: www.hilton.com
Hotel Emion Tokyo Bay: www.hotel–emion.jp/english/index.html
Hotel Okura Tokyo Bay: www.okura.com/hotels/tokyobay
Ikspiari Shopping District: www.ikspiari.com
Japan–guide.com: www.japan–guide.com
Japan Hotel Association: www.j–hotel.or.jp/en/index.html
Japanese Inn Group: www.jpinn.com
Japan Ryokan Association: www.ryokan.or.jp/index_en.html
JR Narita Express: www.jreast.co.jp/e/nex/
Keisei Limited Express:
   www.keisei.co.jp/keisei/tetudou/keisei_us/html/o_express.html
Keisei Skyliner: www.keisei.co.jp/keisei/tetudou/keisei_us/top.html
Metro/Subway information: http://www.tokyometro.jp/global/en/index.html
Mitsui Garden Hotel Prana Tokyo Bay:
   www.gardenhotels.co.jp/eng/prana.html
Nationwide Insurance: www.nationwide.com
Orbitz: www.orbitz.com
Oriental Hotel Tokyo Bay: www.oriental–hotel.co.jp
Palm & Fountain Terrace Hotel: www.palmandfountainterracehotel.com
Phonerental USA.com: www.phonerentalusa.com
Priceline: www.priceline.com
Rakuten Travel: www.mytrip.net/en/index.html
Rentafone Japan: www.rentafonejapan.com
Sheraton Grande Tokyo Bay: www.starwoodhotels.com/sheraton
Skype: www.skype.com
Sunroute Plaza Hotel: www.sunroute–plaza–tokyo.com
Tokyo Bay Hotel Tokyu: www.tokyuhotelsjapan.com
Tokyo Bay Maihama Hotel: www.maihamahotel.jp/en
Tokyo Disney Resort: www.tokyodisneyresort.co.jp/index_e.html
Tokyo Disney Resort guide to get to the resort:
   www.tokyodisneyresort.co.jp/tdr/english/plan/access/index.html
Tokyo Disney Resort guide to get to the resort via Airport Limousine Bus
   Service: www.tokyodisneyresort.co.jp/tdr/english/plan/access/train.html
Tokyo Disney Resort guide to get to the resort via train/subway:

www.tokyodisneyresort.co.jp/tdr/english/plan/access/train.html
Tokyo Disney Resort ride refurbishments:
www.tokyodisneyresort.co.jp/tdr/english/plan/schedule/stop.html
Train/Rail times and prices: http://www.hyperdia.com/
Travelers Series: www.travelersseries.com
Travelocity: www.travelocity.com
Trip Advisor: www.tripadvisor.com
Urayasu Brighton Hotel: http://brightonhotels.co.jp/urayasu–e/
USA State Department: www.travel.state.gov
Wikipedia: www.wikipedia.com
Yahoo! Finance Currency Converter:
http://finance.yahoo.com/currency–converter
Yahoo! Travel: travel.yahoo.com

Index

2

20,000 Leagues Under the Sea, 184, 242, 243, 244, 246

A

Abu's Bazaar, 232
Adventureland, 112
Adventureland Bazaar, 96, 126
Agrabah Marketplace, 183, 227, 232
Airport. *See* Narita International Airport
Alice's Tea Party, 150, 158, 238
American Waterfront, 198
AquaSphere, 185
Aquatopia, 183, 214, 215, 216, 218
Arabian Coast, 227
Ariel's Greeting Grotto, 239
Ariel's Playground, 238, 239
AristoCats, The, 97, 103, 142, 154
ATM, 10, 12, 13, 14, 22, 42, 50, 59
Aunt Peg's Village Store, 213

B

Baby Mine, 97, 142, 154
Barnacle Bill's, 182, 199, 211
Bayside Station, 33, 61, 66, 73
Beaver Brothers Explorer Canoes, 97, 115, 129, 137, 139, 140
Big Band Beat, 182, 199, 206
Big City Vehicles, 182, 199, 200
Big Thunder Mountain, 97, 126, 127, 129, 130, 135, 139
Blowfish Balloon Race, 183, 233, 237
Blue Bayou Restaurant, 96, 112, 119
Boiler Room Bites, 96, 112, 122, 123
Bon Voyage, 32, 78, 81, 109
Bowing, 8

BraviSEAmo!, 182, 186, 190, 191, 246
Breezeway Bites, 183, 214, 218
Buffet, 82, 121, 182, 199
Buffeteria, 82, 217, 245
Buzz Lightyear's Astro Blasters, 172, 173, 174, 178

C

Café Orleans, 96, 112, 120
Café Portofino, 182, 186, 192
Camera Center, 96, 101, 109, 196
Candy Wagon, 112, 126
Canteen, The, 135
Cape Cod Cook–Off, 92, 182, 199, 207, 210
Captain EO Tribute, 169
Captain Hook's Galley, 152, 153
Caravan Carousel, 183, 227, 230
Casbah Food Court, 183, 227, 231
Cash, 12
Castle Carrousel, 146
Cell phones. *See* Phones
Center Street Coffee House, 106
Chiba Traders – Arts and Crafts, 96, 112, 125
China Voyager, 96, 112, 123
Chip 'n Dale Treehouse, 160
Chuck Wagon, 97, 127, 136
Cinderella's Fairy Tale Hall, 180
Cirque du Soleil, 31, 32, 36, 81, 235
Cleo's, 153
Clothing
    Jacket, 25
    Layer, 25, 48
    Shorts, 15
Communicating, 7, 251
Cosmic Encounter, 98, 165, 178
Counter Service, 83
Country Bear Bandwagon, 97, 127, 137
Country Bear Theater, 97, 127, 128
Credit Cards, 11, 12, 14
    AMEX, 13
    MasterCard, 13

Visa, 13
Cristal Arts, 96, 112, 125
Critter Country, 137
Crowds, 23, 24, 26, 28, 31, 51, 102, 105, 108, 111, 117, 156, 161, 248
Crystal Palace Restaurant, 96, 112, 121, 133

D

Daisy's Snack Wagon, 163
Debit Cards. *See* ATM
Delancey Catering, 182, 199, 212
Diamond Horseshoe, The, 132, 134
Dinghy Drinks, 98, 156, 163
Directions, 8
Disabilities, 91
Discovery Gifts, 183, 214, 218
Disney & Co., 96, 101, 111
Disney Ambassador Hotel, 34, 35, 36, 38, 40, 41, 42, 51, 73, 81
Disney Gallery, The, 104, 105
Disney Resort Cruiser, 33, 36, 61
Disney Resort Line, 33, 36, 43, 51, 57, 61, 79
    Monorail Ticket, 33
Disneyland Paris, 1, 2, 32, 95, 101, 116, 143, 181, 214, 223, 228
Disneyland Resort, 2, 4, 23, 28, 29, 52, 59, 80, 87, 93, 247
    Disney's California Adventure, 2, 93, 105, 174, 203, 205, 233, 237, 238, 247
DisneySea Electric Railway, 182, 183, 184, 199, 200, 201, 212, 213, 214, 216, 217
DisneySea Transit Steamer Line, 182, 183, 184, 186, 187, 188, 199, 201, 202, 219, 221, 222
Donald's Boat, 161
Dumbo the Flying Elephant, 146

E

Eastside Cafe, 105
Eating, 9, 90

Electrical Adapters, 10
Embassy, 15, 63
Emergencies, 10, 11, 17
Emporio, 182, 186, 195, 212
Enchanted Tiki Room, The, 96, 112, 117, 118, 126
Exchange Rates, 12
Expedition Eats, 183, 219, 225, 245
Expedition Photo Archives, 183, 219, 226

F

Fantasmic!, 191, 246
Fantasy Gifts, 97, 142, 154
Fantasyland, 141
FASTPASS, 87, 88, 89, 92, 130, 138, 139, 147, 149, 150, 152, 168, 169, 170, 172, 173, 174, 203, 206, 214, 218, 220, 222, 223, 229, 235, 236, 242, 243
Figaro's Clothiers, 197
Flight Time, 6
Flounder's Flying Fish Coaster, 161, 233, 234
Fortress Explorations, 182, 186, 188, 189, 190, 191, 194
Fotografica, 182, 186, 196
Fresh Fruit Oasis, 96, 112, 124
Frontier Woodcraft, 97, 127, 136

G

Gadget's Go Coaster, 160, 161, 234
Gag Factory/Toontown Five & Dime, 98, 156, 164
Galleria Disney, 182, 186, 195
Gazebo, The, 96, 112, 120, 121
General Store, 97, 126, 127, 136
Glass Slipper, The, 97, 125, 142, 154
Golden Galleon, The, 96, 103, 112, 124
Gondolier Snacks, 182, 186, 194
Goofy's Bounce House, 161, 162, 164
Goofy's Drink Stand, 164

Grand Circuit Raceway, 98, 165, 171, 172
Grand Emporium, 96, 101, 108, 111, 195
Grandma Sara's Kitchen, 140
Great American Waffle Company, 96, 101, 107
Grotto Goodies, 183, 233, 240
Grotto Photos & Gifts, 183, 233, 241

H

Harrington's Jewelry & Watches, 96, 101, 110
Haunted Mansion, 97, 99, 142, 147, 148, 149, 172
Hidden Mickey, 33, 36, 37, 38, 40, 42, 43, 44, 48, 50, 51, 52, 56, 57, 58, 61, 79, 81, 83, 92, 95, 100, 101, 102, 108, 115, 118, 123, 139, 144, 157, 159, 160, 162, 172, 175, 178, 185, 187, 195, 196, 208, 209, 216, 217, 220, 223, 224, 232, 233, 234, 235, 237, 238, 239, 243
High Tide Treats, 182, 199, 212
Hilton Tokyo Bay, 60
Holidays, 6, 23, 25, 26, 27, 28, 31, 34, 248
  Christmas, 28, 81, 129
  Halloween, 28
  Japanese Holidays, 6, 25
  U.S. Holidays, 6, 23
Home Store, The, 96, 101, 103, 112
Hoot & Holler Hideout, 97, 137, 141
Horizon Bay Restaurant, 217, 218
Horseshoe Roundup, 97, 127, 132, 134
Hotel Emion Tokyo Bay, 68
Hotel Okura Tokyo Bay, 60, 65
Hotels
  Disney Hotels, 7, 32, 33, 34, 42, 60, 61, 67, 72, 79, 82
  Tokyo Disney Resort Good Neighbor Hotels, 7, 68, 73

Tokyo Disney Resort Official Hotels, 7, 32, 60, 61, 66, 67, 79
Tokyo Disney Resort Partner Hotels, 7, 67, 68, 69, 73
House of Greetings, 96, 101, 111, 196
Huey, Dewey and Louie's Good Time Café, 163
Hungry Bear Restaurant, 97, 127, 134

I

Ice Cream Cones, 96, 101, 106
Ikspiari, 32, 36, 43, 51, 61, 73, 79, 80, 81, 82, 125
Il Postino Stationery, 182, 186, 196
ImageWorks, 98, 165, 178
Indiana Jones Adventure, 183, 219, 220, 221, 223, 226
Insurance, 10, 11, 253
  Travel Medical Insurance, 11
  Trip Cancellation Insurance, 11
Internet Access, 11, 35
It's a Small World, 149, 150, 228

J

Jasmine's Flying Carpets, 246
Journey to the Center of the Earth, 184, 242, 243, 244, 246
JR Lines, 21
JR Maihama Rail Station, 33
JR Maihama Station, 61, 67, 75, 78, 81
JR Narita Express, 75, 253
Juliet's Collections & Treasures, 197, 198
Jumpin' Jellyfish, 236, 237
Jungle Cruise, 96, 112, 113, 114, 115, 220

K

Keisei Limited Express, 75, 253

Keisei Skyliner, 75, 253
Kiosk, 83, 124, 137, 154, 163, 164,
    177, 179, 198, 211, 212, 213,
    218, 225, 226, 231, 240, 241, 245
Kiss de Girl Fashions, 183, 233, 240

L

La Petite Parfumerie, 96, 112, 125
Legend of Mythica, The, 182, 186,
    189, 190, 193
Length of Stay, 30
Liberty Landing Diner, 182, 199,
    211
Lilo's Luau & Fun, 96, 112, 118,
    121
Limousine Bus, 75, 76, 77, 253
Lite Bite Satellite, 98, 165, 177
Lookout Traders, 183, 219, 226
Lost River Cookhouse, 183, 219,
    225
Lost River Delta, 219
Lost River Outfitters, 183, 219, 226
Lucky Nugget Cafe, 135
Luggage, 15, 33, 42, 50, 59, 74, 75,
    77, 79, 136
    Baggage Delivery Service, 34, 61
    Baggage Storage, 42, 59

M

Magellan's, 194, 195
Magic Lamp Theater, The, 88, 183,
    227, 229, 230
Magic Shop, 96, 101, 110
Main Street Daily, 96, 101, 109
Mamma Biscotti's Bakery, 193
Mark Twain Riverboat, 97, 115, 126,
    127, 129, 139, 140
McDuck's Department Store, 212
Mediterranean Harbor, 186
Meet & Smile, 182, 186, 192
Meiji Shrine, 249
Merchant of Venice Confections,
    182, 186, 197
Mermaid Lagoon, 232

Mermaid Lagoon Theater, 183, 233,
    235, 236, 239
Mermaid Memories, 183, 233, 240
Mermaid Treasures, 183, 233, 240
Metro Lines, 20, 21
Mickey & Minnie's Polynesian
    Parade, 118, 121, 122
Mickey Mouse, 56, 57, 83, 92, 100,
    104, 106, 112, 123, 132, 134,
    137, 156, 159, 163, 174, 179, 247
Mickey's House and Meet Mickey,
    159
Mickey's PhilharMagic, 179
Mickey's Trailer, 164
Miguel's El Dorado Cantina, 223,
    225, 226
Minnie Oh! Minnie, 96, 112, 119
Minnie's House, 158, 159
Miramare, 182, 186, 198
Mitsui Garden Hotel Prana Tokyo
    Bay, 68
Monorail. See Disney Resort Line
Monsters, Inc. Company Store, 98,
    165, 179
Monsters, Inc. Ride & Go Seek!,
    173, 174
Music Rhythms, 222
Musica Mexicana, 183, 219, 223,
    225
My Friend Duffy, 92, 182, 199, 207,
    208, 211
Mysterious Island, 241

N

Narita International Airport, 5, 14,
    17, 74, 76
Nautilus Galley, 184, 242, 245, 246
Nautilus Gifts, 184, 242, 246
New York Deli, 182, 199, 210
Newsie's Novelties, 213
Nicolo's Workshop, 197

O

Omnibus, 96, 101, 105, 200

One Man's Dream II – The Magic Lives On, 98, 165, 174, 175
Open Sesame, 183, 227, 231
Oriental Hotel Tokyo Bay, 68
Oriental Land Company, 3, 28, 35, 42, 50, 95
Out of Bounds Ice Cream, 98, 156, 163
Over the Waves, 182, 199, 206, 207

P

Packing, 14
Palm & Fountain Terrace Hotel, 68, 253
Pan Galactic Pizza Port, 98, 165, 176
Papdakis Fresh Fruit, 211
Parades, 98, 184
Park Hours, 28
Parkside Wagon, 96, 112, 122
Party Gras Gifts, 96, 112, 125
Passport, 15, 29, 74, 88
Passports. *See* tickets
Pastry Palace, 96, 101, 110
Pecos Bill Cafe, 133
Pecos Goofy's Frontier Revue, 132, 134
Peddler's Outpost, 226
Penny Arcade, 96, 101, 103
Peter Pan's Flight, 142, 143
Phones, 15, 16
Piccolo Mercato, 182, 186, 198
Pin Trading, 83, 124
Pinocchio's Daring Journey, 145
Pirate Treasure, 96, 112, 124
Pirates of the Caribbean, 96, 112, 113, 114, 119, 124, 228
Planet M, 98, 165, 178
Plaza Pavilion, 97, 127, 133
Plaza Restaurant, 98, 165, 175, 176
Pleasure Island Candies, 97, 142, 155
Polynesian Terrace Restaurant, 96, 112, 118, 121
Poncho, 14, 103, 108, 185
Pooh Corner, 97, 142, 155

Pooh's Hunny Hunt, 150, 151, 155, 158, 216
Pop–A–Lot popcorn, 164
Popcorn, 91, 98, 156, 164
Popping Pod, The 98, 165, 177, 178
Port Discovery, 44, 183, 184, 185, 190, 200, 201, 212, 213, 214, 215, 217, 218, 219

Q

Queen of Hearts Banquet Hall, 97, 142, 153

R

Rackety's Raccoon Saloon, 140
Raging Spirits, 183, 219, 222, 223
Rail Lines. *See* JR Lines
Refrescos, 182, 186, 195
Refreshment Corner, 96, 101, 107
Refreshment Station, 184, 242, 245
Rental Car. See Car
Restaurant Hokusai, 96, 101, 106
Restaurant Sakura, 182, 199, 209, 211
Restrooms, 17
Ride Refurbishments, 29
Rimembranze, 182, 186, 190, 191, 192, 198, 200
Ristorante di Canaletto, 182, 186, 193
Roger Rabbit's Car Toon Spin, 99, 156, 157, 158
Romeo's Watches & Jewelry, 197, 198
Royal Street Veranda, 96, 112, 119

S

S.S. Columbia Dining Room, 182, 199, 208
Safari Trading Company, 96, 112, 125, 126
Sailing Day Buffet, 182, 199, 210

"Saludos Amigos" Greeting Dock, 183, 219, 224, 232
Scuttle's Scooters, 234, 235
Sea Turtle Souvenirs, 183, 233, 241
Seaside Snacks, 183, 214, 218
Sebastian's Calypso Kitchen, 239
Sensoji Temple, 249
Sheraton Grande Tokyo Bay Hotel, 60
Shoes, 14, 213
Silhouette Studio, 96, 101, 111
Sinbad's Storybook Voyage, 228, 229, 231, 246
Single Riders, 89
Skipper's Galley, The, 96, 112, 124
Skywatcher Souvenirs, 183, 214, 218
Sleepy Whale Shoppe, The, 183, 233, 240, 241
Slue Foot Sue's Diamond Horseshoe, 134
Smoking, 35
Snow White's Adventure, 144
Soft Landing, 98, 165, 176
Solar Ray's Light Supplies, 179
Space Mountain, 74, 98, 165, 166, 168, 169, 170, 248
Space Place FoodPort, 98, 165, 177
Splash Mountain, 97, 115, 129, 137, 138, 139, 140, 141
Splashdown Photos, 97, 137, 139, 141
Splendido, 182, 186, 198
Squeezer's Tropical Juice Bar, 123
Star Tours, 98, 165, 166, 167, 168, 176, 215
StarJets, 3, 98, 165, 170, 171, 177
Steamboat Mickey's, 212
Stellar Sweets, 98, 165, 178, 179
StormRider, 183, 214, 215, 218
Stroller and Wheelchair Rental, 100, 184
Stromboli's Wagon, 155
Subtitles, 93
Subways, 75
Sultan's Oasis, 231
Summer Vacation, 23, 25
Sumo Wrestling, 250

Sunroute Plaza Tokyo, 60, 62
Super–Duper Jumpin' Time, 133
Sushi, 9, 10, 21, 62, 106, 211
Sweetheart Cafe, 107
Swiss Family Treehouse, 96, 112, 116

T

Table Service, 83
Taxi, 36, 68, 70, 76
Teddy Roosevelt Lounge, The, 182, 199, 208, 209
Tiki Tropic Shop, 96, 112, 126
Time Zone, 18
Tipping, 14, 33
Tokyo Bay Hotel Tokyu, 60
Tokyo Disneyland Hotel, 34, 35, 50, 51, 52, 53, 55, 56, 57, 58, 59, 70, 73
Tokyo DisneySea Hotel MiraCosta, 31, 34, 42, 43, 44, 46, 47, 48, 49, 50, 51, 73, 82, 186
Tokyo Highlights, 248
Tom Sawyer Island, 97, 127, 129, 131, 132, 135, 136, 189
Tom Sawyer Island Rafts, 97, 127, 131
Tomorrowland, 165
Tomorrowland Terrace, 98, 165, 177
Toon Park, 98, 156, 162
Toon Pop, 98, 156, 163
Toontown, 155
Toontown Delivery Company, 164
Tower of Terror, 182, 199, 203, 205, 213
Tower of Terror Memorabilia, 213
Town Center Fashions, 96, 101, 109
Toy Station, 96, 101, 110
Toy Story Mania, 247
Trading Post, 97, 126, 127, 137
Trains, 75
Transportation, 5, 18, 71, 74
    Bus Routes, 75
    Entering and Exiting, 20
    Tickets, 19, 29, 33, 78, 82
Travel Budget, 30

Travel Warnings, 22
Tropic Al's, 225
Troubadour Tavern, 97, 142, 152
Tsukiji Fish Market, 249
Turtle Talk, 182, 199, 202, 203

U

Umbrella, 14, 17, 24, 162, 231
Upcoming Attractions, 179, 246
Urayasu Brighton Hotel, 68, 254

V

Valentina's Sweets, 195
Venetian Carnival Market, 182, 186,
    197
Venetian Gondolas, 182, 186, 188
Village Pastry, 97, 142, 154, 155
Vulcania Restaurant, 184, 242, 245

W

Walking, 13, 14, 21, 22, 33, 42, 90,
    127, 172, 186, 195, 248, 249
Walt Disney World Resort, 2, 1, 2, 4,
    23, 28, 29, 32, 37, 43, 50, 52, 60,
    80, 87, 93, 142, 168, 205, 215,
    247
    Disney's Animal Kingdom, 2, 93,
        236, 239
    Disney's Hollywood Studios, 2,
        168, 191, 205, 215, 236, 239,
        247
    Epcot, 2, 93, 170, 187, 188, 202,
        203, 221, 228, 243
    Magic Kingdom, 2, 1, 50, 55, 85,
        87, 93, 101, 102, 103, 108,
        113, 114, 115, 116, 117, 121,
        124, 127, 128, 129, 130, 131,
    137, 139, 142, 143, 144, 145,
    146, 147, 148, 150, 152, 157,
    159, 161, 162, 166, 169, 171,
    172, 173, 180, 181, 200, 214,
    219, 220, 246
Weather, 14, 23, 24, 25, 100, 102,
    139, 218
    Fall, 24
    Rain, 7, 14, 24, 25, 102, 151
    Rainy Season, 24
    Snow, 14, 24, 25, 176
    Spring, 25, 26, 27
    Summer, 24, 47
    Winter, 25
Western River Railroad, 96, 112,
    115, 116, 140
Western Wear, 97, 127, 136
Westernland, 126
Westernland Picture Parlour, 97,
    127, 137
Westernland Shootin' Gallery, 127,
    174
Wheelchairs, 100, 184
Whirlpool, The, 183, 233, 237, 238
World Bazaar, 101
World Bazaar Confectionary, 96,
    101, 108, 155

Y

Yen, 4, 12, 13, 19, 34, 54, 62, 70, 78,
    81, 102, 103, 136
Yucatan Base Camp Grill, 183, 219,
    224

Z

Zambini Brothers Ristorante, 192,
    193